DETROIT'S POWERS & PERSONALITIES

TIM KISKA

MOMENTUM BOOKS, LTD.
BUSINESS OFFICE: 2051 WARRINGTON ROAD
ROCHESTER HILLS, MI 48063

DETROIT'S POWERS & PERSONALITIES

Manufactured in the United States of America

Momentum Books Ltd.
Business office:
2051 Warrington Road
Rochester Hills, MI 48063

ISBN 0-9618726-1-6

To my wife, Pat, who was very patient throughout this project.

EDITOR'S FOREWORD

Okay, so you know a Detroit personality—or a power, even—who isn't in this book. There are a number of things I can say about that.

(1) In the post-Warhol age—where newspapers interview my car-wash man about the fortunes of one sports team or another, then print his analysis on page one—the only way to do this thing right is to print an annotated phone book.

(2) I ran into a book on movers and shakers in England. It had fewer biographies than this book. You may deduce that (a) England is smaller than Detroit, (b) Detroiters have more power and/or personality than the Brits, (c) Tim Kiska compiled a reasonably extensive list for inclusion here. The day before these words were written, an incredible scene was played out at a British soccer match. Remember October 1984 and Bubba and the burning police car, Michigan and Trumbull? Bubba was a dilettante. And, except for a few people descended from the first assembly line, Detroit has no royals. So I would have to say that the correct answer above is (c).

(3) Entrée here was determined by humans—Tim, the publisher, and myself—not by computers. That's why Tim's picture is on the jacket, not Ed McMahon's. If we made an error or two in judgment, buy several extra copies as Christmas gifts. That way the next edition can be bigger and better.

You can quarrel about who is in here—and what is said about them and how it's said—but you can't quarrel about birthdates. They're one of the two facts of life that are immutable: check-in and check-out. Some readers will pore over the birthdates; others won't notice them. Editors have to notice.

One most noticeable thing is that some of our subjects have a birthdate that is "not available." We didn't twist arms for this data; we just asked. So don't be too hard on the reticent ones. In some quarters birthdate suppression remains a convention as common as eating with a fork. It is nonetheless bemusing that a male with a bank account as big as the Ritz, and whose life plays out in the news media, will volunteer all kinds of information except this one simple fact — which, if he is lucky, is his only file at the courthouse.

One subject lists her age as 4,000 and has been doing so since before Shirley MacLaine found out how old she was. Several have a birth month and a birth day but no birth year. You can send them a card, but it will have to be generic.

Editors do more than proofread birthdates, of course. For instance, among the 360 or so biographies in this book, I actually wrote one: Lester Knight, the jockey. I happen to think that thoroughbred horse racing is our greatest spectator sport, one where onlookers needn't *pretend* that they are involved. So in return for seeing that "birthdate not available" is spelled correctly about 40 times, I got horse racing represented here. Lester may not be a power in Detroit, but he's a helluva personality.

I think you can see we had fun with this book. It's dead serious in that we tried to come up with a good list and we went to considerable trouble to get facts straight. If your cousin Al is moving here from the East Coast, I can't think of a better way to download his new reference points. On the other hand, it's written in the breezy style of Tim's newspaper column, and you won't need to sit near the unabridged to read it. We want you to have fun with it, too.

About the only mechanical feature you might not figure out at a glance is that any reference to a person who is the subject of a biography elsewhere in the book is highlighted in *bold italic*. The biographies are all entered alphabetically. You can read from A to Z, or backwards, or look for specific people.

A note about Kiska: I've known Tim since he was a copy boy at the *Free Press* and I would stick paper copy on a steel spike and yell "Copy!" and he would take it off the spike and send it through a pneumatic tube to waiting typesetters. There are no pneumatic tubes or paper copy or typesetters anymore, and neither one of us works at the *Free Press*. It was encouraging to get back together for this project and see that, many miles later, Tim has lost neither his enthusiasm nor his integrity.

TOM FERGUSON

INTRODUCTION

We've often heard that Detroit is the biggest small town in America—that there are only 20 people and 20 dollars (10 of it in cash), and that they are simply passed around. The purpose of this volume is to identify these 20 people. (Actually, we've numbered 360.) Then, we've sought to explain where they came from, what they do and why they're important.

Some of the people in this book aren't famous in the least. I avoided those who are amid their 15 minutes of fame. Power and accomplishment received more weight here than glitz. Thus, former Cheeks owner Richard Rollins wouldn't have made it—even at the height of his notoriety. But the less famous Wayne County Prosecutor John O'Hair, who is identifiable by fewer than one in 10 people, merits inclusion. Why? O'Hair is certainly less flamboyant than Richard Rollins, but O'Hair is the man who puts crack cocaine dealers in jail. O'Hair also has a couple of decades of public service beneath his belt.

I steered away from the various society crowds. As far as I can determine, there isn't a single "society" bunch. After two years as the "Yours Truly" columnist at the *Detroit News*, I have come to understand that these people are important to each other, but perhaps nobody else. Thus, some of the folks who hang around the various Birmingham bistros may be amusing, but it's still a puzzle as to why anybody in Trenton would care.

So how did we make our choices? Each person is well-known in his or her particular field. It would have been pleasant to produce a volume in which I could say that 90 percent of the people here are known to the general populace. But that would eliminate almost the entire automotive industry, which takes pains to hide all but a few of its leaders from the press. The auto industry was an especially trying subject. Color or quotability are sins in the automotive world, unless you're Lee Iacocca.

The fact is, Detroit's power grid has no central source of power. To an up-and-coming engineer at General Motors, the person who runs the Chevrolet-Pontiac-Canada division is the center of the universe. He or she couldn't care less about, say, Police Chief William Hart. But to the cop on the beat, there is no percentage in knowing who's ruling Chevrolet-Pontiac-Canada this week.

Covering these various power bases, my beat included the sleazy dives where reporters hang out, the clubs where the power brokers cut their deals, the automotive executive suites, the union halls and the law offices.

My most fervent wish: That 100 years from now, somebody will see the book and get an idea of who ran Detroit in the late '80s. I felt like a cave man scratching pictures on his wall, hoping to give some future Detroiter a clue about what we're doing here.

TIM KISKA

ACKNOWLEDGEMENTS

Several people labored long and hard to make this volume what it is. Special thanks to:

Tom Ferguson, my editor. Thank goodness for Tom. Some of my copy, particularly the stuff written during the post-midnight hours, came out awfully sloppy. Tom fixed that, and raised the quality of writing in this volume higher than I thought possible.

Deputy City Clerk Jeffrey Blaine was especially patient and helpful as I examined city records. He's a rare civil servant with the twisted idea that he's there to serve; writer Paul Lienert (*Detroit Free Press*, *Automobile* magazine) was helpful, both as a friend and as a resource on automotive history; public affairs consultant Alan Feuer was an invaluable resource when it came to politics. And a special thanks to three top-flight journalists: the late Don Ball of the Detroit News, the late Ven Marshall, of Channel 7, and the late Bob Zonka, editor/publisher of the *New Buffalo Times* and a great Chicago newspaperman.

Since I wasn't born with the quality of omniscience, I've depended on a few publications to clue me in as to what happened here in the last 30 years. Actually, I've borrowed lots from numerous sources.

Among the newspapers I've consulted are the *Detroit News*, *Detroit Free Press*, *New York Times*, *Wall Street Journal*, *Automotive News*, *Crain's Detroit Business*, *Michigan Chronicle*, *Detroit Legal News*.

Among the magazines that sat on my dining room table as I worked on this project were *Advertising Age*, *American Film*, *Adweek*, *Automobile*, *AutoWeek*, *Broadcasting*, *Business Week*, *Car and Driver*, *Detroit Monthly*, *The Economist*, *Forbes*, the now-defunct *Metropolitan Detroit*, *Newsweek*, Gale Research Co.'s *Contemporary Authors Autobiography Series*; Gale Research's *Contemporary Authors*; and *Time*.

And, of course, there have been books that gave me a long-range view of events. Among those are August Meier and Elliott Rudwick's "Black Detroit and the Rise of the UAW"; W. Hawkins

Ferry's "The Buildings of Detroit, a History"; Wayne Andrews' "Architecture in Michigan"; Michael Barone and Grant Ujifusa's "The Almanac of American Politics, 1972–1988"; Peter Guralnick's "Sweet Soul Music"; Alfred P. Sloan Jr.'s "My Years with General Motors"; Frank Angelo's "On Guard—A History of the Detroit Free Press"; Earl Blackwell's "Celebrity Register"; David Halberstam's "The Reckoning"; Peter Collier and David Horowitz's "The Fords: An American Epic"; Joel Whitburn's "The Billboard Book of Top 40 Albums"; "Vitale—Just Your Average Bald, One-Eyed Basketball Wacko Who Beat the Ziggy and Became a PTP'er" by Dick Vitale, with Curry Kirkpatrick; "Detroit Jazz Who's Who," by Herb Boyd and Leni Sinclair; "The New Grove Dictionary of Jazz," edited by Barry Kernfeld; and "Heat Wave: The Motown Fact Book," by David Bianco.

Also a word of thanks to Bill Ballenger, Laura Berman, the Rev. Harry Cook, Father William Cunningham, J.B. Dixson, Eleanor Josaitis, Kathy Ryan, Neal Shine and Ron Williams.

T.K.

A

Abraham, Spencer—June 12, 1952; Republican Party tactician.

This fresh-faced lawyer/pollster referees the Bickersons, a.k.a. the state GOP. "The epitome of a non-controversial person," says one Republican of her party's state chairman. That's a plus when Republican politics becomes blood sport, as in the George Bush/Jack Kemp/Pat Robertson presidential primary (translate: moderates vs. conservatives) in 1988. "Anybody who can survive that with his scalp intact," gushes one admiring Democrat, "has got to have something."

Politics is in Abraham's genes. His late mother, Julie, was a Lansing Republican stalwart. Her son's political debut came at age 14 working for the re-election of Governor *George Romney*. At 16 he ran an Ingham County drain commission candidate's campaign. After Michigan State University and Harvard Law School, where he edited the prestigious law review, he returned to Lansing as an instructor at Cooley Law School. Abraham served as pollster on Richard Headlee's failed 1982 gubernatorial campaign before winning the state party chairmanship in 1983, when young conservative types tossed out their more liberal counterparts.

Strategy, not glad-handing, is Abraham's forté. He'd rather fool with direct mail and fund-raising minutiae than press the flesh in Kalamazoo, or wherever. His name is mentioned when important spots open up on the Republican ticket, but he has never run for public office. *William Lucas* considered him for the lieutenant governor's slot in 1986, but settled on Colleen Engler. Abraham did ponder a run for **Donald Riegle**'s U.S. Senate seat in 1988.

His nerd-like image conceals indications of being one of the guys. He is a sports freak, and his collection of Topps baseball cards is complete from 1960-'65. Abraham declared to all at the 1984 Republican convention in Dallas that he had fallen for CBS newscaster Connie Chung. (No hint of scandal there because Abraham is, and was, unmarried.)

Adamany, David—September 23, 1936; Wayne State University's top Tartar.

His closely cropped hair, thin frame and wire-rimmed glasses give him the air of a Trappist Monk. But anybody who has crossed WSU's eighth president knows that Adamany is as tough as a crack house enforcer. During a particularly vicious strike in the fall of 1988, he was characterized as "the most hated man on Wayne State University's campus." Does he mind? Probably not much. He once quoted the late Malcolm Moose, president of the University of Minnesota, as saying: "When treed by a bear, enjoy the view."

So overpowering is Adamany's intellectual aura that one wonders if there is a rod of pure plutonium stuck somewhere in his head. His father, a Lebanese immigrant, owned a restaurant and supper club in Green Bay, Wisconsin. The bookish son graduated magna cum laude from Harvard, picked up a law degree from Harvard Law in 1961, then returned to the Midwest for advanced degrees in political science at the University of Wisconsin.

An expert in political fund-raising, he shuffled between the groves of academe and the jungles of state government during much of the '70s. He worked as an aide to Wisconsin Lt. Gov. Patrick Lucey, and served as the state's revenue chief. There were stops at the University of Maryland and California State University at Long Beach before Wayne State University's board of governors hired him in 1982.

Adamany lives in the president's quarters near McGregor Memorial Conference Center, making him one of the few non-commuters on campus.

Adams, Rev. Charles—December 13, 1936; man of the cloth/man of clout.

Adams has two pulpits: one at Hartford Memorial Baptist Church, where he serves as pastor to the city's biggest Baptist congregation, and one in the *Michigan Chronicle*, the black weekly where he pens a column. Adams used both as springboards to the presidency of the Detroit NAACP in the mid-1980s. There, he hit the front pages leading a boycott of Dearborn businesses after outsiders were banned from the white suburb's parks. Religion and politics form an important nexus in the black community.

Adams sprang from the womb with a calling. Childhood friends remember him attending church on Sundays, then running home to deliver his own power-packed sermons. Educated at Cass Tech High, Morehouse College, Fiske University, the University of Michigan and Harvard Divinity School, Adams polished his preaching skills at a small church in Boston before returning home in 1969 to run Hartford Memorial, a church which has figured prominently in Detroit history. The Rev. Charles Hill, Adams' predecessor, ran Hartford Memorial for 46 years and was an important figure in forging links between the United Auto Workers and the city's black community. Adams inherited the clout. *Mayor Young* pays attention to Adams, checking with him on occasion before making important moves.

A closet opera singer, Rev. Adams can negotiate Verdi's "Aida" with no trouble whatsoever.

Adams, Tom—September 16, 1919; retired but not forgotten.

Before he retired as chairman of Marshalk Campbell-Ewald (now Lintas: Campbell-Ewald) in 1984, Adams was in charge of Detroit's largest ad agency. But his active civic life made him a towering figure among the town's power brokers. He was, for instance, a member of the Wayne State University board of governors and chaired the Wayne County Stadium Authority, which tried—and failed—to have a stadium built near downtown Detroit.

As a student at WSU, Adams was a star halfback and track man. He worked out with the Chicago Cardinals football team, but World War II interrupted a promising gridiron career. During the war, Adams was a torpedo bomber pilot, flying 111 missions in the South Pacific. He caught on with Campbell-Ewald after the war, rising to the presidency in 1958 at the age of 38. There, he was part of the team that created the "See the U.S.A. in your Chevrolet" campaign.

Although he's retired, he still has plenty of fans around town.

Albom, Mitch—May 23, 1958; Free Press sports superstar.

He's the lead columnist on the *Freep* sports pages, and perhaps the highest paid writer at the newspaper. Albom's meanderings on WLLZ-FM's morning show, his constant television appearances and his book ("The Live Albom") make him a mini-conglomerate.

Free Press executives went into a funk when star sports columnist Mike Downey left for the *L.A. Times* in 1985. The *Freep* played the story the way they would have played the death of, say, Winston Churchill. There were Mike retrospectives and Mike testimonials. Enter Albom, whom the *Free Press* snared from the *Fort Lauderdale News and Sun-Sentinel* and who fits quite nicely in Downey's shoes. Somehow, both the *News* and the *Freep* called him for a job interview within six hours of each other. The *News* paid for the flight up, the *Freep* for the flight back. Each paper coughed up for one of his two nights at the Westin. He chose the *Freep* a couple of weeks later.

Every bit as clever and productive as Downey, Albom was thrice named the country's best sports columnist by the Associated Press sports editors—and is the only writer to win the award more than once. The busy Albom was once seen pounding out a column on a portable computer while being driven to a book-signing appearance. His second book, written with **Bo Schembechler**, was scheduled for publication in the fall of '89.

Like many journalists, he got into newspaper work circuitously. He worked as a piano player and singer across the U.S. and in Europe. When he made his career switch in Florida he was not an instant writing star, but did earn a reputation as a wordsmith. And the *Freep* needed somebody clever and young—somebody who wouldn't mind being on the road most of the year.

It's a shame Albom can't enjoy himself more. He's on the road so much that it is said his two roommates require him to show ID on his rare trips back home to Farmington Hills.

Aldridge, Stan—December 21, 1938; hooked on golf.

This Bloomfield Hills industrialist bought Lake Orion's Indianwood golf course in 1981. "When I got into this, I thought I'd fix the place up and sell it," says Aldridge. "Eight years and several million dollars later, I'm still fixing." The place is now so spiffy that it hosted the U.S. Women's Open in 1989.

Aldridge is the perfect example of low-key rich guy. For the record, not all rich folks flaunt their wealth. Some—such as Aldridge—are mortified by even the smallest amount of personal publicity. The only time he made the newspapers (other than his purchase of Indianwood) was when he was named as a possible buyer of the Detroit Red Wings in the early '80s.

Those close to him marvel that a man who is a self-professed horrible golfer can have such a deft touch for golf course architecture. That may be because he has enough sense and restraint to hire the best experts, give them the resources to do the job and insist only that they produce the best. So far, that's what they've done. In a golf-savvy area, Aldridge's Indianwood is drawing raves as a true world-class club with 36 of the most beautiful and heart-breaking holes anywhere. Aldridge just listens to the applause and looks for something that needs fixing.

Anderson, Sparky—February 22, 1934; Detroit Tigers skipper.

When he's on the air with *George* and *Al,* it's like detention room at grammar school. But baseball managers and announcers aren't paid to talk like Oxford dons.

It would be stretching it a bit to rate Sparky Anderson as a mediocre baseball player. He wasn't that good. Of his 11 seasons on the field from 1953 to 1963, only one was spent with a major league club—the 1959 Philadelphia Phillies, for whom he batted .218. That earned him a speedy return to the minors, where he swatted at curve balls another four seasons before turning to coaching in 1964. His five years as a minor league manager sent him to one hot spot, Toronto, and such mere spots as Rock Hill, St. Petersburg, Modesto, and Asheville.

Once he broke into major league managing, Sparky enjoyed untrammeled success: He took the Cincinnati Reds to the World Series during his rookie year in 1970. Anderson lost that one. But there were three more World Series appearances in the next six years, with back-to-back victories in 1975 and '76. The Reds held first place in five of Sparky's first seven seasons. However, even when George Steinbrenner isn't your owner, it's easy to get fired. After sweeping the Series in 1976, the club landed in second place for two consecutive years. Gak!!! Captain Hook got the hook. When the 1979 season began, the Tigers gave Les Moss his first and last shot at managing. Barely out of the gate, he was fired by Tigers president *Jim Campbell* to make room for Sparky.

Everybody knows the story from there: A World Series victory in 1984, a dramatic run to the playoffs in 1987 and a startling departure in May 1989 to recover from exhaustion. At times, it seems that Sparky—not any of his players—is the star of the team. If he sticks around beyond 1992, he'll beat Hughie Jennings' record (1907 through 1920) as the longest-running Tigers manager.

Andrews, Edward F. "Punch" Jr.—(birthdate not available); rocker *Bob Seger*'s keeper.

This rock and roll hustler has managed Seger for two decades. The two met when Punch was booking frat parties at the University of Michigan. The enduring relationship has provided Andrews with enough income for a home on Cass Lake and cash for some heavy real estate investments.

The son of a produce company owner, Andrews learned the work ethic loading fruit on the docks. Says one insider: "He's hot-tempered. But he's very loyal to his early supporters—especially the Nederlanders. That's why you always see a Pine Knob concert from Seger."

Antonini, Joseph—July 13, 1941; the finger on the button of the blue light special.

Joe Antonini runs Troy-based K mart, the world's second-largest retailer. Trailing only Sears in sales, he has a lot to do with how Middle America dresses, what it reads, even what it eats. As chairman, he'll take K mart into the '90s as it tries to wipe out Sears' lead and ward off smart interlopers like Wal-mart.

If there is a biochemical laboratory somewhere that creates K mart execs, Antonini is a product. K mart's corporate culture resembles General Motors'. Executives move from store to store in hopes of taking that extra step up the ladder. Like most top K mart executives, Antonini worked his way up by moving goods on the store floor. Educated at West Virginia University, he started out as a stock boy in Uniontown, Pennsylvania. Nineteen years later he was running K mart's apparel unit, which accounts for about 20 cents of every $1 in sales.

What broke him from the pack was his ability to attack headquarters' central problem. "K mart" had become a synonym for "cheap." He persuaded former Charlie's Angel Jaclyn Smith to lend her name to a fancy new K mart clothing line. And suddenly, K mart shed its synonym. "What the Mustang was to Lee Iacocca," says retail consultant *Fred Marx*, "the Jaclyn Smith line was to Joe Antonini." He was named president in 1986, and chairman the following year.

Analysts credit him with breathing some energy and creativity into the company's marketing. "Before, you might see a K mart circular with maybe a dozen unrelated items advertised on the first page. They'd worry about how much they could get for a jar of peanuts," says Marx. "Now, everything they do seems to be part of a theme. Like 'Back to School' or some such thing. It's very shrewd, and it's all Joe."

Antonini's latest five-year plan envisions K mart overtaking Sears in 1991. His effervescence has made him something of a favorite in Detroit power circles. Unlike the faint of heart who lift a drink at society bashes and leave once the program starts, Antonini feels it's his duty to stay to the end. "It's like he's a Boy Scout," says one observer. He was named to the National Bank of Detroit's board in 1988, which is a sign of having really made it in Detroit. His salary is anything but "K mart." His salary was $925,000 in 1988.

Antoniotti, Steve—September 20, 1947; Channel 2 clean-up man.

Gillett Broadcasting imported this bearded wonder to make sense of the mess left behind by Channel 2's old owners, Storer Broadcasting. The problem was that former general manager Bill Flynn, the George Steinbrenner of Detroit broadcast journalism, had fired the old pros and replaced them with a passel of plastic people from Keokuk. Unfortunately for Storer, Detroit has a preference for the down-home bar fighter image personified by *Bill Bonds*. Ratings plunged. This was not a good situation for Gillett, which bought the station in 1987. What to do?

Antoniotti, who joined the station as a vice-president in 1988, did a lot: He had a hand in hiring roguish sportscaster *Eli Zaret*, who had been stranded at WABC-TV in New York after a successful career at Channel 4 in Detroit; rehired anchorman *Joe Glover*, who had been among Flynn's first sackings; picked up anchorwoman/reporter

Dayna Eubanks, who had been dumped unceremoniously by Channel 7; and fired news director Chris Sloat, who had been a Flynn hire. Whether this will work is anybody's guess. It may take a year or two to tell. If it works, Antoniotti will become famous. If it doesn't, Antoniotti will take his show on the road, as he has done many times before.

Channel 2 is Antoniotti's seventh television station—eighth if you include a previous tour at Channel 2. But nobody can accuse him of lacking Detroit-area roots. After graduating from the University of Michigan (BA 1969, MA 1972) he held producer jobs at Channels 4 and 2 before jumping to Channel 7 as an executive producer. Then he did a decade as a broadcast gypsy. From Channel 7 he headed east to New York City, where he served as an assistant news director at WABC-TV, ABC's flagship station; west to Oklahoma City, where he was news director at KTVY; farther west to Los Angeles, where he served as news director at KNBC; then back east as news director at the NBC affiliate in St. Louis, where he got the call from Gillett.

With his extensive news credentials, Antoniotti would seem to be what Gillett needs right now. A station's news department can bring prestige and millions to its owners—if the ratings are there. All seem in short supply right now. He is straightforward, often answers his own telephone, and is remarkably short on arrogance.

Applebaum, Eugene—November 16, 1936; prescription for success.

This Wayne State University grad founded Arbor Drugs Inc. (the second-largest drugstore chain in the area) in 1963, only three years after winning his pharmacist license. Arbor now has about 84 stores, with each shop bailing in an average of $3-million. That's a lot of aspirin, toilet paper and shoe polish.

Arbor went public in 1986, but Applebaum still owns more than 60 percent of the shares—which makes him very much the master of his own destiny. A good share of destiny also goes to Arbor executive v.p. Markus Ernst, an Applebaum compatriot for more than two decades. Ernst owns about 10 percent of the company for his loyalty.

Archer, Dennis—January 1, 1942; Michigan Supreme Court justice/ retired political maven/future Detroit mayor?

Justice Dennis Archer works a room like an artist works a canvas. He never forgets a name. He has a firm handshake and a few minutes of sincere chat for everyone. The man has accumulated virtually no enemies, but has filled a bag with chits from a lifetime of doing favors and running other candidates' campaigns. *Coleman Young* won't live forever.

The son of an odd-jobs man, Archer attended Western Michigan University. He tutored slow learners in Detroit Public Schools before realizing that it might get him to heaven, but the earthly rewards were a little thin—a thought that sent him to night school at the Detroit College of Law. DCL degree in hand, he moonlighted as a political campaign manager, piloting the late Ed Bell's unsuccessful run for mayor in 1973. Confident of victory over then-state Sen. Coleman Young even before the primary, young Archer sought a meeting with Young's campaign manager, Bob Millender. An old pro who had godfathered victories for many black politicians, Millender must have been amused by the téte-a-téte: Archer, the young upstart, told Millender there'd be a job for Young in the Bell administration if only Young would admit the obvious and drop out. Tsk tsk. Archer's exile didn't last long. He was in sufficiently good odor to run the mayor's 1977 campaign.

When he wasn't dabbling in politics, Archer made a wad of cash working with superlawyer *Larry Charfoos*'s downtown firm. Other attorneys said they'd never mistake Archer for F. Lee Bailey, but found him very likable. Also a dabbler in bar associations (president of the State Bar of Michigan, Wolverine and National bar associations), Archer's appointment to the high court was no surprise when Governor *James Blanchard* filled a vacancy in 1986. Archer's campaign later that year to retain his seat was the first time his name had ever been on a ballot. He will remain berobed as long as he wishes.

Avis, Warren—(birthdate not available); rental car patriarch.

The man who put rent-a-car booths in airports around the world still lives near Ann Arbor. In his 70s, he has become a philosopher/ businessman, running his potpourri of interests from a 300-acre farm and giving advice to would-be zillionaires in books like "Take a Chance to Be First." An interesting title from a man who got rich as No. 2.

Avis cooked up his hot idea when he was an Air Force bomber pilot during World War II. He started his rental car firm at Ypsilanti's Willow Run Airport, and then in Miami, with $10,000 of his own money and a borrowed $75,000. Hertz laughed at the idea of renting cars beside the runway, but was soon forced to run through a lot of airports. Avis took the pile of money he made when he sold out in 1954 and became a business gunslinger—buying into whatever seemed like a good idea at the time.

His credo: "It's best never to take a naysayer's word at face value . . . if you're willing to say yes instead of no—to believe that all things are possible and that nothing is impossible—you'll be amazed at the fortunes and adventures that are waiting to reward a positive attitude."

When he's not in Ann Arbor, he can be found in homes in New York City or at his cliffside villa in Acapulco. As the man says, there are rewards for a positive attitude.

B

Baier, George—October 13, 1956; WLLZ-FM's man of many voices.

Another local boy made good in Detroit radio. His Dick the Bruiser, *Al Kaline*, Popeye and *George Kell* send-ups have made Baier and straight man *Jim Johnson* the longest-running comedy duo on the dial. A little more raw than WCZY-FM's *Dick Purtan*, Baier and Johnson have provided some wildly clever local satire for a decade—five lifetimes in the radio business. A five-year contract they signed in 1988 will make Baier one of the few on-air radio personalities to have spanned the '70s, '80s and '90s.

A 1974 graduate of East Detroit High School, Baier began his career at Wayne State University's WAYN, which can be heard only as far as the student cafeteria. He earned his tuition and spending money pumping gas at a Sunoco station at Outer Drive and Van Dyke. Somehow, Baier found enough time to drop by for a few minutes during WWWW-FM deejay Steve Dahl's morning show. Dahl, knowing a radio genius when he heard one, asked Baier to switch stations—from Sunoco to W4. Baier's raw-voiced Bruiser imitation was an instant hit. When Dahl left for big bucks in Chicago, WWWW-FM program director Johnson stepped in as the smooth-voiced foil. They've been together ever since, with Baier providing an ever-expanding cast of characters. Baier never did finish his formal education.

His power in the business can be illustrated by what happened after he and Johnson left WRIF-FM, where they went in 1979 after quitting WWWW-FM. WRIF managers foolishly ignored the duo during contract time in 1985. The two left for WLLZ-FM, taking their listeners with them. WRIF has tried several combos since then, but the station remains invisible in the top 10 morning ratings.

Baier's life is more like his listeners' than they would ever imagine. Unlike Johnson, he assiduously avoids life in the fast lane. He married a St. Clair Shores girl in 1985, and spends quiet nights in front of a television set. "Maybe I'm one of the few people in media who's had only one wife," he says. He's proud of the fact that most of his salary, rumored to approach $200,000, goes right into a savings account. He's smart enough to realize these things don't last forever.

Baker, Anita—January 26, 1958; Detroit's newest hitmaker.

This diminutive songstress has been on the cover of *Rolling Stone* magazine twice and on NBC-TV's "Saturday Night Live." She has been compared to legend Dinah Washington, and was a constant presence on *Billboard*'s charts from 1986 until this writing. "Giving You the Best That I Got" hit No. 1, which—as far as we know—makes her the only person in Grosse Pointe who can claim such an honor.

A Toledo native who moved with her family when she was still in diapers, she is the youngest of seven children. A graduate of Central High School, she knocked around town with the 10-piece funk band, Chapter 8. It enjoyed small success, but failed to attract national attention. Baker retired to a job as a receptionist for a Detroit law firm, which—dull though it was—provided Blue Cross and paid vacations. An L.A. record company had to do some heavy lobbying to convince her to abandon her fringe benefits. The results can be found in "The Songstress," released in 1982. A legal wrangle with her record label (Ariola) put her on the sidelines for three years. Elektra Records signed her, braved the lawsuits and had her record "Rapture" (1986).

"Rapture," with the single "Sweet Love," put her husky, distinctive voice on the nation's radio stations and earned her two

Grammys. She followed that up with "Giving You the Best That I've Got" in 1988.

Bannon, James—June 9, 1928; Ph.D. (police have degrees).

Bannon, No. 2 in the Detroit Police Department, is cut from a different cloth. He has a doctorate in philosophy from Wayne State University, shows up on newspaper "best-dressed" lists and attends Tom Schoenith's parties. The circumstantial evidence points to hot-dogging, but his 34 departmental citations (including the Distinguished Medal of Valor) indicate otherwise.

An Indiana native, he grew up in Pontiac, dropped out of high school to fight in World War II, then joined the Detroit Police Department at age 21. As a cop, he earned a never-ending shower of awards, some gained after shoot-outs with bad guys. During the '60s, it appeared he might land in the chief's chair. But *Mayor Young* made Philip Tannian king at 1300 Beaubien, and Bannon's career was sidetracked. At one point, Bannon had been relegated to the relatively peaceful Second (Vernor) precinct to keep him away from the seat of power.

When Young fired Tannian in 1976, Bannon was in line for the No. 1 job. Bannon's team-player demeanor in the ensuing years as No. 2 to *William Hart* bespeaks mucho class.

Barden, Don—December 20, 1943; Detroit cable commissar.

Barden's company is wiring Detroit. Finally. Suburban residents had been enjoying their HBO and ignoring their C-SPAN for years before *Mayor Young* finally chose Barden's firm for the job in 1983. The deal looked as if it might unravel several times, but Barden's trucks were up and wiring in the late '80s.

A 1962 graduate of Inkster High School, Barden attended Central State University in Wilberforce, Ohio, with $600 raised from relatives. He started out in the mailroom at American Shipbuilding Co. in Lorain, Ohio, eventually befriending the boss, New York Yankees owner George Steinbrenner. His resumé notes that he spent a decade and a half as a newsman, politician and developer in northern Ohio before he returned home to the Detroit area in the early 1980s as a would-be cable entrepreneur. Romulus, Inkster and Van Buren Township all signed with Barden before he landed the big enchilada of cabledom—Detroit. The deal makes it superfluous to note that Barden Cable is the largest black-owned system in the United States, because it is also the largest single-city system, period.

Bidding on the Detroit award was fierce. Some of Barden's early investors were Dennis Silber, a generous contributor to the mayor's campaigns; Karl Varner, a Detroit architect; and Nansi Rowe, who once ran the city of Detroit Law Department. Two competing groups had their own list of power brokers. The late Ed Bell, one competitor, even brought in actress Jayne Kennedy for a show-and-tell session. When Young finally chose Barden, the decision was challenged in federal court. The two losing firms charged that Barden's financing was non-existent. Judge Ralph Guy Jr. concluded that the other two firms weren't exactly rolling in dough, either, and pointed out that voters could deal with their elected officials if Barden flopped.

Now that Barden has the franchise, he seems to be a bona fide member of the city hall power set. He cemented his ties to Young's administration with his marriage to city finance chief *Bella Marshall* in 1988. They reside in a $300,000-plus home on the edge of the Detroit Golf Club.

Barnes, Ortheia—October 23, 1944; a bridesmaid with major talent.

A lot of people don't know it, but she's one of Detroit's best singers. Always on the edge of just making it, she's had a critically acclaimed LP with "Person to Person" and has opened for the likes of Ray Charles, *Aretha Franklin*, *Stevie Wonder* and Harold Melvin and the Blue Notes. She even sang for the pope when he visited Detroit.

A 1962 graduate of Cass Tech, she studied for a different kind of record business—medical records. Inspired by her brother, J.J., who had a hit record with "Baby, Please Come Back Home," Ortheia thought she'd give the music business a shot.

She's been close. "Without Your Love," a song she recorded with the group Cut Glass, did reasonably well on the disco charts. But disco died, and the group was never heard from again. She has toured with Motown's Edwin Starr, and starred in her one-woman show, "La Diva." Barnes' voice has earned her a cult following. But it hasn't gotten her around the country. Too bad for music fans.

Barrow, Tom—January 12, 1949; would-be mayor.

He's living proof of the ephemeral nature of the political life. When this book was begun, Barrow was riding high as a likely challenger to *Mayor Young* in 1989. By the time we headed for print, the news media—which gaveth—had started to do some serious taking away. Early in '89, newspaper polls showed Barrow hot on Young's trail among voters. Then stories appeared questioning his financial relationship with New Center Hospital, and the papers dragged out new polls showing Barrow's popularity headed south. By the time you read this, he may be in obscurity—or in Manoogian Mansion. Such is politics.

Barrow is a nephew of the late boxer Joe Louis, and a graduate of Wayne State University.

Baskin, Henry—Fiftysomething; quintessential Oakland County legal gun.

He's the man to see if you want a divorce, or a big-time media contract. *Lee Iacocca*, who could have afforded F. Lee Bailey, used the firm of Baskin & Feldstein for his divorce. On the media side, Baskin was TV anchorman *Joe Glover*'s point man when Glover made his move from California back to Detroit in 1988. The Oakland County Bar Association crowned Baskin its president in 1988. He moves and talks like a Hollywood agent. Telephone calls from his office often begin with: "Hey Baby." He is a favorite of local columnists, particularly the *Free Press*'s *Bob Talbert*, because he is so well connected and so quotable. Divorced himself, he was also considered one of the Birmingham area's most sought-after bachelors for a time.

Baskin, a Wayne State University Law School graduate, started out like many attorneys: grubbing for criminal cases in Detroit Recorder's Court, probably the best place in Michigan—maybe the United States—to hone trial skills. Baskin learned his lessons well; some of the old-timers there still remember Baskin 20 years later as a savvy practitioner. But while Recorder's Court is a great place to learn, it's not a place to get really rich. Baskin, an astute student of where the money is, learned what he could learn and worked his way into the lucrative Oakland County divorce trade. He didn't become known for his divorce work during the '70s, however, as much as for his representation of the area's radio and television talent. Dr. Sonya

Friedman, Channel 7's Jerry Hodak and WCZY-FM's *Dick Purtan* all had Baskin deal with their respective managements.

Many a soon-to-be uncoupled spouse has made his or her way to Baskin's office, though it's not always husbands and wives who have used Baskin when they're splitsville. Jerry Schoenith, twin brother of social butterfly Tom Schoenith, hired Baskin to untangle his fortune from his brother's. Into his 50s, Baskin likely will keep his name in prominence for a long time to come. And his daughter, Dana, is practicing with her father's firm.

Battenberg, J.T., III—April 25, 1943; Buick-Oldsmobile-Cadillac Boss-Oligarch-Captain.

He's in charge of building and designing Buicks, Oldsmobiles and Cadillacs, the third B-O-C chieftain (GM president *Robert Stempel* and executive v.p. *William Hoglund* were the other two) since General Motors announced its reorganization in 1984.

A product of General Motors Institute in Flint, he made the rounds of GM's plant system throughout the '70s. He touched down in no less than six cities (Kansas City; St. Louis; Doraville, Georgia; Arlington, Texas; Tarrytown, New York; and Detroit) during those years, working at three plants in three years (1977-'79). Somewhere in there he expanded his intellectual horizons with an MBA from Columbia University, and did Harvard's advanced management program. He acquired a world view with assignments in Belgium and England before being named to oversee the company's Flint product team. It was there he captained the company's $200-million Buick City project, which had been having quality problems. He apparently fixed them to GM's satisfaction, because he was brought back to Detroit (actually Warren, where B-O-C is headquartered) to run the show there in 1988.

Beckmann, Frank—November 3, 1949; sportswrapper.

Beckmann's nighttime sports talk show on WJR is the outlet for fans who like hearing their voices over 50,000 watts. Of course, that doesn't make them any smarter than when their voices reached only to the end of the bar. But Beckmann's show is certainly a healthy escape valve for frustrated fans.

An east side native, Beckmann attended Detroit's Osborn High School, then graduated from Warren Cousino High School. "Some guys wanted to be lawyers," he recalls, "some guys wanted to be rock stars, I wanted to be a sportscaster." He made the rounds at stations in Alpena, Pontiac and Detroit (WKNR, WDRQ, and Channel 2 "for about two weeks") before signing up at 'JR in 1972. He became the station's sports director in 1979.

Beckmann was the voice of the Detroit Lions before they left for WWJ in 1989. That diminishes his clout somewhat.

Belgrave, Marcus—June 12, 1936; man with a horn.

Like most local jazz musicians, he receives more acclaim outside metro Detroit than in. This trumpet/flugelhorn player has worked with Ray Charles, Sammy Davis Jr., Ella Fitzgerald, Charles Mingus and Max Roach. When we tried to reach him for this profile he was doing a two-month gig in Indonesia. It's nice to have a distinctive talent and a distinctive first name. If you want to talk about him with anyone who knows jazz, just say "Marcus."

Belitsos, Michael—August 4, 1951; rising advertising star.

Detroit Monthly included this man-about-town on its list of folks who will run the town's ad community during the 1990s. A 1969 graduate of Grosse Pointe South High School, he wandered after picking up an English lit degree at the University of Michigan. He taught school in Australia—before Crocodile Dundee was hatched—and played flute with the band at the Money Tree. "Some of my friends were in the advertising business, and they would drop by the restaurant to talk shop," Beltisos told *Detroit Monthly*. "I started thinking, 'Hey, I could do that.' "

He certainly does know how to do it. Once he got himself into gear, Belitsos went into overdrive: He spent time at W.B. Doner, Saatchi & Saatchi, McCann-Erickson and J. Walter Thompson before landing his current job as creative chief with Southfield's Campbell-Mithun-Esty agency in early 1988. He oversees the material in Chrysler's Jeep ads, using the twin insights of writer and musician. Belitsos lives with his wife, Terry, also an advertising whiz, in a stunning Grosse Pointe home.

Bell, Norma Jean—(birthdate not available); lady sings—and plays—the blues.

This Chadsey High grad can sing. She can play the piano. But what she can really do is play the saxophone. *Stevie Wonder* and Frank Zappa have had her on their payroll. Nowadays, she runs her own band, which features an energetic mix of urban funk and urban sophistication. Remember those Channel 7 promo ads, "Tell 'em you're from Detroit?" That's Norma Jean Bell singing and playing. No, she didn't get a chance to solo in that commercial, most likely because she'd make *Bill Bonds'* weave stand on end.

Beltaire, Beverly—August 21, 1926; public relations doyenne.

This enterprising PR woman has the social skills of a Pearl Mesta, the chutzpah of a fighter pilot, and the connections of a Henry Kissinger. She used all three to make her company, Detroit-based P/R Associates, one of the area's most successful flacking outfits. Some of her clients have included DuPont, WDIV-TV, Fruehauf and WJR-AM.

A wartime reporter for the *Free Press*, she broke into the PR business when women were an oddity. Her first work station was a rented desk in a telephone-answering firm. She once told a reporter that she made it because she wasn't afraid to take chances. "I don't know how to impress that on people nowadays," she said, "but it really is important if you're going to get your career moving." Part of her attraction is her ability to make anyone feel at ease. Another factor is her honesty. She won't take an account unless she believes in what she's selling. As a result, people believe her, and her list of friends is voluminous. Anybody who tangles with her does so at his own peril.

People have been known to crash Beltaire's office with a demand: "Make me famous." Unless she's impressed with the quality of the person, the answer is "no." She is married to retired *Free Press* columnist Mark Beltaire, the Town Crier whom village elders will recall on the back page side-by-side with Judd Arnett.

Benkert, Bob—August 27, 1939; Birmingham clothier.

The new money in Birmingham/Bloomfield Hills, ever insecure in their newly minted wealth, strives mightily to look like old English landed gentry. Bob Benkert, who owns Birmingham's Claymore shops and Ralph Lauren/Polo outlets, collects money from the nouveau riche trying to look like old cash.

A Grosse Pointe native, Benkert was trained at Wayne State University as an accountant. He went from behind the books to behind a sales counter when he opened the Claymore Shop in downtown Birmingham in 1966. He followed with a Polo shop in 1984, then moved north a few blocks with a bigger location in 1989. Benkert dresses in earth tones and suspenders and collects fine wines as a hobby. We hesitate to say he looks like something out of the pages of GQ. We hesitate, then we say it anyhow. Because he does.

Benton, Philip Jr.—December 31, 1928; Ford Motor Co. auto chieftain.

Benton has done just about everything there is to do at Ford, short of working the line. These days he's chief of the Ford automotive group.

A Dartmouth graduate, he joined the company in 1953 as a cost analyst. Subsequent stops included Ford's chemical products division, the parts and service unit, Europe for a couple of years as the truck titan, the Ford division as general manager, and sales vice-president for North American operations. International operations is where Benton made his mark.

With such a variety of experience, some people at the Glass House think Benton could rise another rung. It isn't lost on anybody that the last two jobs *Don Petersen* held before becoming president were diversified products and executive v.p. in charge of international operations—two jobs Benton has held. Even if he doesn't rise, Benton is still a force. He's on the board's most important committee, finance. He and his wife, Maryann, hosted opera superstar Luciano Pavarotti when he swung through town in the summer of 1988.

Berg, Bob—(birthdate not available); Detroit mayoral mouthpiece.

Mayor *Coleman Young*'s press secretary is the gatekeeper in an administration that dispenses information as guardedly as the pre-Gorbachev Kremlin. Nobody at city hall has ever been fired for not talking to a reporter. The tone is set at the top. Young considers reporters to be necessary nuisances around the City-County Building, and Berg is forced to deal with the media riffraff. He can be extraordinarily helpful, or mildly obstreperous. Whether or not the mayor heeds his counsel is an open question.

Berg's early news experience was gained at United Press International, the journalistic equivalent of a sweatshop. Raised on a farm in mid-Illinois, he joined UPI after studying at Illinois Wesleyan University and the University of Stockholm. Berg did three years in the Des Moines and Lincoln bureaus before becoming UPI Lansing bureau chief in 1969. After four years in that job, and another four as chief of Panax Newspapers' capital bureau, he became Governor Milliken's press secretary. Mayor Young picked him up after Milliken left office in early 1983. He has been Young's press secretary longer than any of his predecessors—a remarkable feat considering the amount of flak Berg has to dodge from both inside and outside the City-County Building.

Berg's job is both easy and difficult. Where most pols are generally accessible but don't say much of importance, Young is the opposite: generally inaccessible but extraordinarily quotable when he does deign to speak. Berg has only one person to please—the mayor. As long as Berg does that, he can keep his job.

Betti, John—January 6, 1931; Ford's executive v.p. in charge of earth and sky.

He runs the company's diversified products operations. That's most of the stuff that doesn't get around on wheels: satellites (from Ford Aerospace); hotels (Ford Land Development, which includes Ford's Fairlane project—more than $1 billion worth of land and buildings); and, at one time, a Brazilian manufacturer of television sets and VCRs.

An engineer by training, Betti (pronounced Betty) has made a lot of stops since his Ford career began. He has been in charge of product development for Ford of Europe and has run the company's power train and chassis operations. Immediately before landing his current job in early 1988, he presided over the company's technical affairs and operating staffs. That was a big job: He spent his days anticipating what the consumer might want, what the government might require in the way of safety, and how to reconcile the two. He was awarded a seat on Ford's board in 1985. Said to be a personal favorite of Ford vice-chairman *Red Poling*, he is another possibility for the Ford presidency.

When he's not pondering his life at the Glass House, Betti involves himself in cultural affairs and charity. He serves on the board of Michigan Opera Theatre, and in 1986 was the United Foundation's Torch Drive general chairman, a job reserved for heavy corporate shooters.

Bidwell, Ben—June 22, 1927; head Chrysler hawker.

Another lieutenant in *Lee Iacocca*'s Ford mafia at Chrysler. When Chrysler needs to trot out an executive who is funny and colorful, Bidwell gets the nod. One Ford official described him to the *Free Press* as a "totally refreshing, candid, straightforward kind of guy." He's hell on the golf course and tennis court, and something of a favorite at local charity events. Chrysler's sales, marketing, and public affairs staffs all report to Bidwell, now a co-president.

Before joining Chrysler in 1983, Bidwell spent 27 years at Ford and two years at Hertz Corp., where he was president and chief executive officer. Iacocca and Bidwell were contemporaries at Ford in the 1950s, though not necessarily friends. Bidwell worked the Ford division's sales office in Boston, while Iacocca worked out of Philadelphia. Under Iacocca's Ford presidency, Bidwell ran the company's Lincoln-Mercury division (1970-'73) and Ford division (1973-'75) before riding to a group vice-presidency at the Glass House, Ford headquarters. Some thought Bidwell would run the place eventually, but RCA Corp. (Hertz's owner) snagged him in time for a palace revolution. The car rental concern was put on the block about the time Bidwell got there. When Iacocca called to offer Bidwell a job at Chrysler, Bidwell was on the next plane out.

Old pals threw a "welcome back" party at the Bloomfield Hills Country Club. "Well, Ben," chided his chum, *J.P. McCarthy*, "you can't sell 'em and you can't rent 'em. What are you doing back in Detroit?"

Bieber, Owen—December 28, 1929; Solidarity House sultan.

He's one of the few guys in town who can make *Roger Smith* flinch. Smith may rule an empire, but the president of the million-member

United Auto Workers can lead Smith's serfs into revolt at the flick of a strike vote.

A native of North Dorr, outside Grand Rapids, Bieber worked the line twisting heavy-gauge wire for automobile seats. Most of his union experience was gained serving workers in western Michigan and the Upper Peninsula. That made him something of a stranger when he was called upon to run the UAW's GM department in 1980.

The first modern-day UAW president who was not one of Walter Reuther's boys, he got the top job in June 1983. The UAW executive board almost chose Raymond Majerus, who died in late 1987. The *New York Times* said Bieber won the job by quiet restraint—"a good example of how it is possible to win while playing by the rules."

He doesn't have the intellectual firepower of former president Leonard Woodcock, who went on to be President Carter's envoy to China. And he doesn't have the charisma of Doug Fraser, his predecessor. Some members criticize the union for going into partnership with the auto companies. Others think there is no sense talking like a Wobblie if the golden goose shows signs of being cooked. Bieber is stuck mediating between these points of view.

Assuming he keeps his job until 1995, Bieber will have led the UAW longer than anyone except Reuther, who ran the outfit from 1946 until his death in 1970.

Bing, Dave—November 29, 1943; jock-turned-businessman.

A prominent name in "Life After *Coleman Young*" speculation. Famous for his All-Star basketball abilities as a Detroit Piston from 1966 through 1975, his life didn't end with the applause. Instead, Bing went out and made himself a bundle in the steel business. What do you get when you have a well-known, highly respected name who also knows how to make money? A formidable mayoral candidate, should he ever decide to go for it.

Bing was the *Isiah Thomas* of his era, dominating the Detroit Pistons from the time he hit town as a rookie from Syracuse University in 1966-'67 until he left for the Washington Bullets in 1975. After finishing his career with the Boston Celtics in 1977-'78, he was back in town. Off seasons had been spent learning business at the National Bank of Detroit or Chrysler Corp. Ron Kramer, a retired U-M and Packers great, helped Bing get into steel. His company now supplies the stuff to the Big Three.

The important thing to know about Bing is that he can play at anybody's poker table—and he brings his own chips. He can tell a ghetto kid to say no, or a Big Three purchasing agent to say yes.

Birkerts, Gunnar—January 17, 1925; national treasure, local secret.

Architect Gunnar Birkerts' national reputation far outstrips his local prominence. He has been feted by the American Academy and Institute of Arts and Letters as "one of the most talented architects in this country today" and named one of America's top 10 architects by the deans of major architectural schools. Birkerts designed the IBM Building, an unusual and effective high-rise at the corner of the Southfield Freeway and Nine Mile Road; downtown Detroit's 1300 Lafayette Building; and the University of Michigan Law School's underground library. Still, it seems that only *Tom Monaghan* realizes we have a genius in our midst.

Born in Latvia, Birkerts arrived in Detroit from Europe via New York and Greyhound bus in the late 1940s—the time of the city's post-war creative boom. He worked with the legendary Eero Saarinen and later Minoru Yamasaki before forming his own firm in 1959. The hallmark of Birkerts' architecture is the creative use of technology. The windows in IBM's Southfield building look like slits, but are covered with material that disperses light inside. The design allows workers to get plenty of sunshine while saving IBM a bundle of money.

So why doesn't he strike out for New York, where he would undoubtedly be a star? He told the *Free Press'* Marsha Miro: "I like it here because it's peaceful, because I'm not exposed to the warfare and cannibalism that goes on on the coasts." He lets his buildings do the talking.

Blaha, George—March 29, 1944; the voice of the Pistons.

When the Detroit Pistons were a lousy basketball team, George Blaha could shout all he wanted and still travel in anonymity. But the team is hot, and Blaha has become a hot item. "People are on him like crazy," reports Harry Hutt, the Pistons broadcast chieftain who produces Blaha's broadcasts on WWJ-AM and Channel 50.

Plunked down as a boy in the wide-open spaces of Marshalltown, Iowa, Blaha grew up listening at night to greats such as Harry Caray (now of the Chicago Cubs) and Bob Prince, the Pittsburgh Pirates play-by-play man. Although he earned a BA from Notre Dame in economics, followed by an MBA from the University of Michigan, he always had it in his head that he'd do sports play-by-play. "I suppose I got those degrees because most of my family has degrees. My father was a surgeon. I needed that one last piece of paper just in case."

Blaha has created a lugubrious lingo all his own since joining the Pistons in '76: "Joey D is two-timed, hits a triple try off the window!" means Joe Dumars is double teamed, but scores a three-pointer off the backboard nonetheless. The man is nothing if not enthusiastic, which earns him criticism as a homer. There are worse sins.

Blanchard, James—August 8, 1942; once boy governor, now a mature party power.

Well into his second term, it appears Jim Blanchard will inhabit the governor's mansion as long as he'd like. The Republicans are too busy fighting each other to develop a credible consensus candidate. No Democrat is bold or crazy enough to challenge him. That leaves Blanchard in the governor's office with the question of how he'll occupy himself for perhaps the next 20 years.

After earning two degrees from Michigan State University (BA and MBA) and a law degree from the University of Minnesota, he spent five years as an assistant attorney general. Voters in suburban Detroit rescued him from a dreary life as a bureaucrat. Opportunity came in the form of disgruntled voters in the state's 18th Congressional District, a weird mix of Oakland and Macomb County suburbs. Imagine speaking to people in Oak Park and Sterling Heights in the same day, and you have the picture. As disparate as these two municipalities are, they chose Blanchard over incumbent congressman Robert Huber, who so offended voters with his intense conservatism that they sent him packing, 59 percent to 41 percent. As a lawmaker, Blanchard helped guide the Chrysler aid package through Congress, riding that to the governorship in 1982. He celebrated his 40th birthday as his party's nominee.

Blanchard has a remarkable ability to recover from his mistakes. His tax increase in 1982 caused voters to recall two state senators and give control of the Senate to the Republicans. Even so, he gained re-election only three years later with a record landslide.

Even his divorce from *Paula Blanchard* was handled intelligently and sensitively. It could have been a messy trial, with reporters crawling over each other to get at the divorce file. Instead, the couple split cleanly, depriving reporters of a look at a marriage-gone-awry.

Facing another two decades on the job, what is there to look forward to? The presidency? The U.S. Senate? He says he'll stay put. For awhile.

Blanchard, Paula—November 13, 1944; on her own and thriving.

Yes, there is life after the governor's mansion. For this former first lady, it's a plum public relations post in Southfield.

A native of Clarkston, she met the future governor when both were students at Michigan State University. She taught fourth grade for two years in suburban Minneapolis while her husband attended law school at the University of Minnesota, and taught second grade when they returned to Lansing. As first lady, she saved Detroit's Thanksgiving Day parade from extinction, and also promoted state products and tourism.

Someday a PR guru will write a thesis on how she and her husband handled the press after the break-up of their 21-year marriage. The press, ever eager for juicy details, found none. The necessary papers were filed, a brief statement was issued, and that was that.

These days she occupies herself as an associate vice-president at Southfield's Casey Communications Management Inc., where she oversees video work and conducts communications training for clients. She also gives speeches on women in the workplace.

Their son, Jay, studies at Michigan State University's James Madison College, which trains students for work in government.

Says Paula: "My life has never been better personally or professionally than it is right now."

Bock, Dr. Brooks—September 19, 1943; emergency physician extraordinaire.

If you've been shot or stabbed, he's the man you want to see. Bock is in charge of Detroit Receiving Hospital's Emergency Medicine section, which is generally recognized as one of the best departments of its type in the country. His operation has been blessed by the American College of Surgeons as a "Level I Trauma Center," which means surgeons would go there if they found themselves in need of quick care.

A 1965 Wayne State University graduate, Bock picked up his M.D. from Wayne State University in 1969 and immediately went to work at Detroit General Hospital. There, he picked up the tricks of treating trauma patients. He was president of the American College of Emergency Physicians (1983–'84). He got his job as emergency medicine's Numero Uno in 1985. Bock has even gone as far as Brisbane, Australia to let the Aussies in on his work. The paper he presented: "Antibiotics in Management of Extremity Fractures Resulting from Gunshot Wounds."

Boisvert, Emmanuelle—August 2, 1963; first fiddle.

She leads the Detroit Symphony Orchestra's violin section, making her the first female concertmaster in a major U.S. orchestra.

A Quebec native who began her studies at the age of six, she arrived here in late 1988 from the Cleveland Orchestra, where she sat in the second violin section. While "second fiddle" may not sound stunning on a resumé, that was only a way station to gain some large ensemble experience. Before Cleveland, she worked with the prestigious Concerto Soloists Chamber Orchestra of Philadelphia. Her strengths include incredible technical command and an authoritative sound. Her predecessor, Gordon Staples, said Boisvert plays like somebody much older than she is—very big and self-assured.

There are links between Boisvert and the late Mischa Mischakoff, who reigned as DSO concertmaster from 1952 until 1968, and who was concertmaster of the NBC Orchestra under a fella named Toscanini from 1937 to 1952. Boisvert studied with violinist David Cerone at Philadelphia's Curtis Institute of Music. Cerone studied with Mischakoff. Says Cerone: "Her playing is really impeccable, which is to say that nothing is out of place in all the right ways."

She auditioned behind a screen, so the dozen judges wouldn't be influenced by non-musical factors such as age, sex or race.

Bonds, Bill—February 23, 1933; TV news Rambo.

Everybody has an opinion about Bill Bonds, the Channel 7 anchorman. Some people regard him as the informed watchdog for the little guy. Others regard him as a pompous, opinionated jerk. Whatever their opinion, Detroiters have been watching Bonds in large numbers for years. Wherever he appears, he is adulated. When Bonds showed at the Detroit opening of "Beverly Hills Cop II" in 1987, one would have thought Bonds—not Eddie Murphy—was the star. When Bonds was hospitalized for exhaustion in 1984, it was front-page stuff for the *Free Press*. So was a shoving match he engaged in at the Radisson Plaza Hotel in Southfield one night in early 1988. In a 12-month period in the early '70s, he was punched out by a teenager and busted for drunk driving. One couldn't imagine that happening to Walter Cronkite, but in Detroit it doesn't necessarily hurt.

Raised at Twelfth and Burlingame, Bonds dropped out of high school in 11th grade to join the Air Force. He later obtained his GED, signed on at the University of Detroit, then grubbed his way to the top via a series of radio jobs. Mayor Jerome Cavanagh mentioned the hard-working Bonds to a WXYZ-TV executive on a plane from New York to Detroit. The young radio reporter was hired, and found a home.

So impressed were executives in the ABC owned-and-operated station system that they made him KABC-TV's anchorman in Los Angeles. That didn't work out. When he returned to Detroit in 1971, he picked up where he left off. Detroiters couldn't buy enough Bonds, so he was tapped for anchorwork at WABC-TV in New York. That didn't work, either. Bonds returned to Detroit in 1976 and has, again, reaped remarkable hometown stardom. As much feared as respected around the Channel 7 newsroom, Bonds is a fiery, complex man. He can be merciless with those who offend him. He is equally capable of kindness and generosity.

Channel 4's *Mort Crim* may have a more serious mind. Channel 2's *Joe Glover* may be a nicer guy. But it's Bonds who keeps bringing 'em into the Channel 7 tent, night after night, year after year.

Bonior, David—June 6, 1945; congressman from the east.

His congressional district hugs the edge of Lake St. Clair, northeast of Eight Mile Road all the way up to Port Huron.

Bonior was born into the political maelstrom. His father was a mayor of East Detroit and served on the Macomb County Board of Supervisors. David served a year as a probation officer and an adoption case worker, then spent four years in the Air Force. After turning in his wings, he served as state representative (1973-'76) from southern Macomb County. He even wrote a 1984 book: "The

Vietnam Veteran: A History of Neglect" — which described how society ignored vets of that era.

His Democratic compatriots in Washington have taken a shine to him. House Speaker Jim Wright appointed Bonior chief deputy majority whip. His constituents seem to like him, too, although his last election was unusually close. Bonior's margins of victory in the last three outings have been 58 percent, 66 percent and 54 percent.

Borda, Deborah—July 15, 1949; maestro of the front office.

This is getting to be an old Detroit story: An arts institution gets into trouble and turns to somebody from the Twin Cities (St. Paul/ Minneapolis) to fix up the mess. It happened at the Detroit Institute of Arts in 1985, and it happened at the Detroit Symphony Orchestra three years later. In the DSO's case, Deborah Borda was brought aboard to repair a situation that had become a public embarrassment. The musicians were on strike in open rebellion against DSO president Oleg Lobanov. The checkbook was getting thin, and people just weren't showing up to hear the music. Borda, who signed aboard in the fall of 1988, but took office in early 1989, is supposed to restore harmony and balance the books.

Her career started in 1975 as GM of a small contemporary music group in Boston called Musica Viva, then as GM for the town's Handel and Hayden Society. She did a stint in San Francisco, then landed in Minnesota to run the St. Paul Chamber Orchestra.

Borda was handed two hats when she got here: She was named executive director of the DSO and manager of Orchestra Hall. Which makes her one of the primo arts figures in town.

Borman, Paul—(birthdate not available); sowing and reaping at Farmer Jack.

Greater power hath no man than he who setteth the price of the Charmin. Borman, who ran the Farmer Jack chain of grocery stores until it was bought by A&P in 1989, decided not only how much the Charmin would cost, but how far one had to drive to get it. Having a Farmer Jack nearby practically guaranteed a neighborhood's viability. Now that Borman's empire has been gobbled up by A&P, Borman won't have direct control. But judging by how much A&P will pay Borman over 10 years—at least $600,000 annually—it's clear they'll listen to him. And, significantly, the Farmer Jack name will remain on the stores.

Many big businesses have humble beginnings, but Farmer Jack's genesis was unusually so. Borman's father, Abraham, started Tom's Quality Market in Detroit in 1927. The younger Borman started as a teenaged stockboy. By the time young Paul was 32, he was in charge of the entire business. Even after going public, Farmer Jack remained in the family's control.

Ah, but things became unraveled. The company lost $28-million in 1987. It also lost money in two of the four preceding years. The clerks walked out for a week in August 1987. A decision to buy 60 Safeway supermarkets in Utah for $70-million in April 1987 turned out to be fatal. What works in Detroit doesn't necessarily work among the Mormons. Even hiring one of the singing Osmond Brothers as a spokesman didn't help. Within a year, Borman decided to sell. Farmer Jack's price was $76-million.

Working for somebody else won't be bad for this former mogul. He got his 10-year deal and the family got almost $16-million. That's a lot of Charmin. And it'll allow him to continue his considerable philanthropic activities.

Bradley, James—January 9, 1914; untouchable vote-getter.

One of *Mayor Young*'s political enemies that Hizzoner can't touch. Young twice suited up surrogates to beat Bradley. But an immutable Detroit political maxim came into play: Once a city clerk is elected, he's in office until the Grim Reaper personally takes his name off the ballot. (This is true on both the city and county level, probably because it's an awfully dull job that nobody cares about, except when the clerk counts votes on election day. On that day, he is everybody's friend. The only exception to this rule is former city clerk George C. Edwards III, who left office one step ahead of the voters after taking so long to count the 1970 election results that he was too embarrassed to run again.)

A real estate and construction man by trade, Bradley knocked around the Legislature for some 20 years before winning his current job in 1973, coincidentally the same year Young took office two floors down in the City-County Building. Bradley's state Capitol career was an unremarkable tour as labor's vote on the House floor. It was in Lansing that state Rep. Bradley and state Sen. Young took to disliking each other — Young believing that Bradley was a dim bulb, Bradley believing that Young was an arrogant bully.

Bradley has stayed out of the news recently. He seriously embarrassed himself in 1981 by taking an ill-advised jaunt to a convention in Louisville while a major Detroit election was in progress. As city voters were deciding whether to increase their taxes, some 47 precincts ran out of ballots. Young's people saw to it that Bradley's whereabouts were well reported. Hoping to take advantage of his weakened foe, Young sent Shirley Robinson—a political novice and the wife of Young crony Elliott Hall—into a race against Bradley a few months later. The electorate forgot all about the election snafu and re-elected Bradley, 56 percent to 44 percent. Young had worse luck when he put up the more experienced state Rep. Morris Hood in 1985. Bradley beat him 66 percent to 34 percent, despite Hood's endorsement by practically every powerful lobby in town.

Bray, Thomas—November 3, 1941; *Detroit News* **opinionmeister.**

This 1963 Princeton grad is curator of the *News*'s editorial page, regularly causing grief for what he perceives as the tax-and-spend crowd in Lansing and Washington, D.C. Former President Reagan got plenty of support. His pages are framed by the philosophy that "social good flows from economic growth." For instance, *News* editorials don't question abortion as much as wonder who pays the bills.

A 1959 graduate of Cranbrook, he earned his BA at Princeton before landing himself a reporting job at the *San Antonio Evening News* in 1963. He quickly got himself a ticket to the *Wall Street Journal*, the mecca of financial journalism. He rested there for 19 years, first as a reporter, then as associate editor, before returning home to Detroit in 1983 as *News* editorial page chief.

Bray's pages emphasize substance and carefully selected fact. *News* editorials do occasionally take a slightly crazy edge, once referring to National Public Radio as National Public Rathole. "We do not want to become intellectually flat," Bray once told a reporter. At the helm since 1983, he's one editorial side executive who hasn't been replaced by Gannett, owner of the *News*.

Brodie, Dorothy—(birthdate not available); municipal handywoman.

When **Mayor Young** needs something done right, he turns to Dorothy Brodie. It was no surprise at city hall when he chose her to run downtown's People Mover. No civic project had more potential for embarrassment. With its cost overruns and construction problems, the Mover had become a joke long before unloading its first carload of Greektown diners in the summer of 1987. Consider the possibilities: If the Mover didn't work, the critics would finally have concrete proof—literally, concrete—that Young ought to retire. But it worked. No civic project has so exceeded its expectations. With its security patrol and cameras, the Mover is probably the safest place in town. The critics will have to find another target.

A Pittsburgh native, Brodie received a bachelor's degree from Pennsylvania State University and a master's from the University of Hawaii, where—like many students—she attended classes in a bathing suit. Young found her in 1979, halfway into his second term, at the U.S. Conference of Mayors. As a mayoral executive assistant, she established herself as the person who knew how to fence with the federal government.

She's a staunch mayoral supporter, but doesn't make a religion of it. Brodie undoubtedly has a great future in private industry, once she decides to leave city hall.

Brogan, Marcie—(birthdate not available); Detroit's adwoman.

While the lines grew long at U.S. Bankruptcy Court in Detroit in 1982, adwomen Marcie Brogan and Anna Kabot went in the other direction: They founded an agency. Today, the shop handles a healthy $15-million in advertising with a client roster that includes Crain Communications Inc., Henry Ford Hospital and Little Caesar Pizza Stations. The Brogan selling point is creativity: She and Kabot placed a red fez on downtown Detroit's best-known statue and put it on a billboard with the caption "Conventions Are the Spirit of Detroit." They won three Silver Caddy awards from the Creative Advertising Club of Detroit for their AIDS campaign.

Brogan, armed with a couple of degrees (BA in English and philosophy from Ursuline College for Women, master's in literature from the University of Detroit), began her ad career in 1971 at W.B. Doner & Co. She sat out much of the '70s in Europe: London and Brussels with Boase Massimi Pollitt (1974-'76), later making trips to Amsterdam and Rotterdam (1977-'80) with Campbell-Ewald. Doner persuaded her to return stateside in 1980.

Fortuitously, Anna Kabot, who had worked with Brogan at Doner in the early '70s, was also returning from seven years with Lintas: Campbell-Ewald in Warren. Two years later, they struck out on their own. Kabot left in 1988 and was replaced by Bonnie Folster.

Brogan, the agency's president, schmoozes with the clients, runs the place, writes much of the copy. A local favorite: the D.O.C. Optique ad which placed a pair of glitzy purple eyeglasses on England's Lady Di. The ad simply read: "Glasses to Di for." Hubby Prince Charles was fitted for tortoise shell frames—in a photograph headlined: "The Tortoise and the Heir."

Brogan's godfather is retired Campbell-Ewald chairman **Tom Adams**. Grateful, the duo threw an "Adams and Eves" party for him at the Music Hall in 1984—an all-woman affair except for Adams, of course. Campbell-Ewald finance chief **Robert Roselle** and the late *News* columnist Charlie Manos crashed the party in drag.

Brooks, Roy—March 9, 1938; he went, he drummed, he conquered.

This percussion master has played with jazz greats such as Yusef Lateef, Horace Silver, Wes Montgomery, Archie Shepp, Max Roach and Dexter Gordon. Some of his best work here has been with his Roy Brooks and the Artistic Truth ensemble and his Aboriginal Percussion Choir.

Brooks took a fancy to a drumming career listening to Lionel Hampton at the Paradise Theatre (now reverted to Orchestra Hall) and the polyrhythmic Pontiac native Elvin Jones at the legendary Bluebird Tavern on Tireman. Not long after graduation from Northwestern High School he got a call from pianist Horace Silver. Silver's departing drummer, Louis Hayes (another Detroiter), had recommended Brooks. That was in 1959. He spent the next five years with Silver's bluesy-boppish band, appearing on four albums. He spent another 11 years with the other jazz greats named above.

So what brought him back to Detroit in 1976? "Better living conditions, and I figured I'd made enough of a name for myself that I could live almost anywhere."

Broomfield, William—April 28, 1922; hard-nosed Republican.

The heavily Republican areas of Birmingham and Bloomfield Hills have been sending Bill Broomfield to Capitol Hill for more than three decades, making him the state's senior congressman. He owes his long run to something that Southern politicians have known for a long time: You don't help yourself by getting in front of an issue. Don't make waves, or cause too much excitement. As part of the woodwork, you aren't in peril of being thrown out. Soon, the seniority adds up and you've got some real clout. Broomfield knows all that. He's so low-key that he forsakes power lunches at Duke Ziebert's for chow in the House dining room with his chief aide. But everybody pays attention to him, for he is now the senior GOP presence on the House Foreign Affairs Committee.

Oakland County voters have been electing Broomfield to office since 1948, when, at age 26, he got himself elected to the state House. When a congressional seat opened in 1956, the pundits assumed the slot would go to state Sen. George Higgins, a popular automobile dealer who was considered a sure thing. Higgins wasn't popular enough, losing to Broomfield in the congressional primary by 1,440 votes, out of almost 40,000 cast. There were a few tight outings after that, particularly in 1958, when he beat a Democratic challenger by six percentage points. But after years of fighting, the Democrats have given up, gerrymandering territory near Southfield to give themselves some representation, and leaving the rest of Birmingham/Bloomfield to Broomfield.

Ronald Reagan could usually count on Broomfield for help, particularly during the Iran-Contra hearings. But when the Reagan administration pushed a proposal to sell AWACS planes to Saudi Arabia, Broomfield said no. Smart move for a congressman who has a strong Jewish constituency. Deep into his 60s, Broomfield may be looking to retirement. When he leaves, he'll depart with almost $450,000 in unused campaign contributions, which he may keep under federal law.

Brown, Peter—April 16, 1948; he engineers the news on cars.

Automotive News, which Brown edits, is required reading among the auto aristocracy here and around the world. The weekly blends arcane statistics—such as which automaker has how many days' supply of cars gathering dust on its lots, sophisticated analyses of executive suite intrigue, and news of companies from General Motors to Audi. Copies are carefully inspected in Germany, Japan and anywhere else mankind builds automobiles.

Before landing his current job in early 1989, Brown was editor and associate publisher of *Crain's Detroit Business*, the weekly that watches the local business community. The town's two daily newspapers used to relegate business news to a few pages wrapped around the stock prices. Coverage was dominated by stories about the Big Three, which is big news, of course. But that changed when Brown and *Crain's Detroit Business* entered the scene. The weekly tabloid brought news of which developer bought what, and which widget maker did what to which widget maker down the block. Now it appears that both the *News* and the *Free Press* have beefed up their business coverage, at least partially because of *Crain's*.

Brown was a rising star at the *Free Press* before **Keith Crain** hired him. Brown's wife had been an art director at Crain's *Detroit Monthly*. Upon introducing Brown to writer David Halberstam ("The Reckoning") at a Grand Prix party at the University Club, Crain told Halberstam: "He doesn't know it yet, but he'll be working for me soon." Crain was good to his word. At a U Club lunch, Crain laid out his philosophy to Brown: "Cover the stuff the papers aren't covering." It was an immediate hit.

The word around the halls of Crain Communications before Brown got the *Automotive News* job was that Crain trusted Brown. When Brown got the *Automotive News* gig, everybody knew for certain.

Burnett, Patricia Hill—September 5, 1920; from Miss to Ms., she's come a long way.

This world-renowned portrait artist and former Miss Michigan and first runner-up to Miss America is the godmother of the feminist movement in Detroit. And an effective one, too. With one foot among the area's artists and one among the area's upper classes, she was taken very seriously when she helped found the Michigan chapter of the National Organization for Women. As for her artistic skills, they are considerable. Philippines President Corazon Aquino, Lt. Gov. Martha Griffiths, Marlo Thomas, Betty Ford, Indira Ghandi, Gloria Steinem and Betty Friedan all have been subjects.

She is a graduate of exclusive Goucher College in Baltimore and the daughter of a socially prominent Detroit family. Her stepfather was Dr. Jean Paul Pratt, head of obstetrics and gynecology at Henry Ford Hospital. In an era when debuts were important, she came out at the Sulgrave Club in Washington, D.C.

Without telling her parents that she had entered, she won the 1942 Miss Michigan pageant. A newspaper account described her as "tall, slender, gray-eyed with a luxuriant mass of dark hair . . . Her personality was so vivid that the majority of the spectators knew almost as soon as she appeared in the line of over 100 contestants

that she would be the winner . . . When the talent selection began
she frankly admitted over the ballroom microphone that her talents
were not the sort to be demonstrated in the fashion of most of the
entrants. She explained she did not sing, dance or play an instrument. She told the crowd that she was an artist and had done some
radio work." (She played the Green Hornet's girlfriend, Gail Man-
ning, among other radio roles. The radio schedule was busy; she
once proclaimed coast-to-coast on the "Lone Ranger" show: "Oh
look! It's the Green Hornet!")

The '70s saw Burnett as a leader in the women's lib movement,
chairing the Michigan Women's Commission. She's now a grandmother with the social skills of a grande dame and the toughness of a
Green Beret.

Burns, Ben—May 30, 1940; suburban newspaper overlord.

Writers and editors at the two big daily newspapers believe all great
Detroit journalism emanates from their offices on West Lafayette.
Ben Burns, who edits and publishes the *Macomb Daily* and *Daily
Tribune of Royal Oak*, doesn't think so.

Before Gannett bought the *News*, Burns was on the newspaper's
fast track. A former all-state basketball star (he's 6'8") with a journalism BA and master's in history from Michigan State University,
he spent time at the *Lansing State Journal, Miami Herald* and United
Press International before landing at the *News* in 1976 as an assistant
managing editor. He eventually rose to executive editor, but was
sidelined when Gannett brought in executive editor *Bob Giles* to run
the show. Gannett boss Al Neuharth tried to put a positive spin on
it. "You can write that the *News* has received an infusion of top
editorial-side talent, the better to enable it to compete with the *Free
Press* and enhance its already pre-eminent position in the market,"
Neuharth declared. "Or you can write that two guys got dumped on.
That's the cynical way of looking at it and I'm sure that's the way
some and even many may view it. But that is not the correct way."
Most people at the *News* chose to interpret the moves cynically.

Burns, who was left in a corner to futz with budgetary questions,
got bored and left 18 months later to run Wayne State University's
journalism program. Two other executives left for Memphis and
Sacramento. About a year into his job at WSU, Burns was summoned by Adams Communications to run the *Daily* and the newly
purchased *Tribune*.

His wife, Beverly, is a partner in the silk-stocking law firm of Miller, Canfield, Paddock & Stone.

Butcher, Mary Lou—see Casey, Jack

Butsicaris, Jimmy and Johnny—"right around 65"; gray foxes of sports bardom.

At one time, Jimmy and Johnny Butsicaris's Lindell AC was called "the poor man's Toots Shor's of Detroit." A hangout for athletes, sportswriters and their groupies, it was also somewhat notorious. This is where former Lion Alex Karras and wrestler Dick the Bruiser had their famous brawl. This is where Billy Martin decked one of his own pitchers. (Jimmy was best man for Billy's wedding.) Although still a hangout for some athletes, the Butsicarises' place now has the air of a museum. Jack Morris's jersey isn't enshrined in the display case there. Instead, one sees Tiger Norm Cash's jersey, and a vast photographic record of past generations' glories.

The saloon was founded near Cass and Bagley, not far from the now-defunct *Detroit Times*, for whom Johnny shot photos. The *Times* crowd, notorious for heavy drinking (the paper had its own chapter of Alcoholics Anonymous) christened it "the sewer." The Lindell ceased to be just another newspaper dive after it moved, slightly, to its current location at Michigan and Cass. It became hip in the '60s, when the Lions still played at Tiger Stadium. An athlete was always bending his elbow somewhere in the room. *News* columnist Doc Greene was often about, and added the "AC" to the name. How tight was Jimmy with the jocks? He often sat on the Lions bench at Tiger Stadium, a practice squelched by NFL commissioner Pete Rozelle. Johnny watched the job during the day, Jimmy at night. Both counted the money.

The bar reached its zenith in 1980 with an Alex Karras-produced CBS-TV movie, "Jimmy B. and Andre." A two-hour account of how Jimmy "adopted" Andre Reynolds, the young son of a Detroit drug addict, it gave the saloon national publicity. The next month, the bar received some publicity of another type: A group of Pontiac cops, probably drunk, got into a fight with the Butsicaris brothers and Andre. For some bar-hoppers, the Lindell began to carry an undertone of violence.

And there is competition now. The Golden Galleon seems to get the Red Wings hockey crowd from Joe Louis Arena. The Lions and Pistons, especially those in search of dates, no longer play either game downtown and can be found at Jukebox Saturday Night in Royal Oak. The only constant in life, and especially in the bar business, is change. But we'd all still like to have 10 percent of the Lindell's gross on a game night.

C

Calvert, Ken—August 30, 1951; symbol of thirtysomething hipness.

This FM morning deejay is the voice of the Baby Boomers. Rock 'n' roll was their beacon of truth and enlightenment in the late '60s and early '70s. But they've grown up now, and their beacon is the *Wall Street Journal*. Rock 'n' roll time is a diversionary hour on the freeway en route to the office. Calvert, as much as anyone, is cut out to speak to these people.

The son of an AC Delco executive, he graduated from Birmingham Brother Rice High School in 1969. Calvert got into radio in 1972, joining WWWW-FM during its hip phase in 1973. He jumped to WABX-FM just two years later, but left the station for CBS Records. Bruce Springsteen was one of the acts Calvert repped, as were Rolling Stones Keith Richards and Ron Wood, who were moonlighting as "The New Barbarians." Fears that his liver would explode prompted Calvert to return to Detroit radio. "I was a little too young and having too much fun," he recalls. "I got out of it because I didn't want to die."

Calvert joined WRIF-FM in 1979, and has been there ever since. Station execs felt strongly enough about his work that in August 1988 they signed him to a three-year contract as their morning man. His friends include *Arthur Penhallow*, adman Peter DeLorenzo (a high school chum) and any number of athletes. He's the PA announcer at Detroit Pistons basketball games, the guy who says "Joe Dooooooo-mars" in such a distinctive way.

Campana, Joseph—March 10, 1937; Chrysler/Plymouth chief.

Only months after *Lee Iacocca* went to Chrysler from Ford, Joe Campana followed. That was 1979. Now, Campana is one of three marketing chiefs at the company. (John Damoose at Dodge and *Joseph Cappy* at Jeep/Eagle are the other two. Some wise guys around Chrysler call them "the Three Amigos.")

Fresh out of Yale University, he ran a Pontiac dealership in Sharon, Pennsylvania. That makes him one of the few automotive people in this book who've actually sold cars one-on-one. ("I'm going to write down a figure . . .") Burnishing his resumé with a couple other degrees from Youngstown State (BS, 1961) and Kent State (MBA, 1962), he jumped to Ford Motor Co. in sales/marketing in 1964. During the next 10 years he also taught at the University of Michigan in his spare time.

He recalls being quite impressed with Iacocca's 1960s efforts in marketing the Mustang. He stayed close to Iacocca at Ford, so it was no surprise when he followed Iacocca down the block. He got there in time to build up the truck operations, then went on to several marketing vice-presidencies before he got his current job in early 1988.

Campbell, James—February 5, 1924; "boss Jim."

A conservative baseball man, he set the tone for the Detroit Tiger's organization. There have been few big-buck trades under Campbell, because that's the way he wants it. While some stadiums broadcast rock music between innings, the Tigers played cornpone stuff like John Denver's "Thank God, I'm a Country Boy." He closed the bleachers once because rowdies there were chanting obscenities. He took heat for that, but nothing so clearly defines the gulf between the age of civility and the age of public urination. But who can argue with the results—two World Series victories (1968 and 1984) and two Eastern Division championships (1972 and 1987).

He played outfield for Ohio State University, where he once ran into a cement mixer while trying to retrieve a fly ball. By the time he finished college in three years in Navy aviation, he was too old to play baseball. So he joined the Tigers in 1949 as business manager of the team's Class D farm club in Thomasville, Georgia. The stands burned down after his first game. He worked his way through the farm system, mostly on the business end, and into the Tiger general manager's job by the end of the 1962 season. There, he caught owner John Fetzer's ear and that of owner Tom Monaghan, who bought the club in 1983.

Baseball is Campbell's life. When the Tigers have an off night, he props a radio on his ledge and catches far away contests.

Cappy, Joseph—May 13, 1934; in the Eagle's nest.

He not only survived Chrysler's takeover of American Motors Corp., he thrived. The last president and chief executive officer of an independent AMC, he now runs Chrysler's Jeep/Eagle division.

Before joining AMC in 1982, Cappy spent 26 years with Ford Motor Co. in sales and marketing. He impressed the folks at Renault enough upon arriving at AMC that they made him a board member in September 1986, and No. 2 exec in December. But his spot in the sun was short-lived: Chrysler bought out Renault and the rest of AMC's stockholders in August 1987.

In a business not known for its sense of humor, he's known to have one.

Carey, Paul—March 15, 1928; middle-inning voice of the Tigers.

Carey's voice is so deep and powerful that one wonders: Is God handling play-by-play? No, it's just *Ernie Harwell*'s self-effacing boothmate and perhaps Detroit's most competent second banana.

The Mt. Pleasant native is the polar opposite of the broadcast gypsy. He joined WJR in 1956, creating the station's high school football and basketball scoreboard. He has worked for WJR in a variety of sports jobs ever since, playing second string to Bob Reynolds throughout the '60s and handling Pistons broadcasts from 1969 until 1973 (and again in '75-'76 and '80-'81). When his reward for loyalty was issued in 1973, it was enormous: a partnership with Harwell.

Tragedy darkened Carey's biggest hour as a Tigers broadcaster. While the rest of the city was in World Series hysteria in 1984 as the Tigers began Game Three at Michigan and Trumbull, Carey was informed that his wife would die soon from cancer. "It was a strange feeling," he once told a reporter. "All I could think about in between innings was her. I was like a robot—just doing things automatically. Then on Sunday, everybody was out there celebrating but all I could think about was what was ahead for us." She died the following March. Paul has since remarried, happily.

Casey, Jack (July 19, 1928) and Butcher, Mary Lou (May 18, 1943); public relations prince and princess.

This husband-and-wife team runs what is arguably Detroit's largest PR agency. Casey Communications Management Inc. billed almost

$4-million in 1988. Since rival Anthony Franco didn't turn in its numbers to *O'Dwyer's Directory of Public Relations Firms*—the official scorekeeper of who's big and who's not—the Casey firm claimed premier PR status in town. Franco disputed that, of course.

Casey got into the communications business early—as in before the sun rose. Barely into his teens, he peddled newspapers in front of an auto parts plant in his native Toledo at 5:30 a.m. He took that corner from 40 papers a day to about 600. When he wasn't hawking papers, he worked as a copyboy at the *Toledo Times*, where he later worked as a reporter after graduating from the University of Toledo. The *Free Press* took Casey on as a reporter in 1956, and he stayed there until he signed on as a special assistant to Mayor Jerry Cavanagh in 1962. He managed Cavanagh's successful re-election campaign in 1965 against Walter Shamie, then bailed out in 1966 to sign on with pal Morris Gleicher's ad agency. The two also ran one of the premier political management firms in the city, steering Richard Austin's '69 campaign for mayor and his successful bid for secretary of state in '70.

What he is most famous for, however, is political prognosticating. Since 1966, WJR's *J.P. McCarthy* has been calling on Casey's expertise in survey techniques to divine the electorate for the station's sizable audience.

Gleicher and Casey eventually split up, and the new place has a lot of corporate accounts. General Motors sends a lot of work Casey's way. His clients, past and present, include Michigan Bell, R.L. Polk & Co. and Audi.

Butcher, a graduate of Lincoln Park High School, joined the *News* in 1966 after graduating from the University of Michigan. She was a key mover in a sex-discrimination lawsuit that cost the *News* more than $90,000. Butcher, who had left the paper to enter PR while the case was pending, took about half of her $22,000 and put it toward a journalism scholarship at U-M.

In 1987, Casey and Butcher sold the outfit to London-based Shandwick PLC. The down payment was $2.8-million.

Castaing, Francois—May 18, 1945; riding *le Jeep*.

Another American Motors Corp. refugee who has survived the transition to Chrysler.

Born in Marseilles, France, just 11 days after the Nazis surrendered, he graduated from the prestigious Ecole National Superieure d'Arts et Metiers. He signed up with Renault in 1970 as a designer of racing engines. Remember the Renault Alliance? It enjoyed a mightily successful launch (Motor Trend Car of the Year in 1983) but ultimately failed. Castaing, as Renault's point man, was a top engineer on the project. By the time Chrysler bought up Renault's interest in AMC, Castaing was a group vice-president for engineering, styling and quality. Chrysler kept him aboard after the buy-out in 1987, making Castaing a v.p. for Jeep and truck engineering. Jeeps being the hot thing among well-heeled drivers who haven't been off the road since they fell asleep at the wheel, Chrysler takes the division very seriously. And giving Castaing one of the top jobs there must mean they take Castaing seriously, too.

Insiders say Castaing, a man of no small engineering ability, is destined for some big things at Chrysler.

Charfoos, Lawrence—December 7, 1935; counsel for misplaced appendixes.

Medical malpractice law has been good for Larry Charfoos. His firm takes up two floors of the Penobscot Building, the yacht he owned was docked in France, and he's married to a glamorous Parisian model. Charfoos earned it all by getting in on the ground floor of the medical malpractice field, which was practically non-existent when he began going after spleen-bashers in the late '60s. Now that med mal has become one of the most lucrative areas in law, the field is awfully crowded. But Charfoos still stands out among the pack, pulling in more than his share of million-dollar-plus verdicts. "We are the modern-day equivalent of gunfighters," he once told a reporter. "Here are the samurai. Here are the gunfighters going to do battle from nine to five." That's the kind of hyperbole a jury gets when it listens to Charfoos. It works.

Before becoming a rich malpractice lawyer, Charfoos was in theater. He practiced law with his father for awhile after graduating from Wayne State University Law School, but abandoned the profession out of boredom. He spent a half-dozen years producing plays, mostly in Chicago and on the West Coast. But the mid- to late-'60s saw the quick disintegration of Charfoos's personal and professional life. His theatrical career crashed, his only child died of leukemia at the age of seven, and his first marriage fell apart. He returned to Detroit and plunged himself into the medical textbooks.

The results began rolling in a few years later when Charfoos became the first Michigan lawyer to crack the $1-million jury award mark. That distinction earned him membership in the Inner Circle of Advocates, an exclusive group of 100 lawyers who have won $1-million or more for their clients in a single case. He has a healthy ego to show for it, notable even in his chosen profession. He once threatened to write a seven-volume series on things like "Rethinking Love," with the last volume entitled "Rethinking Thinking."

Cihelka, Milos—July 24, 1930; Czech, please.

Known simply as "Milos," this Czech immigrant cooks up a storm at Southfield's Golden Mushroom. A hotspot for the Oakland County glitterati, the Mushroom seems to have siphoned business from downtown landmarks like the London Chop House and *Joe Muer*'s. So many Birmingham and Bloomfield matrons shudder at the thought of driving downtown, especially at night. And the Mushroom is just off the Lodge Freeway's Ten Mile/Evergreen exit. And Milos does cook in the same league as just about anybody downtown. *Voila*: a recipe for success.

Milos realized that the chances of becoming a master chef in communist Czechoslovakia—where lobsters and porterhouse steaks are rare—were slim. Noted Milos in a newspaper interview a few years after he arrived in the United States: "I could see myself cooking nothing but stew and hash in some workers' factory lunchroom." So in 1950 he escaped to Germany with a priest and an English teacher in an unexpectedly simple walk through the woods. They anticipated some shooting, but the guards were beat from a previous night's pursuit. It was on to the United States for Milos, who spent time on the East Coast before landing at the Roostertail for nine years. Before joining the Golden Mushroom as executive chef in 1976, he held similar posts at the London Chop House (under the late Lester Gruber) and the Detroit Athletic Club.

Though he wins countless culinary awards, he doesn't receive any stars for diplomacy with his staff. "I'm not the nicest person to work for," he once said. "I'm purposely a tyrant, but I consider myself having a soft heart. I run my kitchen like an army; I'm the general and my employees are the enlisted men. They have to toe the line." Employees have described him as "an S.O.B. on wheels." When sous chefs complain, he has been known to say: "This is no hash house."

Nobody would mistake a Mushroom entree for hash.

Cleo—August 1 (lists age as 4,000); real name Cleopatra Hercules Korgis Abuin, psychic to the stars.

Some Detroiters pay more attention to Cleo than they do to their lawyers or accountants. Her client list, though a carefully guarded secret, is said to include big-time moneychangers and a Ford or two. All told, she has some 8,000 charts on file. She's a favorite of talk show hosts and newspaper reporters, partly because she is wonderfully articulate and engaging, partly because she'll predict anything. With her flowing black hair and caftans of many colors, she makes a great photograph.

Cleo grew up in southwest Detroit, where her immigrant Greek parents were shopkeepers. "Everybody who wasn't Greek was a foreigner," she says. Her father, Hercules, owned a grocery shop near Southwestern High School. He learned English at the feet of an Oxford professor, spoke seven languages, and won every medal imaginable for his World War I combat exploits on behalf of the United States. "My mother and sister were both intuitive," she says, by way of explaining her interest in astrology. There is a lot more to Cleo, however, than reading people's fates. She was a rodeo rider in her youth; wrote a couple of country and western songs ("Devil on My Shoulder" and "Learn to Love"), and is a gourmet cook.

She describes herself as "flamboyant, glittering, dramatic, jazzy, pizazzy, extravagant, sun-child, heart of gold." She is all of those things. Only clairvoyant Cleo could know how many decisions have been influenced by her readings. And she isn't telling.

Cleveland, Clyde—May 22, 1935; occasionally rebellious Detroit city councilman.

Cleveland was tweaking *Mayor Young* at the City Council table even before that kind of conduct was considered okay by his colleagues. Cleveland voted to subpoena documents in the Magnum Oil controversy of the early '80s, thereby alienating himself from the 11th floor (Young's office in the City-County Building). Young's pals tried to strip Cleveland of the state Democratic vice-chairmanship in 1983, but Cleveland decided not to run for re-election. Then Young's machine tried to blow Cleveland out of office in the 1985 City Council election. Politically powerful groups such as the Black Slate and the 1st and 13th District Democratic organizations withheld their support from Cleveland that year, but the voters didn't care. He ran fourth, exactly where he ran in 1981 and 1977. Now it's clear that

Young can't hurt him, and Cleveland does as he pleases. While the mayor backed Michael Dukakis in the 1988 Democratic primary, Cleveland co-chaired Jesse Jackson's Michigan campaign.

Cleveland rose to the City Council in 1973 after working in the trenches of neighborhood politics. During the 1950s and '60s he labored as a welfare worker, and later as a community planner and a project director for New Detroit. Cleveland scored a respectable fifth-place finish in his first council election, but then fell prey to a common political hallucination: Because a candidate is well-known in his neighborhood, he deludes himself into thinking he's famous everywhere. Cleveland, a west-sider, made a stab at Charles Diggs Jr.'s old congressional seat in 1980, running against *George Crockett Jr.* Voters in the largely east-side district were affronted by the west-sider's carpetbagging. They buried him deeply into third place, only nine votes ahead of *Nicholas Hood*'s son, Nick Hood III, who wasn't even 30 at the time. Cleveland has stayed put since.

Will he run for mayor? Don't count him out, especially since he fashioned a rather effective political machine of his own while running Jackson's Michigan campaign.

He once observed after the city's Gethsemane Cemetery-City Airport debacle that "this city can't protect people from crime or drugs, there's no services in the neighborhoods and now even the dead don't get treated like they should." Somebody say "Amen," please.

Cohan, Leon—June 24, 1929; Detroit Edison's top legal gun.

When Leon Cohan was running the state Attorney General's Office, the joke around Lansing was: "If anything happened to Leon Cohan, *Frank Kelley* would become attorney general." While there, Cohan hired a young lawyer as an assistant AG. The young attorney's name was *Jim Blanchard.*

Cohan gave up his 14-year Lansing gig in 1972 for a high-paying legal job with Edison. As general counsel and a senior v.p., he tends to the utility's needs and is a Big Presence in the town's Jewish community. He's a man with quiet influence. Quiet is just the way Edison likes it.

Collins, Barbara-Rose—April 13, 1939; Detroit city councilwoman/mayoral ally.

Mayor Young can count on her for help when City Council gets feisty. In the late 1980s, her vote sustained many a mayoral veto.

Collins got her political start as a lowly member of a Detroit regional board of education, a seat she won in 1970. Always looking for something a little better, she spent the next three years unsuccessfully running for the state House, state Senate and Detroit City Council. Collins came in 15th (third from the bottom) in her first run for council in 1973. Her persistence paid off in 1974, when voters sent the Cass Tech High grad to Lansing as a rep from an inner city district. She finally made the City Council cut in 1981, placing seventh. She remained in that slot in the 1985 elections.

A prominent member of the Shrine of the Black Madonna, she once sponsored a testimonial resolution honoring Louis Farrakhan. When her then-16-year-old son was caught in a curfew check in 1986, she didn't make excuses. "He's not allowed any phone calls and he can't go out," she told a reporter. "He's just going to do his schoolwork for a while."

She still has her eye on something better. Against Young's wishes, she mounted a campaign against Congressman *George Crockett Jr.* in the 1988 Democratic primary. She gave the septuagenarian a scare by coming within 3,000 votes of victory. Incumbent congressmen are supposed to win by more than seven percentage points. The 13th District, which includes Detroit's east side and the Grosse Pointes, hasn't seen the last of her.

Conn, Pam—see Marx, Sue

Conyers, John Jr.—May 16, 1929; tenure personified.

Consider the embryonic state of black politics when John Conyers Jr. was first elected to Congress in 1964. Detroit's mayor, police chief and fire chief were white. So was Highland Park's mayor. The U.S. House of Representatives had only four other black members. Now, all of the aforementioned civic officials are black, and 24 blacks sit in Congress. This would seem to make Conyers a god-father of the black political movement in town, but he's not, really.

Conyers was booed when he tried to restore order at the outset of the 1967 riots. *Mayor Young* stole a lot of his political thunder in the 1970s. He's not particularly effective in Washington because, as analyst Michael Barone writes in "The Almanac of American Politics—1988": "He seems to have soured on everything but his own principles."

His father, John Conyers Sr., was a pioneer official of the United Automobile Workers. The elder Conyers organized Local 7 at Chrysler's Jefferson Plant in 1936, and helped write the union's constitution. With that kind of entree, John Jr. couldn't miss. He beat Richard Austin in 1964 by 108 votes out of 60,000 cast, and hasn't had a close contest since. His share of the vote in both primaries and general elections has never been less than 85 percent. Part of that has to do with the attention he pays to his district, which includes Highland Park and much of Detroit's north end. Part of it has to do with the fact that his is one of the most heavily Democratic districts in the country. It went 86 percent for Walter Mondale in 1984, 93 percent for Jimmy Carter in 1980, and 89 percent for Carter four years later.

In a curious congressional career, he is known for two things: He pushed through a national holiday marking the Rev. Martin Luther King Jr.'s birthday, and he hired civil rights pioneer Rosa Parks as his receptionist. By any traditional measure of congressional power, he has none. With his seniority, however, he could some day be chairman of the House Judiciary Committee, which oversees civil rights legislation.

Coughlin, William (February 26, 1929) and Ruth (December 3, 1943); Detroit's literary couple.

He's a federal administrative law judge by day, a novelist by night. Ruth Pollack Coughlin is the *Detroit News* book editor. His quick laugh and pleasant disposition mask a serious mind and a stiff work ethic. He has turned out a dozen books while holding a full-time job of considerable complexity. She has earned the *News* kudos for her "book and author" luncheons with the likes of Cleveland Amory and *Elmore Leonard*.

Bill Coughlin, the son of a *Free Press* editor, quickly scuttled any plan to follow his father into the newspaper business. A short stint as copyboy at the now-defunct *Detroit Times*, the journalistic equivalent of "Animal House," sent him to the law books. After graduating from the University of Detroit Law School, he worked in the

Wayne County Prosecutor's Office and dabbled in Democratic politics. He was chairman of the Michigan Young Democrats during the late 1950s, and ran unsuccessfully for lieutenant governor on the Democratic ticket in 1960. He told a reporter that he turned to fiction writing on a dare from his first wife. Although she was impressed when Coughlin turned out "The Widow Wondered Why" in 10 days, American publishers were not. A British publisher put Coughlin's effort in print. Nowadays, he commands advances of $750,000 in multi-book deals.

Politics, crime and power—the stuff he dealt with for years as a lawyer—have figured prominently in Coughlin's novels. "The Destruction Committee," his third book, involves a half-dozen Vietnam vets who select a U.S. vice-presidential candidate for elimination. "The Twelve Apostles" takes place in a large law firm.

Ruth Pollack Coughlin was brought up in New Jersey. (Her brother is actor Michael J. Pollard, of "Bonnie and Clyde" fame.) After graduating from Rutgers, she was an editor in New York City's book trade for 18 years before marriage to Coughlin brought her to Detroit. She has become an aggressive promoter of the city, and professes not to miss the Manhattan high life at all. Her *News* profiles of Tom Wolfe and restaurateur *Jimmy Schmidt* were especially memorable.

After work, the Coughlins beat a path to a comfortable home on a dead-end street in Grosse Pointe Woods. Despite the fact that he has sold somewhere between four million and five million books, he still hangs on to the federal jurist gig he's had since 1973. A Depression-era kid, he still has it in his mind that the royalty checks will stop some day.

Crain, Keith—February 19, 1941; publishing suzerain.

Forget *Bill Bonds*, *Bob Talbert* and *J.P. McCarthy*. Despite their outsized paychecks, they're merely hired hands. Keith Crain is the only media mogul in Detroit with his name atop a building. Any conversation in the automotive community on Monday morning assumes that both parties have read *Automotive News*, which belongs to the Crain family. Ditto for the business community and *Crain's Detroit Business*. The town's trendoids take at least some of their cues from his *Detroit Monthly*. That's the Detroit constellation of the Chicago-based Crain Communications galaxy. Stars published elsewhere include *Advertising Age*, and a laundry list of trade journals including, well, *American Laundry Digest*. Financial and circulation chores for all 26 publications are handled in Detroit.

Keith is Ruler of All He Surveys in his building on the eastern edge of downtown. A Chicago native, Crain arrived here in 1971, just a few months after his father's company bought Automotive News. Barely 30 years old when he was named publisher, he had some experience in his family's publishing empire and he genuinely loved cars—especially the kind that you drive around the Baja Peninsula in excess of 100 m.p.h. Asked why he'd want to leave Chicago for a one-horse town like Detroit, he reportedly said: "Because I can ride the horse."

He's not shy about exercising his power. After Crain fired somebody one day, a friend of Crain's told a reporter that the newly unemployed person "had a physical problem." "What was that?" the reporter asked. "Myopia," said Crain's pal. "He couldn't see whose name was atop the building."

Crain's elderly mother, Gertrude, still signs the big checks out of Chicago. Keith currently co-exists somewhat peacefully with his brother Rance, who is editor-in-chief of *Advertising Age* in New York.

Crim, Mort—July 31, 1935; Channel 4's avuncular anchorman.

This sober, serious newsman (except for those godawful puns) has a crate full of Emmys, raises bales of money for charity through the Easter Seal Telethon, and projects a thoughtful, concerned visage for his bosses at Post-Newsweek. He also has given Channel 7's *Bill Bonds* some competition on the 11 p.m. newscast, something that no one would have thought possible before Crim got here in 1978.

Before Detroit, Crim made stops in Louisville, Philadelphia and Chicago, where he anchored the news at WBBM, the Windy City's CBS-owned-and-operated station. In Philadelphia he became best friends with an up-and-coming young anchorwoman named Jessica Savitch; after she drowned, he served as an executor of her estate. Since then, he has taken his citizenship here seriously. He made every effort to learn Detroit's customs and mores, even trading in his Mercedes for a Chrysler. Some 10 years into Detroithood, he still insists on driving American, lately a Ford Mustang and a Lincoln.

Crim isn't as flashy as Bonds. Crim likes a quiet dinner between newscasts, and the puns are as close as he comes to outrageous conversation. If he is anything, he is sincere — almost to a fault. He was once dubbed "Sergeant Sobersides" and Wayne State University Med School students named a cadaver after him.

He is only in his 50s, and one can see Crim aging into a Detroit eminence grise.

Crockett, George Jr.—Aug. 10, 1909; political graybeard.

Crockett is one of those political figures who can honestly claim a ringside seat to history. He was next to *Coleman Young* at the height of the McCarthy madness when Young told a congressional subcommittee where to get off. White voters launched a recall effort when, as a Detroit Recorder's Court judge, he released a group of people from jail after they had been charged with shooting a cop. Crockett has served jail time for his beliefs. He was elected to Congress in 1980 at the age of 71. But "legend" isn't a ballot designation, and voters almost sent him packing in 1988.

Cunningham, Rev. William—February 20, 1930; civil rights dynamo.

No list of Detroit clergymen would be complete without Father William Cunningham, the Catholic priest who helped found Focus: HOPE the year after the 1967 riots. In fact, the city of Detroit wouldn't be complete without Cunningham, a flinty-eyed realist and a dreamer, often in the same sentence.

He has been the foremost local symbol of the Roman Catholic Church's commitment to the oppressed. While his fellow priests do much for the downtrodden every day, Cunningham works on a different level: He plays poker with the big boys. A group of female employees at the Automobile Association of Michigan complained about their difficulties at the corporation. Cunningham masterminded a suit that netted $3.75-million for the women. While people in his neighborhood near Linwood and Oakman were screaming for jobs, he noticed that machine shops around Detroit were screaming too—for trained help. Now Focus: HOPE runs the Machinist Training Institute to connect the two groups. And who did Cunningham bring in to show it off? George Bush, who now sleeps at 1600 Pennsylvania Avenue.

The son of an Irish-American real estate broker, he seemed destined to a somewhat peaceful life as an English teacher at Sacred Heart Seminary. The 1967 riots changed all that. He left his teaching assignment at the seminary in the spring of 1969 to devote full time to the organization, while simultaneously serving as pastor of Madonna Parish down the street. What was once a few dreamers plotting brotherhood schemes at Cunningham's dinner table in the Madonna rectory has grown to a full city block of programs along Oakman. A few people raise their eyebrows: The late John Cardinal Dearden greeted Cunningham once with a knowing "How's *business*?" His superiors once suspended him from his clerical duties when he officiated at the society wedding of a couple who had been married to other spouses.

Cunningham seems to know everybody in town, from bank chairmen to GM graybeards to bag ladies. If he had chosen to do something else with his life, he could have had his pick: real estate zillionaire, adman, anchorman—maybe even television talk-show host.

Currier, Frederick—December 6, 1923; master political pulse taker.

Chairman of Detroit-based Market Opinion Research, the state's biggest private polling and survey research concern, Currier knows the winner of a statewide election days before voters cast their ballots. Gannett Corp., the *Free Press*, Richard Nixon, William Milliken and *George Romney* all have paid big bucks for MOR's expertise. "Information is power," he once told a *Free Press* reporter, "and survey research can be a very powerful tool."

Currier comes from a scientific background. His father was a Grand Rapids psychiatrist/neurologist who cared for governors and senators. After a tour of duty at the *Free Press*, he bought into then-tiny MOR when its longtime owner neared retirement. (Although he left the newspaper business years ago, he still likes to jaw with reporters and editors.) Currier expanded the company's business into state and national politics, and landed large chunks of business from newspapers, advertising agencies and consumer products manufacturers. When Currier joined the firm, it was housed in a tiny Victorian home next to the Detroit Athletic Club. It now occupies two floors of downtown's Marquette Building.

He has a voracious intellectual appetite. Something of a Sinophile, he has traveled to China and publishes a newsletter on obscure facets of Chinese-American relations. He has an uncanny ability to get along with anybody from waitresses to big league political figures. Former Channel 4 general manager Amy McCombs is his third wife. Now that McCombs runs San Francisco's NBC affiliate, the two have a commuter marriage.

Cutraro, Antonino "Nino" — October 27, 1953; immigrant strobemeister.

If you dropped Cutraro, owner of downtown's best-known disco, in the Sahara Desert he'd wind up with the local beer distributorship. He opened Taboo in a vacant tool and die shop, and now the neon party barn draws hundreds on a typical Friday night.

A native of Grammichele in southern Italy, he was studying economics in Rome when he decided to tour America. The U.S. interested him in economics of another kind: the theory and practice of making money. He worked construction, did odd jobs—anything that could earn him a buck. With the help of an investor, he started Taboo in 1985. It instantly became hot, largely because of his aggressive marketing manner. The name "Taboo" had a sexy, slightly dangerous ring to it.

The club made the newspapers when a couple of black attorneys were refused entrance. Cutraro says it was a mistake, but one should remember that cash registers at the late Cheeks disco began ringing when a doorman refused entrance to Channel 7 anchorwoman Doris Biscoe. In the bar business, any publicity is good publicity—unless someone has been shot on the premises. Photos of *Madonna* showing up one night for a party, along with (now-ex) husband Sean Penn, who was on a weekend leave from a California jail, didn't hurt business either.

Always conscious that discos fade in and out quickly (remember Oscar's? How about Cheeks?), Nino is smart enough to extend his empire in case one outpost falls. He opened Royal Oak's Metropolitan Musicafe in late 1988. On the drawing boards for fall of 1989 is Vis-a-Vis in Pontiac, which Nino modestly projects as "the biggest nightclub in the Midwest." He also plans another Musicafe in Farmington Hills.

D

Daitch, Peggy—August 20, 1946; selling cars with style.

She's *Vogue*'s woman in Detroit. That means selling ads to the auto companies for Condé Nast. Since women are becoming increasingly important consumers in the auto market, the male-dominated Big Three are listening to her more and more.

A Detroit native, she joined *Vogue* after serving as an account supervisor at D'Arcy Masius Benton & Bowles. There, she worked on the agency's important Cadillac and Michigan Consolidated Gas accounts. Quite stylish, as befitting *Vogue*'s chief ad salesperson, she's also quite effective.

Daly, Chuck—July 20, 1930; he makes Pistons hum.

The longest-reigning coach in Pistons history, he has also presided over the best era since the club moved here from Fort Wayne, Indiana, in 1957. The team hasn't had a losing season since Daly got here in 1983, and the Pistons are a constant, looming presence at playoff time. He rang the bell, winning the 1989 National Basketball Association Championship.

Consider Daly's job: He deals with tremendous talent and tremendous egos (many of whom earn two or three times what he does), but he somehow manages to keep the ship on course. As he told *Detroit Monthly* senior editor Lowell Cauffiel: "Look, I'm not dealing with just twelve men out there. I'm dealing with twelve corporations. Every guy is the head of his own major corporation. The player makes a million a year. Consequently, you're dealing with the president of his own company. Each day. Every day."

Daly spent 20 years clawing at the door before he took his place as a head coach in the National Basketball Association. He paid his dues as an assistant at Duke (1963-'69) and as head coach at Boston College (1969-'71) and Pennsylvania (1971-'77.) He spent four seasons as an assistant with the Philadelphia 76ers (under pal Billy Cunningham) before signing on as head coach of the Cleveland Cavaliers. He spent 93 days with the Cavs before Pistons chief *Jack McCloskey* (also a Penn coach, 1956-'66) signed him as Detroit's 17th coach.

He's better with the press than most of his peers, and he has a taste for journalism. He's a part-time reporter with his Channel 2 show, "Chuck Daly's One on One."

To appreciate Daly's longevity with the Pistons, consider this: Daly joined the organization May 17, 1983. In the six years before Daly hired on, the Pistons had five coaches and no winning records: Herb Brown (77–81), Bob Kauffman (29–29), *Dick Vitale* (34–60), Richie Adubato (12–58) and Scotty Robertson (97–149).

Dauch, Richard—July 23, 1942; head Chrysler factory rat.

Lee Iacocca sometimes refers to Dick Dauch, Chrysler's manufacturing chief, as "that tough German." It's meant as a compliment.

After the designers, marketers and bean counters finish talking, Dauch, a former Purdue football player (fullback and linebacker), builds Chrysler's cars and trucks. Some 65,000 Chrysler employees call Dauch (pronounced Dowk) their boss. He is blunt and sometimes profane, in the best Chrysler tradition. The company's slogan, "Chrysler builds the best cars and trucks," comes out: "Chrysler builds the best goddamn cars and trucks in the world." With his mustache and gruff demeanor, he resembles Dabney Coleman, the actor who sometimes plays tough corporate executives on the screen.

Unlike many of Chrysler's top people, Dauch never worked at Ford. He began his career in the mid-1960s at General Motors as a shop foreman, the toughest job in the auto industry. Shop foremen put "middle" in the term "middle management," are despised by workers and are kicked by the top managers when things go awry on the line. Dauch still believes the turbulence of the shop floor molds good executives, and insists that up-and-coming manufacturing engineers spend a few years there before retreating to the relative calm of an office.

After 10 years at GM, where he rose to plant manager at Chevy's gear and axle complex, he left to run Volkswagen's U.S. manufacturing operations. He spent five years there before Iacocca personally invited him to join the Chrysler team. Prior to Dauch's arrival in 1980, Chrysler's plants were said to be the worst of the Big Three. They were dirty and outdated. Dauch has cleaned up the operation. A few Wall Street analysts believe Chrysler's manufacturing operations are as good as one will find in the country.

In his mid-40s, Dauch is mentioned as a possible candidate for the top job at Chrysler—not as a successor to Iacocca, but perhaps *Gerald Greenwald* or whoever replaces Iacocca. A few of Dauch's colleagues think he might be a loose cannon. Dauch knows that, and is aware of the dangers. "The squeaky wheel often gets the grease," he once told the *New York Times*, "but sometimes it gets replaced."

Davidson, Bill—(birthdate not available); making it off the glass.

Long before the Detroit Pistons could outdraw the World Wrestling Federation, Bill Davidson took a flyer and bought the franchise.

Now, with Isiah having led the march toward a National Basketball Association championship, who knows what they're worth?

Davidson didn't make his money from hoops. In the mid-'50s he took over Guardian Industries, which was founded by an uncle in 1932 but was facing hard times. By the time Davidson came aboard, the company was almost bankrupt. He pumped a little energy into the place. The company began making glass on its own and entered the photo processing business. In the late '60s, the company went public. Everything Davidson did seemed to work. Sales went up every year between 1973 and 1983, and profits jumped each year but one. Being on the New York Stock Exchange can be a bit of a hassle, however. Pesky stockholders show up at annual meetings with dumb or insulting questions, nosy reporters find out how much you make and your kids ask for a bigger allowance. Davidson put an end to all that by taking the place private again in the mid-'80s with $302-million in borrowed money.

He attends Pistons games, but most of what happens with the team is left to general manager **Jack McCloskey**. Davidson enjoys the scene, but is smart enough to leave the day-to-day dribbling to the pros.

Davis, David E. Jr.—November 7, 1930; Hemingway on wheels.

In an age where newspaper and magazine editors increasingly talk and dress like corporate attorneys, *Automobile* magazine's David E. Davis Jr. stands out. His bearded visage resembles Papa Hemingway. He hunts with European royalty, dresses in London-cut suits, and writes with both elegance and precision. His magazine, housed in Ann Arbor's old Pretzel Bell building, is geared to people who like to drive, drink and travel in style. And it has its followers. *Roger Smith* once left a Knight-Ridder party at the Detroit Club to catch one of Davis's bashes.

The road between the Lintas: Campbell-Ewald ad agency and various auto magazines is marked with Davis's tire tracks. He started in the magazine business in 1957 with *Road & Track*. From there he went to Campbell-Ewald, where he wrote Corvette ads. Says Davis of the experience: "*Road & Track* taught me about magazines and quality standards, and my later experience at Campbell-Ewald taught me how to write." Bill Ziff, owner of *Car and Driver*, persuaded Davis to leave the cocoon for a job at the ailing magazine. Davis spent five years there, where he successfully cured the patient but burned himself out. Davis left again for Campbell-Ewald. This time, he rose to membership on the agency's board, but returned one more time to *C and D* in 1976. That tenure lasted until 1985, when he quit after a tiff with CBS. The story has it that CBS, which had just purchased *Car and Driver* and other Ziff magazines, perused Davis's contract and discovered he was getting filthy rich off the magazine. (Which seemed fair enough. Davis had built *Car and Driver* into the world's biggest auto consumer book.) CBS offered to cut his pay, and Davis quietly excused himself from the company—taking a chunk of the magazine's staff with him. Rupert Murdoch was only too happy to finance Davis's new book and add it to his stable.

Davis is fun to read, is great company, and is said to be extraordinarily well-connected in the auto community.

Davis, Don—October 25, 1938; financially sound.

As chairman of First Independence National Bank, he's riding the crest of the town's burgeoning black economic power. A couple of years ago, he was dealing with saxophone players instead of loan officers.

While growing up in Detroit's Brewster Projects, he took up the guitar. A meeting with the late jazz great Wes Montgomery destroyed Davis's guitar aspirations. Davis told the *Metro Times'* Bruce Britt: "I went over to Wes's house one day and was just astounded with his left-hand dexterity, the way he used his thumb to pick the strings and how he managed chord substitutions." Realizing he'd never rise to Montgomery's level, Davis quit picking and became a record producer. He joined Stax Records in Memphis, producing hits by Johnny Taylor, Robin Trower, the Dramatics and Funkadelics.

After earning a stack of money at Stax, he bought United Sound Systems Inc., a studio in an old house north of the Wayne State University campus. United quickly became the recording studio of choice for Detroit artists and a little-publicized Mecca for national acts. Billy Davis and Marilyn McCoo's "You Don't Have to Be a Star" was recorded there, as was Johnny Taylor's "Disco Lady."

An argument with CBS over money, and a feeling that the music business was passing him by, drove Davis out of the studio. With the cash he'd saved, he bought up almost $700,000 of First Independence stock and became chairman. That's where he's been since 1980, and he says that's where he'll stay.

Demers, Jacques—August 25, 1944; duh man for duh job.

If you are a Red Wing, you play with maximum enthusiasm. (Demers would call it "en-tooo-zee-as-m"). Winning is important, but other things are even more key. Mental attitude. Excellence. If you're a Red Wing, not going to the Adirondacks farm team is important. Get the Jacques Demers picture?

Although he's billed for his success, Demers has had his share of failure and bad luck. His hockey career ended at the age of 17 with a leg injury. He was fired in his first year as an NHL coach when his team, the expansion Quebec Nordiques, slid through a 25-44-11 season in 1979-'80. He stayed with a Nordiques farm club, coaching them through several impressive years. St. Louis gave him another chance in 1983, and he had a successful run with the Blues until the Wings hired him away in June 1986.

While the Demers-coached Blues hit first place in the 1985-'86 Norris Division race with a 37-31-12 record, the Wings' 17-57-6 was the worst in the NHL. Long-suffering fans dubbed the team "the Dead Wings."

They didn't seem so dead after Demers took charge. The Wings improved by 38 points (34-36-10) in his first year (1986-'87), finishing second in the division. They would have been first if Demers' old St. Louis team hadn't beat the Wings in overtime on the final night of the regular season. They did finish first in 1987-'88. The team hadn't done that since 1964-'65, when there were only six teams in the entire league. *The Hockey News* has named Demers coach of the year twice.

In person, he is staggeringly polite and charming. A fan called him on a WJR talk show one night and thanked Demers for letting him have a spot in heavy freeway traffic that afternoon.

All of this, of course, is deeply appreciated by owner *Mike Ilitch* and the fans. He's much in demand for television commercials, where he has been seen shilling for local Dodge dealers. The Wings, eager to keep him around, signed him to a contract in May 1988 that takes him through the 1992-'93 season.

Derderian, Leo—October 12, 1918; the straw that stirs the drinks.

One would never mistake the Anchor Bar, at the base of a geographical triangle comprising the *News*, *Free Press* and Channel 4, for a fern bar. Dark, dank and smokey, it's downright depressing. One could win a Pulitzer Prize and an Academy Award in the same day, walk in for a drink, and feel depressed. But if a place is to be judged by the kind of people it attracts, the Anchor rates high. On some nights legislators, reporters, judges, lawyers and priests bolt back drinks, elbow to elbow. Presiding over all of this like a grouchy lion, or an elderly Bluto Blutarsky, is Leo.

The Anchor, in its heyday and in a basement around the corner, was maybe *the* gathering spot among the rough-edged power set. When the late *News* columnist Doc Greene was alive and drinking (the latter contributed to his death at age 50), the place would routinely bring in a U.S. senator or two, Mayor Jerry Cavanagh and much of the town's Irish political Mafia. The seamy side—gambling—only contributed to the joint's charm. A federal grand jury didn't see the charm of bookmaking, however, and indicted Leo and a host of others in 1971. The paperwork claimed the bar was doing $40,000 a day. (The videotape made by the FBI was said to contain nothing more than a bunch of reporters bitching about their bosses.) The Evening News Association, which had acquired the property in 1970, used the indictment as a convenient excuse to terminate Leo's lease. But Leo got the last laugh. The indictments were voided because then-Attorney General John Mitchell hadn't properly signed the wiretap requests. As it was, only Mitchell did time. And Leo opened a new place in the otherwise-vacant Fort Shelby Hotel.

The Anchor decor includes a gallery of customers no longer capable of drinking because they are now dead. The only color photographs are those of the late Msgr. Clement Kern, who ran nearby Holy Trinity Church for so many years, and the late Channel 7 newsman Ven Marshall. Derderian, an Episcopalian, still supports the church—though he remains bitter about *Cardinal Szoka* removing Father Jay Samonie — Kern's successor—from the parish pastorship.

Leo must be getting on in years. He has been telling patrons that drinking is no good for them.

Devellano, Jimmy—January 18, 1943; living and dying by the draft.

The puckish Jimmy Devellano's life is a small round slab of hard rubber. As he once told *News* reporter Bill Halls: "Actually, I'm not single. I'm married to the Detroit hockey club. The hockey club is my wife, and the players are my children." Nobody who knows Devellano doubts the veracity of that remark. Constantly disheveled, he looks like the absent-minded professor. If he socializes, he might be seen having a drink with a player.

His forté is finding talent in out-of-the-way places. To coach *Jacques Demers*, that's important. Demers once wrote that "the chief scout, to me, is more important than the coach. If you don't draft the players, no coach can work miracles." In fact, Devellano began his career as a scout for the St. Louis Blues in 1967, and switched to the New York Islanders organization five years later. Devellano joined the Wings in July 1982 as general manager. He was *Mike Ilitch*'s first hire, the man who had built the Islanders into a league power.

It hasn't all been great. Fans forget that the 1985-'86 season (once characterized by *News* sports writer Shelby Strother as "The Year of the Dead Thing") produced just 17 victories. About that time, there were rumors that Devellano was in trouble.

But Demers is on hand now, some of Devellano's drafts (notably *Steve Yzerman*) have worked out. And you don't hear talk about dead things any more.

DiBiaggio, John—September 11, 1932; top man on the banks of the Red Cedar.

Michigan State University's president grew up on Detroit's east side, the son of immigrants and the first member of his family to attend college. He once told a group of Italian-Americans that ethnic slurs he heard in his old neighborhood made him think about changing his name. But the joke is on his old bigoted neighbors: They're probably still working the line at Chrysler, while he enjoys a six-figure salary at the state's biggest university.

A dentist by training, he practiced in New Baltimore (that's deep Macomb County) before choosing a career in academe. While still yanking teeth, he picked up a master's degree from the University of Michigan in educational administration. His first job was a humble one: chair of the University of Detroit's Department of Social Dentistry. He left town for stops at the University of Kentucky, Virginia Commonwealth University and the University of Connecticut, which he ran for six years before being named MSU's 17th president.

One of the state Capitol's more entertaining feuds is between DiBiaggio and Governor *James Blanchard*. After all, the Guv is an alumnus who bleeds Spartan green. One MSU board member claims DiBiaggio once called Blanchard a "twerp." DiBiaggio denies it, but the two did clash when Blanchard knocked the MSU president for proposing a tuition increase.

His scholarly credentials don't wow the academic types ("After all," sniffed one professor, "he's just a dentist"), but he's aces at public relations.

DiChiera, Dr. David—April 8, 1935; making overtures to Detroit.

As general director of the Michigan Opera Theatre, he provides the fix for Detroit's opera addicts. Before DiChiera arrived on the scene, opera buffs had to content themselves with an annual visit from New York's Metropolitan Opera—an event greeted with more pomp than the pope's visit to Hamtramck. But now with the MOT presenting five to six productions each year, life is much easier for people who have fallen beneath opera's spell.

DiChiera's main role in life seems to be convincing people that opera isn't only for blue-haired matrons from the best zip codes. "We've got to get rid of these old images of opera," he once told a reporter. "For years some people have thought opera is some fat lady screaming at the top of her voice in a language they don't understand; or that the only people who go are stuffy, in long gowns or blacktie, with lots of jewels, who are going to something they really don't enjoy." Indeed, the MOT has done some, uh, strange things to market itself. In an effort to get publicity for "Kismet," it hired a belly-dancer to gyrate in front of a camel at the Detroit Zoo.

Before MOT, DiChiera ran Oakland University's music department. While he was the Music Hall's impresario (1971-'79), he ran Overture to Opera, the predecessor to the Michigan Opera Theatre. When MOT was formed in 1971, DiChiera became its first—and so far, only—director.

When he isn't dressing fat ladies in Detroit, he directs southern California's Opera Pacific. Orange County's big new money, wishing to prove that they aren't mere nouveau riche philistines, hired DiChiera to lend an aura of aria to the area.

His wife, Karen, is a VanderKloot. Her grandfather was the late William Knudsen, president of General Motors (1937-'40) and chief of the Office of War Production Management during World War II. Karen DiChiera is also a music educator and director of MOT community programs. Their home in Bloomfield Hills echoes with music all hours of the day and night, and with socializing about as often.

Dingell, John Jr.—July 8, 1926; Michigan's most powerful congressman.

A writer once called John Dingell "the junkyard dog of Congress." Dingell, who has represented the downriver area since 1955, probably considered it a compliment. "Yeah, I love a good fight," he once told the *Wall Street Journal*. "I love to swing the meat ax." Other adjectives that come to mind when describing Dingell are "effective" and "smart." He chairs the House Energy and Commerce Committee, which, as the Washington, D.C.-based *National Journal* once wrote, "claims jurisdiction over anything that moves, burns or is solid." The automobile industry, of course, fits all three categories. So General Motors, Ford and Chrysler are extraordinarily solicitous of his moods.

There has been a Dingell in Congress since John Dingell's father, John Dingell Sr., was elected in the 1932 Roosevelt landslide. The elder Dingell apparently shared his son's bluntness. Asked in a 1952 *Detroit News* questionnaire if he held any honorary degrees, the elder Dingell wrote: "No unearned degrees from accredited universities. Many from the school of hard knocks." When the elder Dingell died in 1955 at age 61, his son took his seat.

Since then, the younger (now, not so young) Dingell has earned his reputation for hard work and zest for power. The *New York Times* described him as "a good poker player, not showing his hand before the right time comes to pounce."

Dingell, a hunter, has game heads mounted on his office wall. Several top Reagan officials ought to be included among his trophies. A tussle with Environmental Protection Agency administrator Ann Gorsuch Buford led to her resignation. Rita Lavelle thought she could get away with hiding EPA documents from Dingell's committee. A federal grand jury took a dim view of that and filed criminal charges.

It may be that a Dingell will sit in Congress for at least another generation. His son, Chris, was elected to the state Senate in 1986.

Dixon, Dave—September 20, 1938; Detroit public radio potentate.

His eclectic, off-the-wall mix of music has been a catalyst in WDET-FM's resurgence. On any given morning at 10, a listener might hear New Age music from Australia, bebop, experimental electronic sounds from Germany or funk from Detroit. Aging hipster Dixon ties it together in an effective audio package that bridges several age groups. His six-year stint as a WABX-FM "air ace" in the late 1960s and early '70s gives him two generations of fans. Comments like "My mom and I listen to Dixon—it's the only thing we agree on" are not unusual. That's one reason program director Judy Adams hired him. "He brought new people to the station," Adams explains. "For the post-war baby boomers, his time on WABX was an exciting time. He's a magnet for those people—people upset with the boredom of the '70s and the uncertainty of the '80s." His characterization of commercial radio as "a national disgrace" also endears him to fans.

Birmingham-bred Dixon was a classmate of arbitrageur/convict Ivan Boesky at Cranbrook. He grew up listening to WJR's Bud Guest and rock 'n' roll's Mickey Schorr. "I learned from all of them," Dixon recalls, "and I set as my goal to be as natural as I could." His early radio experience included duty in Big Rapids, Pontiac, Kalamazoo and Milwaukee. Disillusioned with radio, he reconnected in New York with high school pal Noel Stookey, better known as Paul Stookey of Peter, Paul and Mary fame. Dixon wrote the group's onstage comments, plus lyrics to "I Dig Rock and Roll Music" and "This Song Is Love." He still receives royalty checks.

Most Detroiters in their mid-30s wistfully remember Dixon as one of free-form radio's best practitioners at WABX. Rock radio historians still think of it as one of the most innovative eras in radio. After leaving there in 1974, Dixon spent most of the next 10 years hosting all-night movies and television programs on Miami UHF television. His acerbic assessments of the movies he hosted made him a cult figure. Much of what Dixon did was based on Detroiter *Bill Kennedy*'s work. At one time, his gnarled face was as famous as *Bill Bonds*' in southern Florida. But Bell's palsy, a form of facial paralysis, killed Dixon's television career and sent him back to Detroit radio.

He never married. "I'm a very difficult individual," Dixon admits. Many people at the station agree. But Dixon gets results.

Doran, Wayne (May 30, 1937) and Keane-Doran, Maureen (March 17, 1940); duke and duchess of Dearborn.

He chairs Ford Motor Land Development Corp., where he has been instrumental in developing tidy little pieces of property such as the Renaissance Center and Fairlane. She's a Dearborn city councilwoman and may run for mayor one of these days.

Doran joined Ford in 1969 after a half-dozen years with Del E. Webb Corp., where he developed three Sun City communities (some 43,000 acres worth) in Arizona, California and Florida. When Henry Ford II got it in his head that Ford Motor ought to get serious about developing its fallow land holdings, Doran became the company point man.

His wife, Maureen, is far better known, particularly in Dearborn. She was a close friend of the late Mayor Orville Hubbard. (He was at her apartment when he suffered the paralyzing stroke that hobbled him throughout the rest of his life.) For awhile in 1981 it appeared that she might become mayor herself. Somehow convinced that incumbent mayor John O'Reilly wasn't living up to the Hubbard tradition of feisty service for the taxpayers, she took him on in the primary. She picked up enough votes to cause people to wonder if a coup was in the cards, but O'Reilly won the run-off handily. She was elected to her council seat in 1985, and she constantly harps at Mayor Michael Guido.

Keane and Doran married in 1982. They lived in Farmington Hills, but moved after Maureen groused that she had to be back in Dearborn. Her brother, noted surrogate-mother broker and attorney Noel Keane, is also based in Dearborn.

Dow, Peter—see O'Connor, Richard

Duderstadt, James—December 5, 1942; *Bo Schembechler*'s boss.

He rose from the smalltown Midwest to become the University of Michigan's 11th president. As such, he'll wrestle with such problems as making minority students more comfortable and more numerous.

A native of Iowa, he grew up in Carrollton, Missouri (pop: 4,700), where he set a lifelong pattern of over-achievement. When he wasn't earning all A's as a high school student, he played basketball, football, baseball and ran track. A graduate of Yale (1964), and the California Institute of Technology (master's in 1965, doctorate in 1967), he signed on at U-M's nuclear engineering department in 1969. He became dean of the engineering school (1981-'86), which is considered among the country's best, then advanced to provost/v.p. academic affairs. He earned a reputation as an over-achieving administrator at the engineering school. Engineering research grants more than doubled, from $16-million a year to $36-million, under his leadership. The engineering school also moved into a spiffy new facility. "I have a reputation as a steamroller . . . I like to see things happen, and I like to see them happen very quickly," he told U-M regents when they quizzed him on his hard-charging attitude. That answer apparently sufficed. He replaced Harold Shapiro, who left for the Princeton presidency in 1987. (Former U-M president Robben Fleming kept Shapiro's seat warm as interim president until Duderstadt got there.)

The university has been hit with heavy protests from minority students in recent years. Duderstadt's first presidential address dealt with the problem. In 1989, the demonstrations relaxed somewhat and the Wolverines won the Rose Bowl and an NCAA basketball championship. What more could a U-M president ask?

Durant, W. Clark III—May 13, 1949; the politically-to-the-right stuff.

This extraordinarily preppy-looking lawyer may be a power in the Republican Party in years to come. Barely 40, he has been in the forefront of conservative politics for a decade. Unlike some of his ilk, who seem mean-spirited and contentious, Durant comes across more like a friendly young Mr. Chips. It's the bow tie and suspenders, which he wore before they became trendy accessories to young risers, that make him seem a little professorial. As of this writing, he has his eye on U.S. Senator *Donald Riegle*'s seat.

The son of conservative Republican warhorse Richard Durant, Clark was educated at Grosse Pointe University School, Tulane University and Notre Dame Law School. He chose the latter two for strange reasons. Durant, a voracious reader even in high school, had read William Cash's "Mind of the South." That, and ideal golfing weather in New Orleans, persuaded Durant that Louisiana was for him. Notre Dame seemed an odd choice for a fervent Episcopalian. But Durant just happened to be seated one night next to Notre Dame president Father Theodore Hesburgh, who is even more persuasive than New Orleans.

When he joined his dad's law firm, Durant defended indigent clients on grounds it was the best way to get trial experience.

Durant ran Jack Kemp's failed Michigan presidential campaign here in 1987-'88, and was one of four co-chairs nationally. President Reagan thought highly enough of Durant to name him chairman of the U.S. Legal Services Corp. board.

E

Eberhard, Rev. David—January 1, 1934; street-weary but still-kicking councilman.

This red-haired Louisville native was sent to Detroit by his Lutheran overseers in 1959 to close the east side's Riverside Lutheran Church. Eberhard got lost somewhere along the way. Instead of shuttering the place, he mired himself in community civil rights projects and ran for City Council. His debut campaign in 1969 scored him an impressive fourth-place finish, better than any political rookie since. He hasn't done nearly as well in subsequent years, placing eighth, sixth, eighth and eighth in his next four outings. But his seat still seems secure.

He finally closed Riverside after 17 years, when he accepted the fact that his flock had permanently moved to the suburbs. When not at the council table, he now can be found at Historic Trinity Lutheran Church, not far from Eastern Market. His annual Oktoberfest celebration is a big deal, drawing people like the *News'* *Pete Waldmeir* and Channel 7's *Bill Bonds.*

Eberhard, more than most council members, is a creature of the street. As a pastor, he spends much time tending to the dispossessed and down-on-their-luck. He also hits plenty of social gatherings and prides himself on having driven every avenue and alleyway in town. His gruff manner causes some political observers to lump him with more conservative council members, such as *Jack Kelley.* But they're wrong. More often than not, he can be found voting with *Mayor Young*—though he's not as obsequious about it as some colleagues. He is often allied with *Nicholas Hood* and *Barbara-Rose Collins.* Since a 7–2 vote can override a mayoral veto, Eberhard's support has been critical.

Eberhard has given one indication that he'd like to move on. He was knocked off the ballot in 1980 when he failed to file enough nominating petitions for Charles Diggs Jr.'s vacant 13th Congressional District seat. Eberhard was the only white candidate foolish enough to run in the mostly black district. Perhaps the gods were being kind by saving Eberhard the embarrassment of being trounced by *George Crockett Jr.*

Watching the decay, trying to stanch it, fencing with the Mayor's Office, and putting up with the tedium have taken a serious toll. He admitted he was an alcoholic in the early '70s, and spent six weeks in a Washington, D.C., hospital drying out. He told the *Free Press* at the time that "when you first start out in the ministry, you think you're going to convert everyone in the church. When you first start in politics, you think you're going to save the world . . . Now if I do a reliable job and care for my family, I'm thankful at the end of the day."

The father of five sons, he builds finely crafted doll houses when he's not on the road.

Edgecomb, Diane—(birthdate not available); downtown's biggest booster.

Her picture is next to the definition of "Boosterism" in Webster's. As president of the Central Business District Association, she has pushed the health and welfare of downtown Detroit with uncommon dedication. Edgecomb's zeal makes her a bit easy to knock. But she was at the barricades defending downtown's honor while everybody else moved to Troy or Southfield.

Edgecomb joined the CBDA in 1955, working her way up to the group's presidency in 1977. The ethnic festivals were her idea. So was lighting the Ambassador Bridge, which became a reality eight weeks after the first light bulb lit up in her imagination. The People Mover was an Edgecomb idea that teetered on the verge of failure and emerged as a success. Her suggestion that everybody who worked downtown ought to spend $10 a month at the downtown Hudson's wasn't enough to save the day, however.

Although Edgecomb is a Republican, she's one of *Mayor Young*'s biggest supporters and is said to have his ear. Her suggestion that the Civic Center area be renamed Coleman Young International Civic Arena was hooted off the drawing boards.

Elliott, John—June 30, 1931; leader of the city's teachers.

As president of the Detroit Federation of Teachers, he negotiates on behalf of the folks on the front lines: the people who teach in Detroit's troubled classrooms.

Elliott, who has degrees from Wayne State University and the University of Michigan, taught social science at Cooley High School. He had been the union's executive v.p. under Mary Ellen Riordan, but had a falling out with her and challenged her twice in the '70s. Riordan, the wily old pro, crushed Elliott in 1974 and 1978. But when Riordan finally bowed out of the job in 1981, Elliott got the last laugh by beating Riordan's hand-picked slate.

Riordan was a presence in Detroit organized labor; Elliott seems to be less so. He was elected to the No. 2 post with the Michigan AFL-CIO in 1987 after a hard-fought contest, but resigned less than a year later. Some wondered why he went through the trouble in the first place.

Esser, Phil—November 8, 1941; resident baritone

This former 1960's folk singer has made the transition to theater. Arriving here just out of the Air Force in 1964, he became a fixture on the coffee house circuit. But when folk guitar became a little less fashionable, Esser took to the stage with "Jacques Brel Is Alive and Well." That ran from 1973 until 1975, and gave Esser a new career. Wildly entertaining and possessor of a strong baritone voice, he's likely to have a local audience as long as he's able to climb onstage.

Estleman, Loren D.—September 15, 1952; tough-guy detective novelist.

His series of Amos Walker novels are set in Detroit's underbelly. "Motor City Blue" is must reading among Detroit fiction titles. "Downriver" (1988) brought Estleman critical acclaim. "At his best," wrote *New York Times* mystery maven Newgate Callendar, "Mr. Estleman is one of the major practitioners of the tough-guy private-eye novel."

An Eastern Michigan University grad, Estleman took a liking to cops while working the *Ypsilanti Press*'s police beat. Unlike most journalists who blather incessantly about leaving newspapers to write fiction, Estleman actually did it. From the outset of his newspaper career, he thought of himself as a writer who merely worked at newspapers to pay the rent. So he had no problems when he cut the umbilical cord in 1980 for a full-time career writing books.

Amos Walker is the basic cigaret-smoking, booze-soaked, slink-around-town private eye pioneered and popularized by Dashiel Hammett and Raymond Chandler. Walker lives slightly beyond society's fringes, but keeps his ethics intact. How tough is Amos Walker? "There is an Irene waiting somewhere for every one of us," Walker remarks in "Every Brilliant Eye," "to hand us a martini . . . and pillow us with her breasts and say, 'There, there, they just don't know what they've got in a man like you.' The trick is to recognize her and cross the street when we see her coming. By which time, of course, it's too late." A good part of Estleman's fictional output reeks of trail dust rather than city saloons. He has written 13 westerns—an interesting parallel with Detroit's other master of Motown mayhem, *Elmore Leonard*, who also has dabbled in the Wild West.

Estleman, in fact, lives a rather quiet existence in Whitmore Lake. He works on a 1923 Underwood typewriter, making only occasional trips into the evil Big City for local color tours. Novelists are usually dead or pensioned before they get around to bequeathing their papers to their alma maters, but Estleman's are housed at EMU.

Eubanks, Dayna—June 7, 1957; anchor in new waters.

Trained at Channel 7, she rose from street reporter to Diana Lewis's replacement at the anchor desk. When Eubanks' contract wasn't renewed, the firing received the sort of press coverage normally given, say, an assassination or the trading of a popular point guard. Now she's at Channel 2 and hoping to rise again.

There are two schools of thought on why her contract wasn't renewed at Channel 7. One holds that she didn't sufficiently kowtow to anchorman *Bill Bonds*, the news department's Sun King. The other holds that she was so abrasive and arrogant that it made others—including Bonds — uncomfortable. Whatever the case, nobody can deny that she hustled.

As in the case of her partner, *Joe Glover*, her fate rests with the viewers' remote controls. If enough switch to Channel 2, she will have been in on the ground floor of one of the most remarkable turnarounds in local TV news history. Otherwise, she'll be out of work.

Ewald, Ted—September 29, 1924; wealth well-spent.

He's a good example of quiet, effective old money. Ewald's father, a founder of the Campbell-Ewald ad agency, left his son with a pile of money. Instead of squandering it on booze and women, he puts youngsters through college—some 60 of them at any given time. (One of Ewald's alumni is David Olmstead, one of the three HOPE candidates in 1988's Detroit Board of Education race.)

Ewald attended the exclusive Philips Exeter Academy prep school while George Bush attended rival Andover. Ewald remembers Bush as "Poppy."

Something of a sportsman, he's minority owner of the Detroit Pistons. He also managed a couple of boxers until one of them, Sonny Banks, died as a result of injuries sustained in the ring.

He doesn't advertise his money. He just does good things with it. Some of the town's nouveau riche could study Ewald's example.

F

Farbman, Burton (February 12, 1943) and Suzy (birthdate not available); *real* estate.

As a kid, this Troy real estate developer figured he'd like to be rich when he grew up. Now he is grown up and his firm, Farbman/Stein and Co., does just about everything in the real estate field. In the market for an apartment house? You can buy one through Farbman's shop. Want to use somebody else's money for the transaction? Farbman's company might find it for you. And after the deal is complete, Farbman's company can run it for you. From each of these scenarios, the Farbman coffers grow a bit more. After a while, it adds up.

A native of Detroit's west side, he graduated from Mumford High School and Wayne State University, working for a time during his college years as a digger for Rose Builders. Farbman's real education, however, came during stops at Burton Title and Abstract Co., Advance Mortgage, then Schostak Realty. While at Schostak, he and Lee Stein met, then quit the place to start their own shop in 1977. The well-connected Stein, a mover in these parts, died 10 years later from a heart attack, barely aged 52.

At this point, Farbman isn't spectacularly well known. He tends to do things quietly, the way he helped restore the historic Wayne County Courthouse. His wife, Suzy, writes for *Detroit Monthly* magazine, keeps a hand in larger literary and social projects and seems to know everybody in town. The two are part owners of The London Chop House, as well as a few square miles of scenic land in upstate Michigan.

Ficano, Robert—July 19, 1952; Democrat with badge.

This western suburban politician-turned Wayne County sheriff made an ill-advised run for the Wayne County executive's office in 1986—and failed dismally. But don't write him off. Voters like a little gray in their leaders' hair. Ficano, in his mid-30s, has none. With his mustache, he still looks a Jaycee officer. Appearing on television to explain every major drug bust made by his department, he'll be very well known before he's gray.

Although he lacked a law enforcement background before taking his current job, Ficano did have Democratic Party credentials. The U of D Law School grad chaired the 2nd District for the Democrats and was County Clerk *James Killeen*'s deputy for two years. When Sheriff *William Lucas* left to become county exec with two years left in his term, Lucas ignored the fine print in the Michigan Constitution on who picked his successor: The decision was made by the county clerk, prosecuting attorney and chief judge. It just so happened that Ficano worked for one of the three officeholders — Killeen. Killeen, who has a seemingly insatiable appetite for political mischief, persuaded Chief Probate Judge Joseph Pernick to go along with the Ficano-for-sheriff plan. There wasn't much Prosecutor William Cahalan could do. Ficano's appointment was debated for three months in court before he could legally report to work.

When Ficano ran for county executive in 1986, he was clobbered by the older, more experienced *Ed McNamara*. And when Ficano ran for re-election to the sheriff's post in 1988, opponents seized on the '86 campaign as proof that Ficano doesn't really want to be sheriff. But nobody pays much attention to such things, and Ficano skated back into office unscathed. He has not remained unscathed by McNamara, whose running battle with Ficano became the standard news story out of county government. Chief Wayne County Circuit Judge *Richard Kaufman* took the jail out of Ficano's control and gave it to McNamara in early 1989.

Fink, Neil—August 23, 1939; top dog criminal defense lawyer.

Fink has argued some of the biggest criminal trials in Detroit. He successfully defended alleged mob figures such as Anthony Zerilli and two Giacalones—Vito and Anthony (Tony Jack). He wasn't quite as successful defending coed killer John Norman Collins or Vista defendant Sam Cusenza. Nevertheless, the U.S. Attorney's Office plays close attention when Fink takes a case.

The son of a Hudson's clothing salesman, Fink learned everything he knows within Detroit's city limits. He attended Mumford High School, the University of Detroit and the Detroit College of Law. He joined up with Joe Louisell, a legendary Detroit criminal defense lawyer who was the attorney of choice of mobsters in distress during the '50s and '60s. Louisell's dramatic style would astound even devotees of Broadway courtroom dramas. Louisell made trips to the water cooler during final arguments. With H_2O in hand, he'd tell the jury why his clients would go free. Often, they bought it. From his mentor Fink inherited an energetic, emotional, sincere appeal punctuated by show-biz flair. If Fink were tall, blond and square-jawed, straight out of "L.A. Law," the package wouldn't work. In fact, Fink is of barely medium height, curly haired and slightly overweight. You wouldn't pick him out of a race track crowd. His package plays well with jurors. He was once cited in "The Best Lawyers of America."

His forté is getting in the faces of government witnesses. The feds regularly make deals with rapists, swindlers and cons so they'll tattle on other bad guys. Fink's job is to make crooks-turned-federal witnesses babble—or worse. One such offending witness began spitting up blood during Fink's cross-examination. "My finest hour," brags Fink.

Fisher, Charles III—November 22, 1929; authentic Detroit blueblood.

As chairman of National Bank of Detroit (the state's biggest bank) and a third-generation director of General Motors Corp., this dignified, understated Grosse Pointer is the essence of quiet power in Detroit.

A dissection of the Fisher family gene pool is necessary when discussing "Chick" Fisher. His grandfather was Charles Fisher, second of the seven Fisher brothers—as in Fisher Body, as in the pack of Ohio grease monkeys who helped build General Motors into a Chrome Colossus. Granddad did a 10-year stint on GM's board, eventually unloading (as his brothers did) much of his GM stock. (The brothers' shares would be worth about $1 billion if they had kept them.) Oh, yes. The Depression had wiped out most of the banks in town, so the first Charles Fisher served on the board of NBD when it was founded in 1933. GM, goodness knows, needed a place to stash its money.

Charles Fisher III's dad, Charles Fisher Jr., was a GM board member from 1954 until his death in 1958, and was a constant presence in polite and powerful society. Fisher Jr. was named president of NBD in 1938, the month before his 31st birthday. Known as "Chick" — like his son—he was a director of Detroit Edison and Michigan Bell. Even though Fisher was a Republican, Gov. Frank Murphy made him state banking commissioner in 1936. Franklin Delano Roosevelt similarly overlooked Chick's party allegiances and made him a director of the Reconstruction Finance Corporation in 1935.

Which brings us to the present-day Charles Fisher III. A Georgetown grad, he added a Harvard MBA to his wall in 1953 before joining Touche Ross. Five years later, not long after his father's death, he joined NBD as an assistant v.p. He didn't inherit enough stock to control the place, but he had enough clout to run it. (In fact, if one took away the stock owned by board member Irving Rose, Fisher would still hold more shares than the rest of the board members combined.) No questions were asked when CFIII was named to the NBD presidency in 1972, or as CEO of both the bank and NBD Bank Corp. in 1982.

Fisher's 1988 salary was on the sunny side of $1-million ($1,088,813 to be exact). And the bank has kept on the safe, profitable course it has always steered. Which gives it assets more than double its nearest competitor.

Fisher, Max—July 15, 1908; ancient power broker.

Forbes magazine claims this octogenarian businessman is worth at least $340-million. But Fisher's ever-growing pile of money is trivial compared with his clout. He can raise presidents, prime ministers and CEOs on the telephone at will. When the Detroit Red Wings needed help getting hockey player Petr Klima into this country from eastern Europe, Fisher gave the U.S. State Department a little nudge. The calls go both ways. When the late Henry Ford II was busted for drunk driving in 1975, Ford was on the horn to Fisher pronto.

The son of an immigrant Russian peddler, Fisher attended Ohio State University on a football scholarship. He began in his dad's oil business, trading this and buying that until the company he owned—Aurora—was the largest independent oil company in the Midwest. He sold Aurora to Marathon Oil in exchange for stock in 1959.

When U.S. Steel (now USX Corp.) bought Marathon 23 years later, Fisher traded in his dusty stock certificates for some $200-million in fresh dollar bills. He made another killing when he and pals *Al Taubman* and Henry Ford II anted up $337.4-million for the Irvine Ranch, 77,000-acres of southern California that stood smack in the middle of a major population shift. Each pocketed about $100-million when they sold their shares only three years later.

These days, his far-flung business interests include an 11.5 percent stake in Sotheby's, the auction house; an impressive chunk of Manufacturers National Corp. stock; and part ownership in the Riverfront Apartments.

At age 80, he shows few signs of slowing down. Fisher was with George Bush on the ground floor of Bush's 1988 campaign, raising more than $1-million when it really counted — during the presidential primary, when a Bush presidency was a chancy proposition. Certainly, Bush will pick up the phone when Fisher calls.

Fitzgerald, Jim—August 5, 1926; Emily's very talented grandfather.

In terms of heart and range and perception, Fitz surely ranks near the top of the city's newspaper columnists. He might unleash unexpurgated vitriol against the Municipal Parking Authority one day, then write lovingly about his granddaughter Emily the next.

Fitz didn't become a Detroiter until he turned 50. Upon graduation from Michigan State University in 1951, his uncle Sam McCool (press secretary to former Michigan governor Murray Van Wagoner) hooked Fitz up with a job at the *Lapeer County Press*. "Actually he didn't want me to get a job in Detroit because he thought I'd move in with him," Fitz says. The temporary job in Lapeer lasted 25 years, 15 of them as editor. Former *Free Press* editor Mark Ethridge tried to hire Fitz as an editorial writer in the late '60s, but Fitz didn't take the job for the oddest of reasons. "After the interview, I was supposed to meet my wife in front of Hudson's. But I got lost." That scared him off from urban life for a few more years. He signed on a few years later (1976) as a columnist.

Since he lives in a high rise near downtown Detroit, commuting isn't a problem. He walks from his apartment to his desk in the middle of the *Freep* newsroom, which makes him a different duck among Detroit columnists. An unusual number of them work from home on computers, far removed from contact with their colleagues. Rubbing shoulders with the people who report real stories seems to be out of the question. Not so with Fitz. He is generally accessible to the public by telephone, and is exposed to newsroom banter and insights every day.

He is one of the few *Free Press* columnists who expressed some reservations about the Joint Operating Agreement, and he sided with editorial page cartoonist Bill Day when *Freep* management stopped Day from making fun of then attorney general Ed Meese while he pondered the JOA. That gained him heat from the corporate suits at the *Freep*. On the other hand, he wound up telling the JOA's most visible opponent, state Sen. John Kelly, to kiss his ass. One can only conclude that Fitz is his own man.

Fitzpatrick, Sean—September 28, 1941; heartbeat of Campbell-Ewald.

This cigar-smoking vice-chairman/director of creative services for Lintas: Campbell-Ewald was the force behind Chevy's "Heartbeat of America" campaign. It won crates of awards for the agency, and helped Chevy sell a few cars.

He didn't start out life wanting to be a huckster. "I really wanted to be Robert Penn Warren or Ernest Hemingway; not Ogilvy or Bernbach," he once wrote. After graduation from Hamilton College in New York, he worked as a reporter in Bloomington, Indiana. Any lust he had for the newspaper business cooled when (a) a paper he joined in Albany went on strike, and (b) two job offers in Manhattan evaporated when one person he was dealing with died and the other paper also died. Goodbye newspapers and hello advertising.

He spent a year each with Ketchum and Grey, then a decade with J. Walter Thompson. He tried his hand at movies (working on "The Great Santini" and the "Walking Tall" pictures), but missed advertising. His work on the Toyota account drew the attention of folks at Campbell-Ewald, and he was hired to do for Chevy what he had already done for the Japanese.

The "heartbeat" ads were produced, at least in part, because of Fitzpatrick's creative energy. "He was a one-man Cuisinart," recalls one colleague. "He didn't care where an idea came from, he threw everything into the mix."

Underlings say he's capable of being a Southern gentleman one moment, an executioner the next. The New York sharpies thought enough of Fitzpatrick's work to pick him as a judge for the International Advertising Film Festival at Cannes. "I thought you had to be a legend in your own time to be chosen a judge in Cannes," he joked.

Fontes, Wayne—February 17, 1939; a new era, or a new goat?

Here's a depressing statistic: The Lions won their last championship in 1957. Anyone who enjoyed that championship season as an energetic 25-year-old is about to retire without enjoying another one. For a lot of reasons, the Lions haven't been able to do what the Tigers, Pistons and Red Wings have been able to do: win. Enter Wayne Fontes, who was named coach by owner *William Clay Ford* a few days before Christmas in 1988. Will Fontes be a hero? Or another in a herd of goats.

Fontes spent nine years in the Tampa Bay Buccaneers organization as a defensive backs coach, defensive coordinator and assistant head coach before coming to Detroit as defensive coordinator in 1985. Coach Daryll Rogers sloughed to an abysmal 14–40 record before Ford invoked the mercy rule and elevated Fontes. The Lions finished the season with just two wins (against the lowly Green Bay Packers) in their last five games. But new signs of life in the corpse's eyes were enough for Ford to give Fontes a shot.

Will he be another Monte Clark? Another Tommy Hudspeth? Another Rick Forzano? The last winning Lions coach was Joe Schmidt, who ran the place from 1967 through 1972. He retired with a 43–34–7 record.

Ford, Edsel II—December 27, 1948; Ford crown prince minus arrogance.

This Ford scion has a self-effacing sense of humor that makes him extraordinarily popular—both among his colleagues and among the town's social set. Some say his wife, Cynthia, keeps him humble. As general sales manager of the company's Lincoln-Mercury division, he's a good way up the corporate ladder. The drama of whether he'll make it to the top—or, indeed, if he even wants to make it to the top—will provide grist for automotive columnists for years.

The only son of the late Henry Ford II, Edsel has distinguished himself from his father with his genuine love of automobiles. He totes stacks of auto magazines whenever he travels.

He joined the company in 1974, the year after he graduated from Massachusetts' Babson College. He jumped around the company, becoming ad manager at the Ford division; general marketing manager at Lincoln-Mercury two years later; then general sales manager two years after that. The word among ad types is that Edsel allowed the Young & Rubicam ad agency to get creative with Lincoln-Mercury's ads—far more creative than most auto companies would have allowed.

Edsel was extremely close to his father. Some wondered whether Dad had pulled strings to move his son up through the ranks, but Edsel might have risen somewhere even without the mogul's help. He joined the company's board in 1988. Asked if this would provide him with such a lofty position that others in the company would be afraid to speak with him, he said: "I look down on no one."

Ford, Josephine—July 7, 1923; the silent Ford.

"Dodie" Ford, as she has been known most of her life, is the only Detroit woman who makes the *Forbes* magazine list of the country's richest people. The sister of **William Clay Ford**, she owns almost 18 percent of Ford's Class B stock, which makes her the second-biggest stockholder. In her 60s now, she grew up at a time when heiresses didn't venture into the executive suites or boardrooms. Except for a few charity bashes, she leads a low-key existence.

Her husband of the last 40 years-plus is Walter Buhl Ford II, a pretty substantial guy in his own right. A Yale grad who just happened to have the same last name as his bride-to-be, he is descended from a family that was rich and distinguished long before the Model T. Walter Buhl Ford II's family was involved in banking, and his mom was a Brush, the venerable Detroit family after which the street was named. He's president and chairman of Ford & Earl Associates, a design firm, and has been a director of Comerica Inc. for 25 years. He's also thick with the Founders Society crowd at the Detroit Institute of Arts.

Ford, William—August 6, 1927; a quarter century in Congress.

No relation to the automotive family, the shipping family or the golf-playing ex-president, this Ford has represented western and southwestern suburbs since 1964. Longevity has given him a bit of clout in Washington, D.C.: He chairs the Post Office and Civil Service Committee, and holds the No. 2 slot on Education and Labor.

He worked western Wayne County politics to get where he is

today. As a young lawyer, Ford was a justice of the peace in Taylor, city attorney in Melvindale and a delegate to the same Michigan Constitutional Convention that launched the career of one *Coleman Young*. He'd been a one-term state senator when his congressional district was split in two in 1964. He picked the western half, ran, and won.

Though his district is schizophrenic when it comes to voting for Democrats, Ford hasn't been in serious trouble out there: His district racked up 16 percent for George Wallace in 1968, and liked Ronald Reagan in both 1980 and 1984. But Ford usually rolls up 70 percent-plus margins, though his 1984 campaign saw him in an unusually close race against Gerald Carlson, who was so far right as to be identified by the local press as a Nazi.

Ford, William Clay—March 14, 1925; much-maligned Lions owner/ Ford Motor Co.'s biggest stockholder.

While brother Henry Ford II was a busy business patriarch, William Clay Ford was busy building a fortune. As of spring 1989, William Clay Ford owned 7.7-million shares of Class B stock (the stuff reserved for Ford family members), almost 21 percent of the total. A quick trip to the calculator shows that dividends alone were $18-million in 1988.

The youngest of Edsel Ford's three sons, he attended Yale, excelled as a sportsman, and married Harvey Firestone's daughter Martha in a heavy-duty society wedding. But family elders decreed that Henry Ford II would run the company, so that's the way it was. Brother William, a fan of automotive design, occupied himself at the drawing board. Instead of running Ford Motor Co., he found a way to occupy himself with the purchase of the Detroit Lions.

When Ford got into the football business in the late 1950s, he was one of some 144 feuding stockholders. The boardroom in-fighting was so ferocious that pads were appropriate attire for annual meetings. Two failed palace revolts in as many years during the early '60s were launched by a guy who plotted for control of the Lions from a back room of—naturally—the Detroit Athletic Club. Ford put an end to all that by shelling out $6-million for control of the team in early 1964. Some of the bickering stockholders walked away with $250,000 or more, which isn't bad even by 1980s standards.

Most people know Ford as owner of the Lions. In the late 1980s, that was not a good thing to be as the team suffered seasons of 5-11,

4-11 and 4-12 in 1986, 1987 and 1988. The team has not won a championship in three decades, and fans have lost interest. The 80,638-seat Silverdome looks empty at times. The tradition once carried by the likes of Joe Schmidt and Alex Karras is only a memory, and Bobby Layne is dead. How long William Clay Ford will take to fix this mess is—well—it's an old question.

Ford, William Clay Jr.—May 3, 1957; great-grandson on the move.

Okay, you're the only son of Ford Motor Co.'s biggest stockholder. What do you do? Sit back and cash your dividend checks every three months? Go to work for Firestone, which your family has an interest in? Or grab your Tylenol and jump into the competitive world of the automobile business? William Clay Ford Jr. chose door No. 3.

Before joining the company in 1979, "Billy" showed few signs of wanting to claim a spot at Ford. He signed up only after bagging a BA in history from Princeton. He spent a couple of years at Ford, then returned for a master's in management from the Massachusetts Institute of Technology. According to Peter Collier and David Horowitz's "The Fords: An American Epic," the decision to go automotive was a surprise to Billy's father. "Are you sure that's what you want to do?" the elder Ford asked when informed of his son's decision during a game of pool. "Well, you don't have to do it on my account," the elder Ford counseled. "Life's too short to be miserable. Do what you want. But do it well."

Most, if not all, accounts indicate that Billy has done well. He became a product planner in advanced vehicles development, a unit that houses a great deal of corporate gray matter and has zero tolerance for dilettantes. Ford subsequently worked at Ford's New York/New Jersey district sales office and joined the international finance unit in 1985. Later, he set sail for Europe, where he ran Ford of Switzerland, not a bad pin on the company map. But he returned to Dearborn in 1989 to run the company's heavy truck engineering and manufacturing division.

A note on Ford's proxy statement indicates Billy is treasurer of the Detroit Lions. Whispers in sports circles indicate he might take over when his father steps aside. The Lions could do much worse. Fans think they are.

Fortinberry, Glen—November 22, 1927; advertising's acquiring mind.

He runs Detroit's largest locally based ad agency, the Ross Roy Group. Actually, Fortinberry runs a collection of agencies he has assembled since becoming chairman in 1983. Like a kid with a new Lego set, he has been busy acquiring other shops and attaching them to the original Ross Roy unit, founded back in 1926.

A Northwestern University grad and ex-U.S. Navy salt, he came to Ross Roy after 15 years with J. Walter Thompson. Among his JWT chores were two tours as head of the agency's Detroit office (1964-'68 and 1971-'75).

While he was settling into a job as vice-chairman at JWT, two of Ross Roy's principals were looking for a successor. Founder Ross Roy was into his 80s at the time (he died in 1983), and longtime president John Pingel was nearing retirement. New blood was needed. Fifty-two-year-old Fortinberry made the switch in 1980, coming in as president and CEO and getting the chairman's seat in 1983 after Roy died.

Hand on the checkbook, or hand on the stock transfer forms, it didn't take long for Fortinberry to start building his collection: He acquired Ohio's Griswold Inc., Chicago's Lerner Scott Corp. (a direct mail house) and Canada's Commercial Associates and Medcom Advertising. And that was just in 1985. He took Manhattan's Calet, Hirsch & Spector the next year, and added Ann Arbor's Group 243 (the Domino's ad agency) in 1988.

He seems to favor London-made doubled-breasted suits, which give him the look of a banker rather than a slick ad guy. K mart, Blue Cross and Blue Shield of Michigan, and a couple of utilities (Detroit Edison and Ma Bell) are among the accounts tended from the company's spiffy new glass and granite building nestled on 13 acres of woods and streams near Woodward and Long Lake Road in Bloomfield Hills.

It all adds up to more than $600-million in billings each year, enough to put Ross Roy 23rd in *Advertising Age*'s roster of ad shops.

Four Tops, the—Levi Stubbs, Renaldo "Obie" Benso, Abdul "Duke" Fakir and Lawrence Payton (birthdates unavailable); Motown mainstays.

The Tops' driving vocals and meticulous choreography made this group the linchpin of the Motown sound. Their get-together was happenstance at a 1954 high school party. A friend asked them to sing together, and the four guests liked it so much that they met the next day and made the arrangement more or less permanent. But they didn't call themselves the Four Tops. At first, it was "The Four Aims" because—as they told friends—they were aiming for the top. A wise-guy record producer told them that sounded too much like the Ames Brothers, so they went for it all. It certainly sounds better than the Four Career Goals.

The group spent 10 years traveling the Miami/Las Vegas club route before anyone paid much serious attention. They also went through four record labels before finding a home with Motown in 1963. Their forté was interpreting tunes penned by the Eddie Holland/Lamont Dozier/Brian Holland songwriting team. A baker's dozen of these tunes hit *Billboard*'s Top 10 list between 1964 and 1971. "I Can't Help Myself (Sugar Pie Honey Bunch") spent two weeks on the top of Billboard's charts in 1965. "Reach Out I'll Be There" spent a pair of weeks at the top in October 1966. Both tunes were recorded in less than a day.

When the Holland/Dozier/Holland team walked away from Motown in a royalty dispute, so did the Tops' high-octane sound. The group left Motown in 1972, went through several record companies in the '70s, but finally did the Prodigal Sons routine and returned to Motown in 1983.

Stubbs' throaty, urban baritone was the voice of the funnily ferocious man-eating plant "Audrey II" in the film "Little Shop of Horrors." Fakir and a cousin bought the troubled Lansdowne floating restaurant in 1988. As a group, the Tops are no longer hitmakers, but they have plenty to keep them going: They spend some 200 nights each year on the road.

Frank, Alan—June 2, 1944; *Mort Crim*'s boss.

Both as programming chief and as general manager, he has had an immense personal imprint on Channel 4's look and style.

Post-Newsweek was confronted with a problem when it acquired Channel 4 in 1978: A Fortune 500 company had invaded a city that doesn't take well to out-of-towners. Frank, hired as program manager in 1979, fixed that. He helped manage the catchy "Go 4 It" campaign, hired **Dick Purtan** for a few comedy specials, and let community hotshots know that the station's door was open if anybody had a gripe. Suddenly, Frank and company didn't seem like outsiders any more. He foisted Sonya Friedman on the TV world, but everybody makes their mistakes.

Before joining WDIV, Frank made stops at San Francisco's KPIX-TV (1972-'74), Boston's WBZ-TV (1974-'75) and Baltimore's WJZ-TV (1975-'78). With his Detroit programming victories beneath his belt, Post-Newsweek had him working in a Big Corporate Job (v.p. of programming and production, which meant whispering in the ears of the general managers of all four P-N stations) before he came back to replace Amy McCombs as No. 1 at Channel 4.

Franklin, Aretha—March 25, 1942; Queen of Soul.

She is a national and local treasure, rating somewhere up there with the Grand Canyon and the Lafayette Coney Island. Her sound synthesizes the street, the church, the urban black neighborhoods of the North, and the pain of everyday life. While her career has had its peaks and valleys, the peaks (and 21 Top 40 *Billboard* records from 1967 through '86) have been enough to place her in the rock 'n' roll Hall of Fame.

Franklin bore the heavy yoke of having a legend as a father. The Rev. C.L. Franklin, pastor of the west side's New Bethel Baptist Church, was a folk hero in Detroit. Dubbed "the Man with the Million Dollar Voice," he could command $4,000 for an appearance. Mahalia Jackson, Clara Ward, Sam Cooke and Lou Rawls would drop by C.L.'s house during Aretha's early years. (When her father died, some 10,000 people attended the funeral.) Aretha sang in the church choir, and cut a gospel album for Chess Records when she was barely 12.

She was only 18 when she was signed for Columbia Records by the late John Hammond, talent scout for all eras who also discovered Bruce Springsteen, Bob Dylan, Count Basie and Lionel Hampton. Columbia made a mess of her career, giving her show tunes and shlock to sing—sort of like asking Horowitz to play "Louie Louie." It almost killed her. Atlantic Records got smart, signed her, and locked her up in a studio in Muscle Shoals, Alabama. The results were songs such as "I Never Loved a Man (The Way I Love You") and "Respect." When the late Otis Redding, possibly the best soul singer ever, heard her version of "Respect," he said: "I just lost my song. That girl took it away from me." She was in business.

Like a few female artists, she allowed her husbands to manage her career and make shambles of her work. During the late 1970s, some thought Franklin might be down for the count. She is currently unmarried, and her brother Cecil runs the show.

She suffers the misfortune of being a shy person in a business populated by glad-handers, leeches and sycophants. She doesn't suffer these intrusions well. People take her entourage as a form of snobbery. In fact, it's her way of protecting herself. She lives quietly in an elegant, aquarium-filled house in West Bloomfield.

Fredericks, Marshall—January 31, 1908; the green giant's creator.

The "Spirit of Detroit" statue in downtown Detroit is his. So is the 27-foot Christ figure at the Indian River Catholic Shrine near Mackinaw City and the 30-foot marble eagle near the Veterans Memorial Building. *News* arts critic Joy Hakanson Colby described him as "Detroit's most visible sculptor." To that, add "successful."

A native of Rock Island, Illinois, Fredericks studied at the Cleveland School of Art. He broadened his perspective beyond Cuyahoga County by studying in Sweden, Germany, France and Italy before finally settling here in the 1930s at Cranbrook.

His work is done from a small studio in Royal Oak.

Fretter, Ollie—April 15, year unavailable; from clown suit to gray flannel.

So what if Ollie Fretter spent years playing the clown appliance peddler on late-night Detroit television? Ollie Fretter can laugh, because he's one of the newer millionaires in town.

Cleveland-born Fretter got a degree from the University of Michigan in electrical engineering before he started a repair shop with $600 borrowed from his uncle. "Good old Uncle Preston," Fretter joked with a *Free Press* reporter. "He's about 80 years old now and lives in Cleveland. He says he wished he'd have taken a piece of the action instead of me borrowing the money and paying him back." Fretter spent some eight years fixing appliances before he decided to sell a few.

His hallmark, of course, was those zany radio and television ads of the '70s. Fretter can claim "I'll give you five pounds of coffee if I can't beat your best deal" as his personal addition to the Detroit hawkstering lexicon.

But things are different now. Fretter's firm sells stock. Wall Street graybeards don't think much of investing heavy bucks in a company run by a guy who does wacky ads, so local television lacks its once omnipresent pitchman.

Frey, Glenn—November 6, 1948; Berkleyite-turned-L.A.-cowboy.

He did what so many Detroit-area high schoolers in the '60s wanted to do: Frey ran away to California and became a rock star. Along the way, his band, the Eagles, injected a country feel into rock.

The '70s were the decade for Frey and his Eagles. The group had seven albums on *Billboard*'s Top 40 LP chart between 1972 and 1980, including four No. 1's. The Eagles also managed five No. 1 singles. "Eagles/Their Greatest Hits 1971-'75" went platinum upon release, and spent more than a year on *Billboard*'s charts. "The Long Run" enjoyed a long run of nine weeks in the top spot in late 1979 and early 1980. That was about it for the group. They recorded one more album ("Eagles Live") and disbanded.

Despite his success, Frey and the group got little respect from the rock writers. As Kit Rachlis wrote in the *Boston Phoenix*: "I dislike the Eagles with the same adolescent fervor that I reserved for the BMOC in my prep school and for many of the same reasons: fear, politics, style, envy. If the Eagles weren't good at what they did—if they weren't so successful that they've come to epitomize southern California rock—they wouldn't be worth disliking so much . . . a band that arouses this much vitriol must be worth something."

Explaining why the band broke up, Frey told the *L.A. Times*: "I started the band, I got tired of it and I quit." Frey enjoyed a measure of solo success in the '80s, though nothing like he enjoyed as a young Eagle. Since the band's breakup in 1982, he's had three albums on the Billboard charts. At one point, he opened for singer Tina Turner to — as he put it—earn a little drinking money. "Smuggler's Blues" had a "Miami Vice" plot written around it. (Frey played a spaced-out pilot.) "You Belong to the City" was another "Miami Vice" theme.

As an Eagle, he looked like a thin, bedraggled desert rat. But no longer. He got himself into body-building, and even appeared in a Vic Tanny ad telling viewers: "The first rule is you've got to show up."

Fridholm, Roger—March 18, 1941; the braumeister's lieutenant.

Fridholm is *Peter Stroh*'s right-hand man, only the second person ever to sit in the president's chair at the brewery. (The other was John Shenefield, who served in 1967 and 1968.)

A graduate of the University of Michigan Business School, he rose at Stroh as quickly as a well-shaken can of pilsner. He joined the company in 1978 as v.p./planning and development. Two promotions followed (one that year, another the next) and yet another in 1982, which put him where he is today. Fridholm is said to be the brain behind Stroh's daring acquisitions of F.& M. Schaefer Brewing Corp. and the bigger Jos. Schlitz Brewing Co. Fridholm is smart enough to know that in brewing it's proliferate or perish.

He's married to the former Henrietta Barlow, an ex-v.p. of programming at Channel 56. She has her hands full as chairperson of Music Hall.

G

Gardner, Samuel—November 27, 1931; gone private and doing well.

This hyper-energetic lawyer gets the nod when *Mayor Young* needs outside help. Gardner co-chaired Young's Detroit Casino Gaming Study Commission in 1988, which is as close as Young gets to trusting any lawyer. When he's not helping city hall, he mostly gets rich. That's something he hadn't had a chance to do during his 14 years on the Detroit Recorder's Court Bench.

A Northern High School grad, he thought about a medical career while attending Wayne State University. A sister talked him into a teaching career. That didn't work, so he tried Wayne State University Law School. That took.

Before his election to Recorder's Court in 1972, he practiced at one time or another with J. Robert Gragg (now a Wayne County probate judge), *Dennis Archer* (now a Michigan Supreme Court justice) and Elliott Hall (now a Ford Motor Co. vice-president). The kind of guy whose transmission seems permanently stuck in passing gear, he was elected chief judge of the court by his colleagues in 1977. Gardner left the bench 10 years later to help the ailing Ed Bell in his practice. (Bell, with whom Gardner had been a partner in the early '70s, died in 1988.)

Gardner isn't seen in court a lot, though he did help defend former Michigan National Bank chairman Stanford "Bud" Stoddard when Stoddard was accused of fraud. He mostly supervises his firm, which is conveniently located across the street from the Renaissance Center.

Garrison, Frank—December 28, 1934; leading light in labor and Lansing.

Garrison, president of the state AFL-CIO, exercises clout both here and in the state capital. State Democratic Party chief *Tom Lewand* has his job at least partially because of Garrison. Questions about Lewand's intention to continue with his law practice while running the state party were set aside when Garrison said: No problem. If it was okay with Garrison, it was okay with the Democrats.

Before his election to the presidency of the federation in 1986, Garrison ran the UAW's Community Action Program. That meant politicians from here to Ironwood would visit Garrison in hopes of jarring loose a few extra campaign bucks from the UAW CAP funds. Garrison succeeded the late Sam Fishman at the helm of the AFL-CIO.

George, Michael (December 20, 1932) and Sharkey (January 1, 1922); power in the dairy case.

They are the pillar and the post of the local Chaldean community, some 50,000 strong. The brothers' power base is Melody Farms, the state's largest family-owned dairy. According to *Crain's Detroit Business*, 1987 revenues totaled $92.4 million. Sharkey is chairman of the board; Michael is president.

Mostly, they have anted up a lot of start-up money to people entering the grocery business. As a result, they have more chits around town that probably anybody else in this book.

Their father began with a grocery store when there were few Chaldeans in the area.

Giles, Robert—June 6, 1933; Gannett's man in Detroit.

He was sent here as the *News* executive editor in May 1986, three months after Gannett bought the paper from the Evening News Association. Since then, the *News* seems more lively, a little more rock 'n' roll, and a lot less ideological. Giles presides over his troops with a Zen-like calm that makes him impossible to read. Associates say they remember Giles flustered only once: While at the helm of Gannett's Rochester, New York, newspaper, a reporter wrote that a local nuclear power plant was about to blow. It wasn't true, so Giles assigned two reporters to do a front-page story that explained how the mess occurred.

He started out in 1958 as a reporter at Knight-Ridder's *Akron Beacon-Journal*, rising through the ranks. The paper won a Pulitzer in 1971 for its coverage of the shootings at Kent State University. After a change in top management at the Akron paper, Giles joined the *Rochester Democrat and Chronicle* (and *Times-Union*) newspapers when they were still Gannett's flagship paper—pre-*USA Today*.

Unlike the Ben Bradlee-Abe Rosenthal buccaneer style of management, Giles' approach to newsroom command is somewhat academic. He has written a book on newspaper management, replete with quotes from White House wizards and wartime generals.

Gilmour, Allan—June 17, 1934; unorthodox thinker at Ford.

Gilmour, a Ford executive v.p. and member of the Office of the Chief Executive, stunned reporters during the *Automotive News* World Congress in 1986 by admitting he didn't know everything about cars. "People simply aren't following their old buying patterns," he remarked. "They're buying vans and light trucks instead of station wagons, causing Ford and other companies to underestimate the van market consistently. There was a time when you bought a Chevrolet, then you moved to a Pontiac, then you moved to an Olds. If you became rich and famous, then you moved to a Cadillac. Is that how the fleet for the family progresses nowadays?" He wasn't sure. That kind of refreshing candor shows that Gilmour is open to something besides conventional thinking—which has gotten the Detroit auto industry in such trouble with its customers.

Gilmour, a finance man by training, sounds rather like a professor from his alma mater, Harvard University. A grad of the University of Michigan Business School, he fell in with J. Edward Lundy, the pre-eminent finance man of his generation at Ford. The Lundy protégé was named the company chief financial officer in 1986, took over as chief of international automotive operations in 1987, then moved up another rung to his current job in May 1989. Some say he's only a few steps away from the chairmanship.

Gilmour's power can be seen by what Ford did and didn't do in the mid-1980s. While GM spent billions on EDS, Ford made no wildly adventuresome splashes. Part of that reticence, which seems smarter as time goes on, can be traced to Gilmour's philosophy. "When one is diversifying, it is remarkably easy to buy. All you need is money. But it is not nearly as easy to manage after one has bought . . . it's a lot easier to buy these outfits than it is to sell them if you would like to do so down the road."

A lifelong bachelor (like his mentor, Lundy), he lives in Dearborn not far from the Glass House.

Glover, Joe—December 11, 1938; Channel 2 savior?

Channel 2 is hoping Glover's return to the anchor desk will resuscitate the station's weak ratings. He is competent and straightforward, much less mercurial than Channel 7's **Bill Bonds** and less stuffy than Channel 4's **Mort Crim**. Mercurial and stuffy have been doing well.

An East Coast native (born in Delaware, raised in Massachusetts), Glover anchored the news at Channel 2 from 1974-'83. He was doing a creditable job when he was axed in one of the station's numerous purges. It was one of general manager Bill Flynn's daffier moves. Flynn had inherited a moderately successful lineup of Glover, anchorwoman Robbie Timmons, sportscaster Ray Lane and weatherman Sonny Eliot. They were replaced with less-than-flashy talent. By the time Flynn and his wrecking ball had gone, the ratings were so bad that—as former *Free Press* critic Bettelou Peterson once remarked about another operation—one wondered if more people listened to the police radio.

Glover had worked in San Francisco and Sacramento, so when KSBW-TV in Salinas/Monterey came calling in 1983, he snapped it up. Life during the hiatus couldn't have been all bad. When he returned to Detroit in July 1988 he had thinned out a bit, and somehow he looks healthier than when he left. We'll see how he looks in two years.

Some things haven't changed during his five-year break: Glover moved back to the same home in Birmingham.

Goodman, Ernest—August 21, 1906; blue-collar counsel.

This octogenarian attorney has been in the thick of civil-rights and union battles for 50 years. Goodman defended union officials in the '30s and '40s, Communists in the McCarthy era of the '50s, Black Panthers in the '60s and '70s. He even defended "dime-a-dance" halls. A judge reportedly told him in the '30s: "You know, Ernie, we all think a lot of your legal ability and some day we'd like to decide a case in your favor, so why don't you represent something other than a union?"

A graduate of Wayne State University Law School, Goodman set up the first integrated law firm in the state. One of his partners was the late Robert Millender, who later played a key part in sending *Mayor Young* to Manoogian Mansion. Goodman's became the law firm of choice for union officials who were being harassed in fights with management. He was one of the UAW's top lawyers between 1939 and 1947, and in 1948 supported the Michigan Progressive Party, which pushed the candidacy of Henry Wallace. (A young Coleman Young was a Progressive candidate for state Senate.) In 1975 he spent six months preparing a defense for a black prisoner accused of murder, kidnapping and conspiracy in the Attica Prison uprising. His client was acquitted, and all related cases were dismissed.

Although Goodman has slowed somewhat, he keeps his hand in. He represented a group of demonstrators who had been jailed for picketing the Williams International defense contracting plant in Oakland County, successfully arguing their case before the Michigan Supreme Court. His firm is still going great guns from its offices in the Cadillac Tower. His son, Bill, is a partner in the firm.

Gordy, Berry—November 28, 1929; he launched Motown on $800.

He harnessed Detroit's energy, engraved it on vinyl and sold it 'round the world. The Europeans can claim Bach, Brahms and Beethoven as their contributions to culture. Thanks to Gordy and his Motown Records, we can claim *Stevie Wonder, The Temptations* and *The Four Tops* as our proud offerings. Big deal, you say? Then why do half the bistros in Paris play Motown music when they want to liven things up?

Gordy, an overachieving factory worker, started Motown with an $800 loan from his family. The promissory note is still on display in the Motown Museum, not far from the New Center area. Gordy was smart enough to line up some major league song writing talent (*Smokey Robinson,* for instance), then proceeded to work everybody around him to exhaustion. The word among moonlighting Detroit Symphony Orchestra musicians was that they could play string backgrounds until they dropped. This didn't win Gordy any popularity contests among employees, but it certainly gained the record company success. He lost even more friends when he moved the company to Los Angeles in 1972. People here are still critical of the move, but L.A. *is* the undisputed record capital of the world.

The transplant didn't work as well as it should have. Motown didn't develop talent as effectively as it did in the '60s. Gordy ended up selling the label to MCA Records in 1988. But there are indications Gordy is readying himself to conquer yet another world. He sold the record division to MCA, but he kept the company's film/ television unit. Its most recent offering was CBS-TV's "Lonesome Dove," which made a mint for the network. You can bet Hollywood will pay attention the next time Gordy gets on the horn.

A reclusive man, Gordy rarely speaks to the press. He still has a Detroit connection—he never sold the mansion he owns in the Boston-Edison area of Detroit.

Greenwald, Gerald—September 11, 1935; the next Iacocca?

Lee Iacocca doesn't plan on leaving Chrysler until at least 1991. But his anointed successor appears to be Greenwald, the tall, stately, patrician chairman of Chrysler Motors.

The son of a Missouri chicken farmer, Greenwald joined Ford's Edsel division upon graduation from Princeton in the late 1950s. Despite shipping out on the automotive equivalent of the Titanic, Greenwald was regarded well enough for posting to Paris, Brazil, London and Caracas during the next 22 years, mostly in financial positions. Greenwald had a comfy job running Ford's Venezuela operations when Iacocca invited him to join Chrysler in the difficult days of 1979. Iacocca explained his attraction to Greenwald this way: "Jerry has the talent and the know-how of the entrepreneur who can analyze a problem and then move on to solve it. He doesn't talk things to death—he acts." In other words, Greenwald is the perfect Iacocca guy: a blunt-talking ex-Ford official who doesn't live for committee meetings.

Henry Ford II and *William Clay Ford* personally tried to talk Greenwald out of leaving. But the thrill of joining a company that was a candidate for bankruptcy court was just too much. Perhaps it reminded him of his days at Edsel.

Most accounts of Chrysler's financial recovery credit Greenwald as the chief architect. Iacocca was the company's public face, *Steve Miller* dealt with the bankers, and Greenwald held the place together.

His wife, Glenda, cuts a wide swath through Detroit society. While Greenwald was busy tending to the automotive business, she earned a couple of degrees in English literature from Wayne State University, studied at the Sorbonne in Paris and ran art galleries on two continents.

Though it looks like Greenwald will get Iacocca's office, there is a problem. As Chrysler vice-chairman Miller once said: "I don't think anybody's going to have the nerve to tiptoe down to Iacocca's office the day he's sixty-five and tell him it's all over."

Grettenberger, John O.—July 25, 1937; chief dude at the Cadillac ranch.

Tall, silver-haired, and very dignified—he looks like he belongs on the 16th green—Grettenberger is central casting's version of a Cadillac guy. Although Cadillac is nowhere near other GM divisions in volume, Caddy's profit margins are Fat City. It is also GM's "image" nameplate. Hence, a job of both glitter and substance.

A native of Okemos, Grettenberger signed on as a clerk in Oldsmobile's Los Angeles office in 1963. He planted plenty of pins on the company map during the next two decades: Oklahoma City, Milwaukee, Newark, Houston, Japan and Germany, mostly for the Oldsmobile division, always in the sales and marketing end. GM corporate fathers summoned him home in September 1983 for a top job at Oldsmobile. Grettenberger had barely warmed his seat when GM's brain trust brought him down from Lansing to run Cadillac four months later.

The line around GM had always been, "How smart do you have to be sell Cadillacs?" Until the 1960s, the answer was "not very." But that was then. Now, Mercedes-Benz, BMW and other European automakers skillfully work the top end of the market, and Lincoln-Mercury is on a roll. And with the Japanese entering the game, Grettenberger and his successors will have to be very smart, indeed. At one time, Cadillac was *the* car to own if one had more than a couple of quarters to rub together. These days, even the drug dealers don't buy Cadillacs. They prefer German craftsmanship.

In 1986, Grettenberger presided over the introduction of the Cadillac Allanté, which was supposed to lure back a few Mercedes buyers. The Allanté is certainly a creative idea: The body is by the Italians, and everything else is assembled in Hamtramck. But it didn't meet sales projections and was branded a turkey by the press. While the Allanté didn't sell well, perhaps because of its stiff $54,700 retail price, the experts still say it's one heckuva car. Maybe Grettenberger's staff shouldn't have broadcast such unrealistic sales estimates. They had been telling reporters that Caddy might sell 6,000 in 1987. The bottom line was less than half that, giving *Ward's Automotive Reports* an opportunity to dub Allanté "the biggest disappointment in 1987."

Grettenberger is still young enough to climb another notch. Whether he'll do so is anybody's guess.

Griesdorn, Tom—December 7, 1949; the boss at Broadcast House.

There are probably better jobs in Detroit than having **Bill Bonds**, **John Kelly** and **Marilyn Turner** demanding raises at the same time. But that's WXYZ-TV general manager Tom Griesdorn's lot in life.

He came up though the financial side of broadcasting. Before joining Channel 7 as controller in 1982, he spent five years in the ABC owned-and-operated television station division as a finance man in Chicago. ABC's people in New York sent him here in 1982 to manage the checkbook. Channel 7 general manager Jeanne Findlater liked him so much he was named assistant general manager in 1986. When she looked for a replacement for herself later that year and early the next, she settled on Griesdorn. She told friends she never would have left if Griesdorn hadn't been up to her standards.

An Ohio State University graduate, he has strewn his office with scarlet and gray colors. Despite spending most of his life contemplating a calculator, he gets high marks from the staff for decency and civility. Whether or not that counts with the hard-nosed suits at Scripps Howard Broadcasting is another question.

Guarascio, Phil—June 28, 1941; GM's ad czar.

If you'd like to see really quick movement, pick out the advertising executives in a room and watch them when Phil Guarascio enters. He oversees General Motors' $1-billion ad budget—"which explains why when I pulled out a cigar," he once told the New York Ad Club, "there were seven or eight lighters in my face before I even looked up."

Guarascio spent his entire two-decade ad career at Benton & Bowles (now DMB&B), which handles GM's Pontiac and Cadillac accounts. He rose at B&B from media buyer to hotshot and board member by 1984. Legend has it that GM chairman *Roger Smith* noticed that certain ad execs were becoming millionaires handling the General's accounts. Smith figured he'd tighten the money spigot. GM spent somewhere in the six-figure range with head-hunters trying to find the right guy. They landed on Guarascio. Much to the amusement of his friends in the Big Apple, he made the trip from New York City to Detroit in the fall of 1985.

Despite the belt-tightening, head-knocking nature of his job, Guarascio managed to garner some respect here in town. "He's really liked by the ad people," says one observer. "He's a fairly tough guy, but he's the highest guy at GM to understand advertising. He has a high degree of credibility, understands what they can do and can't do. Before it was not 'Can you do better?' It was 'Can you do it for less money?' "

New York fairly oozes from his expensive Italian suits. But now that he has been in the hinterlands for awhile, he has become something of a Motor City booster. "There's a lot that I miss about New York," he chided his friends back East. "I miss trying to grab a taxi at six o'clock on a rainy Friday night. I miss getting stuck on the Long Island Expressway without something to read—like 'War and Peace.' And I miss having to take out a second mortgage for dinner at Arcadia and two orchestra seats for 'Phantom of the Opera.' "

H

Handleman, David—November 23, 1915; in the middle of the music business.

The founders of the Handleman Co., the country's largest independent wholesale record distributor, are brothers David, Joe, Paul and

Moe, Central High (David and Moe) and Northern High (Paul and Joe) grads who got the company off the ground with the help of their father, Phillip. Almost every time you buy an LP, cassette, compact disc or book at K mart, you're putting a few dimes in the Handleman family fortune. With their 15 percent interest in the Troy-based company, which had sales of $560-million in 1988, they are worth plenty.

Moe and Paul both retired in the '70s, but remained on the board. David, into his 70s, is still very much active, serving as chairman and chief executive officer of the company. He's also a shaker with the Detroit Symphony Orchestra and is seen at an occasional social engagement. He received B'nai B'rith's Great American Traditions award in 1984.

Haney, Marce—June 7, 1922; a casting of thousands.

She's probably the best talent agent in Detroit. "I can't help but be the best," she insists. "I'm the only agent in Detroit." Well, maybe south of Eight Mile Road.

Marce (short for Marcella) Haney grew up in Detroit, graduating from Nativity of Our Lord High School and Marygrove College. She took up her current line of work during an eight-year hiatus to Chicago, where her late husband had been transferred. When she returned to Detroit in 1961, she noted that there were few agents for the industrial films and occasional feature movies shot in the city. So she hung out her shingle in the Book Mansion on the east side and called herself an agent. She has moved her shingle to downtown's David Stott Building, but her work remains the same.

She hired 1,000 extras for a day's work on "Collision Course," shot in Detroit in 1987. But we haven't seen the result, because the movie hasn't made it to the big screen, at least not as of this writing. Her work was seen in "The Rosary Murders," which she helped cast. From her 23rd-floor office she can see the entire city. And, she says, she's having one heckuva time.

Harlan, Carmen—November 4, year unavailable; the silk in Channel 4's fabric.

Articulate, smooth, unflappable Harlan complements *Mort Crim*'s somber narration and flippant patter at the Channel 4 anchor desk. Anchor teams, especially in local television news, are an exercise in balance. When it clicks, it usually involves a mixture of wit, wisdom and demographics. White male anchor with black female is a familiar anchor tandem. After seating a series of experiments next to Crim (Kai Maxwell, Ben Frazier, Jennifer Moore,) Channel 4 honchos finally settled on Harlan in the fall of 1981. The combo seems to have clicked.

A 1975 graduate of the University of Michigan, Harlan started out as a news/public affairs director on WWWW-FM in its rock 'n' roll days. WLLZ-FM's *Jim Johnson*, then her colleague at W4, recalls her falling asleep at her typewriter. Channel 4 picked her up in 1978 as a general assignment reporter. She got her anchor spurs on the noon news in 1979. Harlan's strength seems to be her range: She's capable of reading the heavy-duty stories, but can perform pretty well on the heart-tuggers.

Crim and Harlan are close. They often dine together quietly after their early evening newscast. Or sometimes, not so quietly. On one excursion they received a standing ovation from fellow diners as they paid their tab—more proof that the real celebrities in this town are the TV newsoids.

Harlan and her husband, Joseph Cobb, who is a regional v.p. for ABC/Children's Publishing, are a model of contented Motown Yuppiedom.

Harper, Jim—September 3, 1953; younger, blonder *Dick Purtan*.

He's WNIC-FM's morning man, program director and suburban Detroit's idea of hip—marginally dangerous, but never offensive. He looks and sounds like a young, slightly bent arbitrageur who spent some time listening to rock 'n' roll instead of business school lectures.

As a teenager growing up in Hamtramck, Harper was a big fan of Detroit's old WKNR-AM, better known as "Keener 13" to fans of early-'60s radio. So hypnotized was Harper with the craft that he hitchhiked to Ypsilanti's WYNZ-AM and begged for a job. The owner, impressed by Harper's chutzpah, awarded him a weekly teen show. Harper was hooked. Other teenaged jobs included trips to WHMI in Howell and WAAM in Ann Arbor. A gig at WCAR-AM came two years after his 1971 graduation from John Glenn High School in Westland. But it was WNIC-FM, where Harper landed as a morning man in 1977, that put him in Detroit's public ear. His show was part comedy, part pabulum rock.

His bold experiment occurred when he teamed with friend Lorraine Golden in 1985 to run WDTX-FM. (The bank required a commitment from Harper as a morning deejay before they'd lend the money for Golden to buy the station.) The two tried an interesting Hipper-Than-Thou approach, pledging to air music Detroiters couldn't hear elsewhere. It was to be cutting-edge stuff, like the innovative programming of WABX-FM in the late '60's. (Interestingly enough, WDTX-FM occupied the same spot on the FM dial.) But the head-bangers didn't like Harper, and Harper's fans didn't like the music. Ratings didn't take off immediately, so the station— maybe too soon—abandoned the format and returned to basic soft rock. Three years later Harper returned to his old job at WNIC-FM. He requires a foil as part of his act. These days, it's deejay Chris Edmonds.

Despite Harper's hijinks, he's a scholar when it comes to Detroit radio. On occasion, he has hosted reunions of washed-up deejays. Harper supplements his income by doing a car ad or two.

Harris, Julie—December 2, 1925; overachieving Grosse Pointer.

TV viewers know her as Lili Mae Clements on CBS's "Knots Landing." Broadway fans know her better as the actress who has won five Tonys, which places her in the "Guinness Book of World Records." She has portrayed Emily Dickinson in "The Belle of Amherst" and Mary Todd Lincoln in "The Last Days of Mrs. Lincoln." She repeated the role that established her on stage when she made her screen debut in 1950's "The Member of the Wedding." Classic film buffs know her best for her role opposite James Dean in 1955's big one, "East of Eden."

Harris's background is pure Grosse Pointe. Dad was a Yale-educated investment banker who lost a good deal of money in the Depression. Nevertheless, there was enough to send her to Detroit Country Day School. Harris caught the acting bug by hanging around the Punch and Judy Theatre in Grosse Pointe Farms and the Cinderella on Jefferson Avenue, both of which are now defunct.

Now into her 60s, Harris still looks a dozen years younger.

Hart, William—January 17, 1924; Detroit's top cop.

There is no more important service in Detroit than police protection. And no other city department has taken more heat. Mayor

Louis Miriani lost his job to Jerry Cavanagh in 1961 because Detroit police were too quick to rough up the town's black citizens. *Mayor Young* was elected in 1973 largely for the same reason. Detroiters, first white and then black, fled to the suburbs primarily because of crime. As this is written, a campaign is mounting against Coleman Young because Detroiters are worried that the cops just aren't doing their job.

Hart was anointed by Young in 1976 after feuding between Police Chief Phil Tannian and executive deputy chief Frank Blount tore the department asunder.

A native of Detroit, Hart was raised in West Virginia and Pennsylvania. He joined the department in 1952, and spent time undercover busting organized crime figures. His career was in gear when Young took office in 1974, but it went through the roof with Young in charge. Hart was an inspector in 1971. Three promotions and five years later, he was running the entire department.

1300 Beaubien has been calmer since Hart's ascendancy, but Police Headquarters is still a first-rate migraine for Young. Some of Hart's young cops have been caught moonlighting as burglars.

Harwell, Ernie—January 25, 1918; the voice of summer.

Since Ernie Harwell began broadcasting Tigers games in 1960 we've had four mayors, eight presidents and two riots — if you include the one outside Tiger Stadium after the team won the 1984 World Series. But some things never change. Every spring and summer, we have Ernie Harwell narrating our baseball games.

The elements of his success are twofold: He's more reporter than editorialist, and he's a student of the game. Feelings are rarely injected, opinions rarely ventured. On or off the field, he is the classic Southern gentleman. Even the strangest pencil-bearing geek is treated with consideration, if not respect. Which makes Harwell the karmic opposite of Kirk Gibson. Harwell's peers think a lot of him, too. They elected him to the Baseball Hall of Fame in 1981, which puts him in the company of broadcast greats like Mel Allen and Red Barber. His collection of baseball memorabilia, some 3,000–4,000 books and nearly 90,000 clippings, rests in the Detroit Public Library's Burton Historical Collection. When he's not adding to that lode, he writes song lyrics and reads books. His own "Tuned to Baseball" has sold 65,000 copies and still sees action in the bookstores.

If the fans who gather around the WJR trailer parked near Tiger Stadium before Opening Day every year are any indication — and most of them weren't even born when Harwell started with the Tigers—he can stick around as long as he wants.

Hearns, Thomas—October 18, 1958; he coulda been somebody.

Well, he *did* become somebody. After all, he won titles in five divisions (welterweight, junior middleweight, middleweight, super middleweight and light heavyweight). And he brought new interest in boxing to Joe Louis' hometown, where the sweet science had been down for the count for decades. But in the strange modern world of boxing, where a single defeat diminishes a star to just another main event, Hearns lost three big ones. As this book went to press, he fought former vanquisher Sugar Ray Leonard to a draw. But this is twilight time, and even a victory would not rewrite history.

Manager *Emanuel Steward* discovered a young, tall, gangly kid with an uncommonly long reach on Detroit's west side. Steward, Hearns and a west-side gym, Kronk, became world-famous as a result. Under Steward's guidance, Hearns recorded 17 straight knockouts working his way up the pro ranks, winning his first title from Pepino Cuevas in Detroit in 1980. The rise of the Motor City Hit Man was over in the 14th round, September 16, 1981, when Leonard—holder of one welterweight title—put away Hearns, holder of the other. Later losses to Marvin Haggler and Iran Barkley were punctuation marks to his story.

Whatever the outcome of the proposed fall 1989 Hearns-Leonard rematch, the Detroiter will be remembered as a world-class fighter, if not a great one. He has designs on a new career in acting. Thanks to Steward, Kronk, his own prodigious skills and the amazing earning potential of top boxers in the age of closed-circuit TV, Hearns won't need the money.

Heathcote, Jud—May 27, 1927; it's not easy being green.

This Augustus Caesar-coiffed hoops maven rekindled interest in basketball at Michigan State University. A North Dakota native, he was educated at Washington State and was coaching at Montana when MSU hired him for the 1976-'77 season. His mission: fix the basketball program at MSU, which had been stunned in the mid-'70s when coach Gus Ganakas's players walked off the court complaining of racial problems.

Heathcote didn't rekindle interest in basketball, he torched it. MSU won a Big Ten basketball championship in 1977-'78. A year later he won the NCAA championship with Earvin "Magic" Johnson. Their 75–64 championship victory over Indiana State and Larry Bird is still considered a classic. Heathcote's team showed another glimmer of hope in the 1985-'86 season, when a Scott Skiles-led team beat Georgetown in tournament play before losing to Kansas in overtime.

The word was that Bill Frieder could recruit and Jud could coach. With Frieder gone from Michigan, maybe Heathcote will get more talent to manage.

Helterhoff, Hal—May 31, 1942; head G-man.

Since he took over as special agent in charge of the FBI's Detroit office, the place has tightened up a bit. Under Helterhoff's predecessor, Ken Walton, some agents felt free to grow beards and dress like *Tom Selleck.* "Some of these guys looked like they were undercover, even when they weren't undercover," recalls one insider. Not so under Helterhoff, a by-the-book kind of guy.

A native of Beaver Dam, Wisconsin, Helterhoff did stints in Baltimore, Omaha, Cleveland, New Orleans, St. Louis and Washington, D.C., before taking over the Detroit bureau in April 1988. Many cases that came to trial in 1989, notably that of 36th District Court Judge Leon Jenkins, had been developed when Walton was in charge.

One reason Walton left was that he was a bit too colorful for the taste of U.S. Attorney Roy Hayes, who reportedly resented Walton's swaggering style. But both are gone now. The legacy of that tiff is Helterhoff, whom nobody could find the least bit offensive. In other words, the perfect FBI chief.

Henderson, Erma—August 20, 1917; first among equals on the Detroit City Council.

She'd like to move into Manoogian Mansion, the official mayoral residence. But the current resident doesn't give any indication he's about to leave, so Henderson must content herself with leading the nine-member Detroit City Council. Meanwhile, she has turned almost as many pages off the calendar as *Coleman Young* himself.

But she is tempted. Henderson filed for the mayor's race in 1985, then changed her mind three days later. If Henderson ever decides to make the leap, she could give Young headaches. Henderson's strength is her knowledge of the city's grass roots: She knows every church group and coffee klatch, and has moles feeding her information from every corner of the City-County Building.

Henderson grew up in Black Bottom, on Detroit's east side, during the Depression. Most of her career was spent as a secretary, though she dabbled in politics. She placed 15th when she first ran for council in 1969, more than 50,000 votes out of the money. What a difference a few years can make. With the death of Robert Tindal in 1972, she beat future colleague *Jack Kelley* in a special election. She was the first black woman to hold the job, and only the third woman ever on the council. When she ran one year later, she placed an impressive third. It's been first place ever since—three straight in 1977, 1981 and 1985.

Henderson shows signs of becoming increasingly resentful of Young's sometimes harsh, sometimes mushroom treatment of the council.

Hermelin, David—December 27, 1936; mogul with a Palace to prove it.

His crowning business achievement is the Palace of Auburn Hills, which Hermelin built along with longtime friends and business partners *Bill Davidson* and *Robert Sosnick*. For a time, Hermelin and friends owned WWJ-AM and WJOI-FM, which they bought for $39-million in 1985. The group peddled the stations to CBS in 1989 for $58-million.

A 1958 grad of the University of Michigan Business School, he was a partner in his father's insurance firm while investing wisely. One thing led to another, including enough nickels for him, Sosnick and Martin Goldman to buy into the first phase of Stroh River Place.

Hermelin's unbounded energy is on display as he sits next to Davidson at Pistons games. Hermelin is the one bobbing and weaving with every shot. He's a Big Presence on the local charity circuit, too. His wife, Doreen, is heavy into community and Jewish causes, and received B'nai B'rith's Great American Traditions Award in 1987.

Although he peddled WWJ to CBS, Hermelin is still in the media business. He and a couple of other investors bought WMCA-AM in New York, one of that city's top talk stations, which they purchased for an undisclosed sum in 1986.

Hertel, Dennis—December 7, 1948; all in the family.

This congressman represents Detroit's eastern suburbs: from the Grosse Pointes up to Sterling Heights, and west to Madison Heights/ Hazel Park.

His father owned a restaurant and was president of a local Kiwanis club. The elder Hertel never ran for public office, but his sons made up for that oversight. Dennis's older brother, John, has been a state senator (1974-'82), a Wayne County commissioner (1973-'74, 1983-'86, the last two years as chairman) and a Macomb County commissioner (1988-present). Younger brother Curtis has been a state representative since 1981.

Dennis Hertel spent six years in the state House before running for Congress in 1980. Hertel hasn't had a difficult time since his first election, when he ran against former Channel 2 anchorman Vic Caputo in 1980. The 14th is the classic ticket-splitting district. Although Democrat Hertel hasn't had a difficult time, the district voted for Ronald Reagan in 1984 and George Bush in 1988.

Hill, Chato—March 29, 1949; creative tornado.

Chato Hill's claim to fame is the classic series of "Hank and Phil" spots he created for Highland Appliance in the early '70s. Recognizing that an appliance shop might have a credibility problem selling high-tech stereo gear previously available only in specialty stores, Hill and his colleagues at the W.B. Doner ad agency beat everybody to the punch and had Highland make fun of itself. Remember the Hank/Phil exchange? Phil: "You are a stereo expert." Hank: "An authority, a buff, an aficionado, if you will." Phil: "And what qualified you as a stereo expert?" Hank: "Why I've been into stereo . . . since it was mono." That's the Hill style: humor-tinged advertising that makes a point.

The son of ad man/baseball writer Art Hill, he broke into the business while attending Western Michigan University. He worked in the Doner mailroom, but was promoted within two weeks to write ad copy. "I think I still hold the record for getting out of the mailroom," Hill says. "I'd drive around writing ideas and drop them on people the next morning." Word quickly spread that Hill was something of a zany, but one who knew what he was doing.

As is fairly common in his business, he became an ad gypsy, flitting from agency to agency: Campbell-Ewald, McCann-Erickson and Doner (twice). Hill snoozed through entire work days at Campbell-Ewald. His favorite trick, he says, was sleeping slumped against the office door so he would awaken if somebody tried to enter the office.

Colleagues' descriptions of Chato Hill include "innovative" . . . "willing to take chances" . . . "ability to find new ideas" . . . "one of the best radio comedy writers in the country" . . . "a punk Renaissance Man" . . . "a nut."

These days, he and partner Bruce Broder are hired creative guns: If an agency needs a typewriter that'll turn out funny copy, they write a large check and let the pair have at it.

Hill, Commander Gil—November 6, 1931; Detroit's best-known cop.

He played Eddie Murphy's constantly agitated boss in "Beverly Hills Cop" and "Beverly Hills Cop II." Being on the large screen made him more famous than any of his real-life homicide roles in the '70s and '80s. It also earned a lot of jealousy from his superiors. These days, Hill runs the department's special services division, which includes identification, science labs, evidence technicians and the court section. He also does a lot of community work and talks to kids on the street, which is what he really enjoys. One gets the impression he doesn't get a lot of credit for that around city hall.

The son of a domestic who later moved to Washington and worked as a Pentagon clerk, he went to high school in the capital and spent time in the Air Force. When he was discharged, he came here to stay with friends. He joined the Police Department in 1959 as a patrolman and worked his way up to the homicide section in 1970. He became slightly famous when he busted a fellow who murdered two youngsters in a botched extortion attempt. Cops usually hate reporters, or at best mistrust them. Hill believes reporters have a job to do like everyone else, and he talked to them as human beings. He got a lot of good ink.

Film director Martin Brest wasn't casting when Hill showed him around Detroit to scout locations in 1984, but Brest was smitten. As he later told former *Detroit Monthly* senior editor Matt Beer: "I was struck by his warmth and humanity. At the same time, he had this strength and force about him." Soon Hill was on the screen as Inspector Todd, the foil for Murphy's smart-aleck Axel Foley. On the night "Beverly Hills Cop II" opened in Detroit in 1987, it seemed as though Hill owned the town.

Simultaneously, he somehow ran afoul of some mayoral lieutenants. Hill admits that though he's a fine street cop he lacks something as an administrator. At any rate, he was sent to his new, relatively minor job. Hill didn't mind that much. No midnight calls. No stiffs to deal with. He has an enormous bag of chits and he's famous. As of this writing, he was prepared to cash in a few by running for City Council.

Hoglund, William E.—August 22, 1934; he gave Pontiac a U-turn to success.

This second-generation GM man might be in one of the company's two top jobs when *Roger Smith* retires in 1990. Hoglund is a rare combination of bean-counter and car nut. He holds a BA from Princeton, class of '56, burnished by an MBA from the University of Michigan, '58. In a company that prefers home-grown talent, he's been there all his adult life. Hoglund looks good in front of a television camera, and can actually deliver a joke. His experience is broad and deep: treasurer's office, practice at the helm of a car division (Pontiac, 1980-'84, and later Saturn in 1985-'86) and a group (Buick-Oldsmobile-Cadillac, 1986-'88).

Hoglund was born in Stockholm, Sweden, where his father was serving one of his overseas GM postings. The younger Hoglund's turnaround of the company's Pontiac division in the early to mid-1980s is part of company folklore. By the time Hoglund got there in 1980, the division was confused and headed for a terrible slump.

"How did they get where they were?" asks one GM executive. "Remember what Pontiac was during the 1960s? It was the flame-throwing, 400-horsepower muscle car dragging up Woodward. Pontiac comes roaring into the '70s and it's circle-the-wagon time—emission standards, fuel economy, gas interruptions with price hikes. Pontiac had no firm direction — trying to guess and get ahead. They tried to out-price Chevy and out-velour Buick. Dealers didn't know what to sell, customers didn't know what to buy." But it didn't fool Buick, Chevy or Pontiac customers. Pontiac sales went from a record 896,980 in 1978 to less than 800,000 in 1979 to barely 600,000 in 1980.

Hoglund, fresh into the job, locked all of Pontiac's hotshots in an Ann Arbor hotel until they decided exactly what Pontiac wanted to be. The result was a precisely spelled out image statement everyone burned into their brains and the rebirth of the "We Build Excitement" division: sporty cars and roadability, which customers saw reflected in the revolutionary though now-defunct Fiero and still-popular Grand Am. Higher-ups tried to kill the Fiero several times, but Hoglund kept getting the car back in the product lineup to inject some flair into the division.

The numbers rose from sales of 483,149 in 1982 to an impressive 841,441 only four years later. Hoglund's reward was the prestigious Saturn president's job, which opened up tragically after Joseph Sanchez died three weeks after getting the post in 1985. Hoglund was barely warm in his seat at Saturn when he got the Buick-Oldsmobile-Cadillac chief's job. These days, as executive v.p., he rides herd on GM's automotive components group and the power products and defense operations group.

The best thing that recommends Hoglund is that he truly enjoys cars: Engineers tell of Hoglund showing up at a test track during his days at Pontiac. The engineers expected him to do what most GM satraps do when they appear for a test drive: cruise around the track at a very slow speed and say "Carry on, men." Instead, Hoglund drove the wheels off the vehicle and said: "I like this car."

Holley, Rev. James—December 5, 1943; activist maverick.

Rev. Holley never met a demonstration—or a television camera—he didn't like. The pastor of Detroit's Little Rock Baptist Church marched on Channel 4 to protest the demotion of anchorman Ben Frazier; planned a march on Dearborn to protest its ban on outsiders in city parks (the march was later called off), and accused the Pistons of playing "plantation basketball" in the suburbs.

A graduate of Nashville's Tennessee State University and holder of a Ph.D. from Wayne State, he was dean of students at the now-defunct Shaw College when asked to take over the Little Rock pulpit in 1972. He gained further visibility when he founded the Detroit Chapter of PUSH (People United to Save Humanity), the home base of the Rev. Jesse Jackson.

Holley is considered something of a maverick or even a loose cannon by elders in the black community. Holley supported *William Lucas*, a black Republican, in his gubernatorial bid in 1986 while most of the black power structure in town lined up for Democrat *James Blanchard*. His plans for a march on Dearborn also angered a few older black leaders, who thought Holley should wait until negotiations with Dearborn city fathers were completed. Conspicuously absent from Holley's anti-Dearborn protests was *Mayor Young*.

Holley's voice has been heard in the fight against gambling and the "airplane" pyramid scheme. And where a television camera goes, you may be certain Holley isn't far behind.

Hood, Rev. Nicholas Sr.—June 21, 1923; senior politician/preacher.

Detroit City Council's longest-serving member, Hood was first elected in 1965. (*Mel Ravitz* arrived in 1961, but took an eight-year sabbatical from 1974-'81.) At the time of his election, Hood was the council's only black member, and just the second black ever to serve. During the early to mid-1970s, he looked like a possible successor to *Mayor Young*. There is evidence, however, that his time has passed.

Possessor of a divinity degree from Yale University, Hood was appointed pastor of Plymouth Congregational Church in 1958. He worked the civil rights vineyards through the 1960s (he was a presence at the founding of the Southern Christian Leadership Conference in New Orleans) until the voters gave him his current job. Able to draw votes from black constituents, his softspoken and noncontroversial nature drew votes from the city's white precincts as well. This appeal gained him second-place finishes in both 1969 and 1973.

When Council President *Carl Levin* announced he would not run again in 1977, most city pols assumed Hood would be the top vote-getter. That would mean presiding over the often contentious, sometimes raucous nine-member body, and automatic viability as a future mayoral candidate. But voters tossed water on Hood's political fires. He placed not first, not second, but third. *Erma Henderson*, who had been elected only five years earlier, outhustled Hood to a first-place finish. *Maryann Mahaffey*, energetic and omnipresent on the campaign trail that year, beat Hood by seven votes. While he placed second in 1981 and 1985, he hasn't been able to come within 20,000 ballots of breaking Henderson's hold on the top slot.

Perhaps as a result of his stalled career, Hood seems to have lost some of his drive. He isn't out front on issues, usually siding with colleagues **David Eberhard** and **Barbara-Rose Collins** in backing the mayor.

I

Iacocca, Lee—October 15, 1924; the puzzle behind the pentastar.

He is a working-class hero who earned $21.5-million in one year. His face is so well-known that ads don't even bother to identify him. But he does little night life, preferring to beat a path home after a long day. He is considered a genius for saving Chrysler from the scrap heap. But the company appeared to falter in the late 1980s. Is the stumble a momentary blip? Or did Iacocca think short-term when he cut product plans in the '80s? It'll be years before anybody unravels this guy.

Asked what it was like working for Iacocca, Chrysler manufacturing boss **Richard Dauch** once told NBC News: "It's great, if you can stand the beatings." Iacocca can push people beyond their capabilities. When Chrysler's brain trust argued about an extended warranty program, not many people in the room wanted it. Manufacturing types would have been content to forget the cars once they were out the factory gate. Financial types argued the program was too costly. The marketing folks liked it, but they aren't taken as seriously as the boys in financial or manufacturing. But the warranty program went through because Iacocca's vote was equal to the sum of everybody else's. "This is the only way I know of to turn the heat on you guys," he told the crowd.

Iacocca deserves credit for seizing the public relations initiative after his firing by Henry Ford II in 1978. He saved Chrysler, of course. Then he wrote a book that couldn't miss with the masses. The tome had an awful "Mom, the rich guy is picking on me" tone to it. Iacocca was the son of an Italian immigrant. Henry Ford II was a rich, overweight mogul. Hard to mistake old Henry for a sympathetic character.

But Iacocca's press seems to be turning. He appeared as the bad guy in Robert Lacey's book on the Ford dynasty, and appeared even worse in Peter Collier and David Horowitz's "The Fords: An American Epic." Iacocca was portrayed as an arrogant, pushy character who forgot who owned the company.

Who knows how history will treat Iacocca? Henry Ford II's autobiography will hit the bookstores in 1990, so we may get a glimpse from the grave of what the jowly monarch thought of his former employee. Or maybe not, if Ford is true to his "Never complain, never explain" motto.

Ilitch, Mike—July 20, 1929; shortstop with a hockey team and a ton of pizzas to go.

Another guy who earned his sports franchise the hard way — tossing pizzas. Ilitch's Little Caesar Enterprises Inc. is maybe one-third as big as *Tom Monaghan*'s Domino's Pizza Inc. But $908-million or so in sales, which is what Little Caesar parlors rang up last year, isn't small provolone. Ilitch was able to buy the Red Wings for undisclosed millions from the aging Bruce Norris in 1982. Not bad for a guy who washed out of the Tigers farm system as a shortstop.

Which is where our story starts: Ilitch's baseball career had ended when he convinced a west-side bar owner that money could be made selling pizzas out of the saloon. Soon, there were other places. Before he knew it, Ilitch was stacking money with the best of 'em. A hard-core baseball freak, he apparently wanted to buy the Tigers. But Tigers owner John Fetzer secretly did the deal with Tom Monaghan. So Ilitch settled for the Red Wings, which hasn't turned out so bad. There are so many third-generation hockey fans in town that even when the Wings are terrible (as in the 1985-'86 season, when they won only 17 games) the Joe is full. And with the Wings winning, the only problem is getting a ticket to stand in the aisle.

He is a lot more reclusive than Monaghan, possibly because a nut made a kidnap threat against one of his children. The nut was ultimately apprehended and tossed in a clink by federal authorities, but the experience has skewed Ilitch toward discretion. There isn't much celebrity schmoozing for him, either. (Though he has been known to pal around with Channel 7's *Bill Bonds*, a friendship that was cemented long ago.) Ilitch's reopening of the Fox Theatre in fall 1988 could go a long way to reclaiming the north end of downtown. Otherwise, Ilitch hides his cash beneath a bushel basket and hangs around with his family, most of whom work for the organization.

Inatome, Rick—July 27, 1953; hardware store for the '90s.

He rode the home computer boom all the way to the bank. But unlike some of the Silicon Valley crowd who became rich and burned out, Inatome still rides high. Inacomp is in 18 states now, with some $300 million in sales in calendar 1988.

A native of Warren, Inatome graduated from Michigan State University in 1976 not knowing what he wanted to do. He found the answer in his own home. His father, Joseph, an engineer, kept computers around the house. Inatome found them interesting and opened a small shop in Clawson to sell them. Soon there was another, and another. And soon he had gone public. Those who bought stock in the early days became millionaires.

Like most entrepreneurs, he doesn't do a 9-to-5 kind of day. Meetings might start at 5:30 p.m. and run until after midnight. If he orders pizza, the executives all ante up a buck or two to cover the bill. Definitely not the company-sponsored three-martini lunch.

Even though Inacomp stock trades publicly, a major portion remains in family hands.

J

Jeanes, William—February 19, 1938; *Car and Driver*'s commander-in-chief.

His influence is felt throughout the automotive industry in a thousand subtle ways. As editor of the world's largest automobile magazine, this tall, courtly Mississippian speaks directly to 950,000-plus car buffs every month. But it is Jeanes's indirect influence that gets the attention of auto moguls. A rave *Car and Driver* review lends credibility to national television ads touting the latest piece of hardware. Wall Street auto analysts read his magazine, then tell their big-spending clients whether GM is doing its job. Newspaper reviewers take his cue and advise car buyers accordingly. One can't attach numbers to that sort of power.

He graduated from Millsaps College in Mississippi, where his father owned a Detroit Diesel Allison franchise. Jeanes was his dad's sales manager until he joined *Car and Driver* as feature editor in 1972. The next 12 years were spent shuffling between ad agencies and automotive enthusiast publications, the usual drill for his field.

In 1975, he jumped into advertising at Campbell-Ewald, then to J. Walter Thompson/Detroit (where he worked on the Ford account) and other places. He quit the ad business eight years later for a career in free-lance writing, picking up kudos for his work on the Buick and Cadillac Allanté catalogs. He landed at *Car and Driver* in late 1987.

Few writers can match the stylishness of his prose. In person, he's unfailingly polite. The only thing he asks is that you don't call him "Bill."

Jeanes's wife, Susan, is as much of an automotive buff as her husband. She's now *Car and Driver*'s executive art director, having filled similar posts at *AutoWeek* and *Automobile*.

Johnson, Glenn—October 30, 1922; links lord.

This Grosse Ile insurance man is a five-time Michigan Amateur golf champion. He files every score, every practice stroke, and has a wall of awards that inspires awe.

A natural athlete, Johnson won nine letters in football, basketball and baseball as a high school student in Grosse Ile. Johnson played quarterback at Michigan State College (later Michigan State University) in 1941-'42 and 1945. After college he turned to sailing, and was first mate on the boat that won the 1957 Port Huron-to-Mackinac race. Johnson didn't take up golf until he was age 26.

After he clinched his first amateur championship in 1954, a competitor loudly claimed that Johnson was the "worst champion Michigan ever had." So Johnson won again in 1955. Just to spite the naysayers, he won again in 1956, '58 and '61. The last championship is part of golf lore. Johnson was four down after nine holes, but then won five of the next six. One thing about Johnson—he knew how to do it with style. He'd load his Cadillac convertible with some eight outfits — one for each round.

A little older now, he's still big on the links, a major presence in senior tournaments. Johnson had been inducted into the Michigan Sports Hall of Fame, but declined to accept the nomination when it turned out that Commissioner Nick Kerbawy had pushed Johnson's name through to sell more tickets at the organization's banquet. His accomplishments on the links leave no doubts about his qualifications.

Johnson, Jim—July 30, 1952; WLLZ-FM air ace.

Johnson's smooth soothe plays straight man to mimic *George Baier* on WLLZ-FM's morning show. While Baier cuts up, Johnson provides order and continuity. He's the "pipes" of the outfit, a rock 'n' roll Dean Martin to Baier's Jerry Lewis. Off the air, now that former WRIF-FM colleague *Arthur Penhallow* has gotten older and cut back on the booze, Johnson's fast-lane antics help keep the local radio roster from becoming boring.

A graduate of Redford's Thurston High School, he flitted through Central Michigan University on a football scholarship. "I mostly majored in chasing women and playing football," Johnson recalls. Between games and dates, however, there was time for radio. The summer after his freshman year, he worked a marathon 3 p.m. Sunday-6 a.m. Monday shift at WEXL-AM. He'd introduce preachers in the afternoon and spin country and western twangers in the post-midnight hours. He did all-night or weekend gigs in Lansing and Flint, commuting from Mt. Pleasant, before abandoning his football scholarship for the promise of big money ($10,000 a year) at WVIC in Lansing. That's where Johnson got his first dose of the unfriendly side of the radio biz—fired after three months because the station manager said he couldn't afford him. From 1973-'74 he worked at WILS-FM in the capital.

Like a lot of radio careers, Johnson's was built on a series of small, seemingly inconsequential events. "I joined WWWW-FM during the summer of 1975, working weekend and vacation shifts," he remembers. He soon got the morning shift, then went to mid-days, then got afternoons and the program directorship, then hired Steve Dahl. When Dahl left for Chicago in January of '78, Johnson hooked up with Baier, who had been discovered by Dahl, while the station looked for another morning man. "We're still looking," Johnson says. Johnson's two messy marriages have made the gossip columnists very happy. He's a lot more apt to hit the discos than Baier.

Think of WLLZ's "J.J. & the Morning Crew" as a rock band. Baier is the lead guitarist—astounding with his pyrotechnics, improvising constantly. Johnson is the drummer, providing a framework, a foundation for the screecher to work from.

Jones, Ernie—June 18, 1915; father of XVI.

He's responsible for bringing Super Bowl XVI to Pontiac in 1982. As chairman of what is now the D'Arcy Masius Benton & Bowles ad agency, he oversaw the spending of millions of bucks on behalf of Cadillac and Pontiac (two of D'Arcy's biggest clients) on network television. The National Football League, dependent as they are on big-buck automotive advertising to pay the bills, listened oh-so-carefully when Jones made his pitch to bring the Super Bowl to Detroit. As a result, the NFL played its first cold-weather Super Bowl here in town. Pansy sportswriters groused about the winter weather, but this town had one heckuva time.

An alumnus of the University of Michigan (class of '38), Jones joined what was then the MacManus, John & Adams agency in 1939. He opened the agency's New York office in 1950 and ran the Detroit office from 1955 until his retirement in 1983. An erstwhile trumpet player at U-M, he liked to guest-conduct musical organizations such as the Detroit Concert Band and the Vienna Chamber Orchestra. Jones still does concerts with buddy Victor Borge. He was one of two ad agency guys in the '70s (the other being *Tom Adams* at Campbell-Ewald) who made some real civic contributions.

Jordan, Charles—October 21, 1927; top GM designer.

Amazingly, when Jordan took charge of design in 1987 he became only the fourth person in General Motors history to hold the job. Being chief designer at GM is a bit like being elected pope: It's a long climb, but the tenure is terrific. And you can claim quite a lineage. Jordan's predecessors were Harley Earl (1927-'58), William Mitchell (1958-'77) and Irvin Rybicki (1977-'86).

Jordan's link with GM was forged early. A native of Whittier, California, he won the Fisher Body Craftsman's Guild model competition, picking up a four-year scholarship to MIT. GM picked him up right after graduation, sending him through a succession of jobs including junior engineer, Cadillac chief designer and chief of exterior design. A tall, lanky, very distinguished-looking fellow, Jordan is popular with the automotive enthusiast magazines because he is, well, an enthusiast. Proof: He has owned two Ferarris.

Further proof: When William Mitchell died in the fall of 1988, Mitchell's family wanted a funeral cortege that included all of Mitchell's personal favorites. Jordan put it together: a 1963 silver Sting Ray coupe, a 1938 Cadillac 60 Special, a 1963 Buick Riviera, a 1967 Cadillac Eldorado and a 1980 Cadillac Seville. It had class.

K

Kaline, Al—December 19, 1934; a legend as No. 6.

This shy Tiger joined *George Kell* in the television booth in 1977, just three years after capping a 22-year career on the playing field—all with the Tigers. He's no Vin Scully behind the microphone, but he is an acknowledged baseball expert who has become comfortable on the air. He knows the game better than anybody in the city, and doesn't hesitate to criticize a player—in either uniform—who blows the fundamentals.

As tennis mothers of the 1980s pushed their daughters to excel with a racquet, Kaline's dad pushed him to excel with a bat and glove. His high school years were a never-ending string of doubleheaders and tripleheaders in the punishing Baltimore heat. Scout Ed Katalinas signed an 18-year-old Kaline for the Tigers in the 1953 season. Ted Williams spotted Kaline as a hitter of unusual talent. Williams knew for certain two years later when Kaline became the youngest player ever to win a batting title. He ran up a .340 average, far outhitting legends such as Mickey Mantle, Willie Mays and Stan Musial.

"The worst thing that happened to me in the big leagues was the start I had," Kaline later recalled. "This put the pressure on me. Everybody said this guy's another Ty Cobb, another Joe DiMaggio. How much pressure can you take? What they didn't know is that I'm not that good a hitter. They kept saying I do everything with ease. But it isn't that way. I have to work as hard if not harder than anybody in the league."

On the field, he was practiced grace, the work ethic personified, known simply as "Six." Off the field, he was somewhat standoffish with his peers. The 1968 world champion Tigers were a wild pack of party animals. Kaline would often retreat to his room. When he retired in 1974, his season's average, RBI's and home runs all were diminished by age, but good enough to lead the team. He took a .297 average into the Hall of Fame in 1980.

Kaline lives quietly—very quietly—in Bloomfield Hills. He fits the conservative Tigers organization very well. And if he ever criticized his employers from the booth, viewers would surely choke on their Ball Park franks.

Kan, Michael—July 17, 1933; deputy of art.

He's *Sam Sachs II*'s No. 2 at the Detroit Institute of Arts. A native of China, Ken earned three degrees from Columbia University (BA in art history, MA in art history, another degree in philosophy of art history) and joined the Brooklyn Museum as acting director in 1974. He signed on as the DIA's deputy director in 1976.

Kasdan, Lawrence—January 14, 1949; copywriter's role model.

It seems that every frustrated Detroit ad writer has a screenplay in his desk drawer and dreams of becoming Lawrence Kasdan. The scenario: writing screenplays by night and laboring at Southfield's W.B. Doner ad agency by day, Kasdan through the early 1970s could barely interest an agent in representing him, let alone convince a producer to put his work on film. But with "The Empire Strikes Back" in 1980, Kasdan was on his way toward being filmdom's hottest writing talent. His screenwriting credits include "Continental Divide," "Raiders of the Lost Ark" and "Return of the Jedi." His directing and writing stamp can be found on "Body Heat," "The Big Chill," "Silverado" and "The Accidental Tourist."

He showed promise early. As a student at the University of Michigan in the late '60s and early '70s, he picked up four prestigious Hopwood Awards for his writing. (Previous winners include playwright Arthur Miller and novelist Marge Piercy.) A Hopwood looks good on one's mantel, but it can't be entered on a bank deposit slip. So Kasdan bided his time in advertising, which he despised, fueling his determination to skip town and pursue his real goal: film. "Continental Divide" put him on the map as a craftsman with original material. Four studios tried to land the script before Universal turned it into a movie with the late John Belushi.

He then sold two scripts within three months. Now Kasdan's happy problem is how to make the telephone stop ringing. He's a top gun in Hollywood and could probably peddle his grocery list.

The '90s will find him behind the camera as often as behind a typewriter. "I have never really liked writing," he revealed to *American Film* magazine. "It's the loneliest work in the world. I hate being alone in a room, and I was alone all the time for seven years while I was trying to sell something. I thought, 'If I can ever get out of this writing racket, I'm going to hang around with people.' And that's what directing is."

Married to his wife, Meg, since 1971, he still makes trips to Detroit to visit his in-laws.

Kaufman, Judge Richard—September 5, 1951; more than a name.

Many laughed when 29-year-old Richard Kaufman was elected to the Wayne County circuit bench in 1980. They blamed his election on his name, inherited from his father, the well-known Judge Charles Kaufman. The younger Kaufman's detractors wondered how smart a guy only three years out of law school could be.

Plenty smart, it turned out. Six years later, he had earned such respect that his fellow jurists—a sometimes unruly lot of 35 robed egos—elected him chief judge in 1986. That means he's in charge of the tedious details of running Wayne County Circuit Court. In addition, lawyers who want trials delayed have to come begging to Kaufman. That's power.

Kaufman, a 1977 graduate of Wayne State University Law School, spent his short stint in private practice with Phil Colista, probably one of the most respected lawyers in town.

To Kaufman's credit, he hasn't shrunk from the tough cases. He took control of Wayne County Jail (long a textbook case of bad management) away from Sheriff **Robert Ficano** and gave it to County Exec **Ed McNamara**. When **Mayor Young** tried to have a paternity case sealed so the public couldn't get a look at it, the mayor's clout didn't carry the day. Kaufman said no.

Keane-Doran, Maureen—see Doran, Wayne

Keith, Damon—July 4, 1922; power on the bench and in the wings.

He may be the pre-eminent man behind the scenes in Detroit. Judge Keith called a pal, Federal Communications Commissioner James Quello, when he heard WJR was moving to Troy. A few phone calls later, WJR unpacked its bags and announced it was staying put in the Fisher Building. When Wayne County Community College and its president, Reginald Wilson, were fighting over—well, gee, who remembers any more?—Keith got the two factions behind closed doors and knocked a few heads. Soon, Wilson was gone and things went back to what passes for normal around WCCC.

Keith, who sits on the U.S. Court of Appeals for the 6th Circuit in

Cincinnati, is the grandson of a slave. His father moved to Detroit from Georgia to work on the line at Ford. Realizing that his son could do better, the elder Keith pushed his son into college. While earning degrees from West Virginia State College, Howard Law School and Wayne State, Keith waited on tables, cleaned chapels, sold fruit and chopped trees. He emptied wastebaskets for $25 a week at the *Detroit News* while waiting for his bar exam results.

He became a power in town not terribly long after passing the state bar examination. He was appointed co-chair of the Michigan Civil Rights Commission, had posts with the Wayne County Board of Supervisors and practiced with Nathan Conyers, Joseph Brown and *Myron Wahls*. (The three went on, respectively, to run a large auto dealership, hold a judgeship in Detroit's 36th District Court, and sit on the Michigan Court of Appeals.) President Lyndon Johnson named Keith to the U.S. District Court bench in 1967. From that outpost, he ruled that unrestricted government wiretapping is illegal.

Attorney General John Mitchell had labored under the mistaken impression that he could order wiretaps at any time, in any place. Mitchell fought it to the U.S. Supreme Court, but lost. Keith was appointed to the appellate bench by Jimmy Carter in 1977.

He is only a few years from semi-retirement, and no dais in town is complete without him. His friend, *Coleman Young*, joked that Keith's Cincinnati court was about to place his picture on milk cartons in an effort to find him.

Keith and his wife, Rachel, a physician, live in a Palmer Park home and are famous for their annual Thanksgiving Day dinner. Most every power broker in town is around the table on that day.

Kell, George—August 23, 1922; "He hit that one a mile, *Al.*"

His gentle Arkansas twang is the television voice of the Tigers. He climbed into the Tiger Stadium broadcast booth for the 1959 season. Except for sitting out the '64 season, he's been there ever since. Straw polls regularly put him on top of the heap with Detroit sports fans. And with baseball ratings sky-high in town, this Southern gentleman ranks as a genuine celebrity.

The son of a small-town barber turned farmer made his major league debut in 1943 with the Philadelphia Athletics. In four seasons with Connie Mack's team, he never hit over .300. But when the right-handed third baseman joined the Tigers in 1946, .300-plus became his standard. In 1949, he was named to the All-Star team and took the American League batting crown from Ted Williams in a wild finish. Kell passed the sharp-eyed Boston slugger on the last day of the season with two hits (a single and a double off Bob Lemon of the Cleveland Indians) in three at-bats. The unlucky Williams went 0–2 against the Yankees in New York. When the numbers were crunched an extra decimal point, Williams averaged a miserly .3427 to Kells' .3429.

Kell was traded to Boston in 1952. A *News* account of the trade characterized him as "the best third baseman in Detroit history. He also was the highest-salaried Tiger at $42,000." This Arkansas Traveler wasn't through traveling: It was on to Chicago in 1954, then to Baltimore (where he met future Tigers radio announcer *Ernie Harwell*) in 1956. With Kell finally in age's grip, he retired from the Orioles with a lifetime average of .306. He was also the only player ever to play at least 200 games for each of five teams.

But Kell never really left baseball. He spent 1958 with CBS helping Dizzy Dean and Buddy Blattner. When Tigers announcer Mel Ott died in an automobile accident after the 1958 season, the still-popular Kell got the call. He finally made it to the Hall of Fame in 1983.

Kell doesn't need the Tigers' money. He has an auto dealership in Arkansas, has been buddy to several Arkansas governors, and even did a stint on the Arkansas Road Commission. In a state with an unusual (by Michigan standards) number of dirt roads, this is no small deal. The only possible answer: He needs the game.

Kelley, Frank—December 31, 1924; an AG for the '60s, '70s and '80s—so far.

Just think about this for a second: Attorney General Frank Kelley has held his job since 1962, which makes him the state's senior elected official of all time. In fact, no other state attorney general in this nation has stayed in one place for such a long time.

There has been a Kelley in Democratic politics for much of this century. His father, Frank E. Kelley, ran a west-side saloon that served as a watering hole for the county's Democratic pols. When the elder Kelley died in 1954, the funeral procession was said to be five miles long. Kelley set up a law practice in Alpena, which is about as far as one can get from Grand River and Quincy without going into the Upper Peninsula. Gov. John Swainson persuaded

Kelley to come back into politics in 1962. Kelley landed himself a 52 percent victory, and hasn't left since.

He loves to beat up on the state utilities, and has a special love for teeing off on Blue Cross and Blue Shield. If he is known for anything beyond longevity, it's for setting up respectable environmental and consumer protection divisions.

Even so, his political future begins and ends where he sits. Kelley lost a 1972 U.S. Senate race against incumbent U.S. Sen. Robert Griffin. Busing was a big issue that year. Kelley even argued against it before the U.S. Supreme Court. But Griffin just happened to scream louder, so Kelley lost, 53 percent to 47 percent. From time to time there are rumblings that he'll take a spot on the Michigan Supreme Court. But those rumblings have been false, so far.

Kelley, Jack—February 9, 1926; highly excitable city councilman.

He is nothing if not blunt. On one occasion he characterized one of *Mayor Young*'s aides as "a fat ass." Another offending mayoral aide was dubbed "the dink." The mayhem Kelley commits upon the English language and his colleagues leads some observers to conclude that he isn't very smart. But while his IQ might be a subject of debate, one thing is not: Kelley is exceptionally well-informed, and has better links with the neighborhoods than just about anybody in city hall. People are "pals" and he'll do just about anything to help them.

A former carpenter and union man, he was a vociferous supporter of Jerry Cavanagh during Cavanagh's run for the mayor's office in 1961. Kelley's loyalty was rewarded with a job in the city's Building Department. Which was fine with Kelley, until he decided he'd like a City Council job. It took him four tries to find success: He placed 11th in 1969 (only about 6,000 votes out of the money); in 1972, he lost in a special election against *Erma Henderson*. Voters finally gave him what he wanted in 1973.

Kelley's early years in office read more like a police blotter than a council agenda. A barroom fight with a retired cop in 1975 earned him a well-chronicled trip to jail. He went dry soon after, and has made red pop his trademark ever since. His 1977, 1981 and 1985 races all landed him respectable fifth-place finishes. Kelley's outbursts, which have become increasingly frequent in the late '80s, reflect frustration with what he sees around him. He feels that the city has fallen apart while the folks in the Mayor's Office fiddle.

Kelly, John (October 7, 1927) and Turner, Marilyn (February 5, year not available); the King and Queen of local TV.

Their morning talk show on Channel 7 is among the last vestiges of local non-news programming in Detroit television. At one time, Channel 4 had Sonya Friedman, while Channel 2 had J.P. McCarthy. But as the '80s faded away, station owners found it easier and more profitable to buy syndicated programming from Hollywood. Even the Kelly/Turner show was under fire: Channel 4's Geraldo Rivera made inroads into the couple's ratings. Only Channel 7 general manager *Tom Griesdorn* knows if the decade-old show will continue into the '90s.

Kelly (real name: John Kelin) originally signed up as a newsman on Channel 2 in 1965. He and Jac LeGoff (now of Channel 4) practically owned the Nielsen ratings book in the late '60s and early '70s. When Channel 7's owners, the American Broadcasting Co., decided to get serious about Detroit, one of the company's first hires was Kelly in 1972. Meanwhile, Turner—a native of Windsor—had been doing weathercasts on Channel 2. She made the switch from 2 to 7 in 1973. With a *Bonds*-Kelly-Turner-Ackerman combo in the saddle, Channel 7 grabbed the ratings lead from Channel 2.

But doing the news night after night became tedious—"I was burned out," he said. So the couple got themselves a talk show in 1977. Intellectuals like to poke fun at Kelly & Co. But when one of 'em writes a book, the begging begins. "*Dutch Leonard* mentioned us in his last book," says he. "Life is complete."

Kennedy, Bill—June 27, 1908; matinee idol emeritus.

This longtime Detroit movie host, now in retirement, was a bit player who brought a star quality to his TV role.

A Cleveland native, he joined WWJ-radio as a newscaster in 1936. He went to Los Angeles as a newscaster in 1941, but it wasn't long before Warner Brothers signed him. Kennedy did some 100 movie roles between 1941 and 1945, none of them memorable. He played one of Bette Davis' lovers in "Mr. Skeffington," and he burned Ingrid Bergman at the stake in "Joan." Kennedy's best line was "My God, we've burned a saint." Maybe God punished him for the transgression, because Kennedy never really caught on in Hollywood. As he once told a *Free Press* reporter: "My agent told me I was the sophisticated actor type and not to accept any roles beneath my dignity. Well, I went around being dignified for eight months—

didn't get one acting job." Kennedy even anchored the news for a couple of years at the CBS owned-and-operated television station in Los Angeles, but lost his job when CBS chose to hire a real newsman.

Burned by the business, he did walk away with a storehouse of knowledge which he parlayed into a successful afternoon television career in Detroit. He did "Bill Kennedy's Showtime" on Channel 9 for 13 years, and "Bill Kennedy at the Movies" on Channel 50 for 14 years, ending in 1983. He drove a Rolls Silver Cloud II between work and home in Grosse Pointe.

Viewers called in with trivia questions. Kennedy supplied answers from the vast databank of useless information stored in his head and a pack rat's collection of "B" movie still shots. He now lives in Palm Beach, where he still owns a Rolls. Too bad there aren't any more Bill Kennedys. The new generation is *so* bland.

Kessler, William—December 15, 1924; virtuoso in concrete.

This Harvard-educated building design virtuoso has better luck snaring commissions out of town than on his own home turf. The rejuvenation of the Fox Theatre was a recent notable exception. Buildings which bear the emphatic Kessler signature include the Detroit Science Center, the Center for Creative Studies near Wayne State University and Detroit Receiving Hospital.

The Pennsylvania-born Kessler studied with the best. His tutors included Mies van der Rohe at Chicago's Institute of Design, and Walter Gropius at Harvard. "Two years," he told his wife on the way to Detroit, where he took a job with the famed Minoru Yamasaki in 1953, "and we'll be out of here." Almost four decades later, he's still around. Kessler teamed with Phil Meathe in 1955 and went on to build a string of magnificent homes. The late W. Hawkins Ferry, who wrote the definitive guide to Detroit buildings, hired Kessler to design his Lake Shore Drive digs in Grosse Pointe Shores. That's like Miss Manners hiring an etiquette coach. Former Gov. John Swainson's summer home in Manistee is one of Kessler's, too, and usually makes the cut in discussions about the snazziest homes in the state.

One of Detroit's best design duos split in 1968, with Meathe walking to head up Smith, Hinchman & Grylls. Kessler's office, in a century-old building near Greektown, offers a view of two Detroit hulks he despises: the Blue Cross and Blue Shield Building and the Renaissance Center. No wonder he sometimes looks depressed. That countenance is cheered when he sees two of his favorites: Yamasaki's ANR Building on Woodward and the old Wayne County Courthouse.

Kienzle, William X.—Sept. 11, 1928; Father Koesler's father.

An ex-Roman Catholic priest, Kienzle now writes mystery novels. His first, "The Rosary Murders" (1979), was made into a 1987 film starring Donald Sutherland, Charles Durning, southwest Detroit and Holy Redeemer Church. Since "The Rosary Murders," he has methodically turned out one book per year. The main character in each is a fictional sleuth by the name of Father Robert Koesler, a 60ish Catholic priest who wears two hats: one as pastor of a church, the other as a once-a-year detective. Koesler, Kienzle says, "is about where I would be had I remained a priest." Except for solving homicides, of course.

Like Father Koesler, Kienzle developed his literary skills as editor of the *Michigan Catholic*. Although he didn't want the job when the late John Cardinal Dearden shoved him into the editor's chair in 1962, it gave Kienzle marketable skills when he left the priesthood 12 years later.

"Never did I become disillusioned with the priesthood," he wrote of his 20 years (1954-'74) wearing a Roman collar. "But, over the years, I grew increasingly disenchanted with Church law on marriage, especially the canonical procedures regarding divorced Catholics who wished to remarry. I became convinced these procedures were demeaning, embarrassing, unnecessary, unfair and unjust," he wrote in an autobiographical sketch for Gale Research's *Contemporary Authors Autobiography Series*. "When I became convinced I could no longer subject people to these procedures . . . I most reluctantly concluded it was necessary to leave."

He married within a year. His wife, Jàvan, a former *Free Press* copy editor, is his editor, adviser and assumedly the source of some of the *Freep* verisimilitude on the pages of his novels. Kienzle has a system. He starts a novel in November or December, writing in longhand. Jàvan edits the text and runs the day's output through a typewriter. He finishes by May, fiddling with the book and doing promo work through the early summer. He breaks for leisure reading in July. "I start to panic around August for another idea," he says. Then, he starts the process all over again.

Some of his works include "Death Wears a Red Hat," "Mind Over Murder" and "Shadow of Death." Each was published by the same Kansas City book house (Andrews & McMeel) that took a chance with "The Rosary Murders." "For a person who was trained to baptize, preach and stuff like that," Kienzle says, "trained for nothing else whatsoever, this is pretty good."

Killeen, James—July 4, 1923; experienced and green, green, green.

He's a classic example of how the Irish Mafia works in this town. Wayne County Clerk Joseph B. Sullivan was about to assume a post on the Wayne County Circuit Court bench in 1973. Chief Judge Joseph A. Sullivan (Joe B.'s brother-in-law) and Judge Thomas Foley approached Killeen, a 23-year veteran of the U.S. Justice Department, about taking the job. His Irish friends maneuvered it through a group of Wayne County judges, many of them Irish and lifelong friends of Killeen. "A reporter asked me if being Irish had anything to do with my appointment," Killeen recalled, "then she ticks off the names: Brennan, Sullivan, Foley. And I say, 'Well, by golly maybe there is something to this.' "

If Tip O'Neill had been born in Detroit instead of Boston, he'd be Jim Killeen. (In fact, each is white-haired and considerably overweight.) The son of an Irish immigrant and Detroit schoolteacher, he grew up near Dickerson and Kercheval on the lower east side. The family produced a crop of kids who were classically Irish in their chosen occupations: Father Joseph Killeen is pastor of St. Blase in Sterling Heights; brother George is a Macomb County commissioner (1984-present) and a former Wayne County commissioner (1970-'84). Jim can claim two Irish occupations — cop (for the Justice Department) and politician. During those years at Justice, when he became an ardent fan of the Kennedy family, he dabbled in national politics.

Although the county clerk's job may sound like a boring one, it does have its moments. Killeen is chief election official for the state's largest county. As such, he has a large office on the second floor of the City-County Building. And he is the official keeper of all sorts of political information, such as who gave how much in campaign donations to whom. And as any schoolboy knows, information is power. *Mayor Young* couldn't be found the night Ronald

Reagan was elected to the presidency in 1980. Where was he? Camping out in Killeen's office.

King, John L.—February 15, 1950; bookworm.

If you really love the printed word, his used-book emporium on the western edge of downtown Detroit is a dream. Both the *New York Times* (in the person of columnist William Safire) and the *Wall Street Journal* have praised John L. King Books as one of the five best shops in the country. He has four floors of literary output, from varying editions of Gibbons' "Rise and Fall of the Roman Empire" to arcane books about Detroit. The author of this book has purchased four tomes on Jimmy Hoffa from John King, and wistfully realizes that one day these very words will rest next to a used copy of "The Pontchartrain Murders," or some such.

"I'm the product of a broken home," explains King. "Lots of times, such people become juvenile delinquents. Sometimes, they become bookworms. I chose to be a bookworm." King liked books so much that he chose them full-time after washing out at Wayne State University. "I suppose if I were a Winkelman and had a lot of money I would have gone into new books," King says. "But I didn't have any money, so this was the only route available to me."

He's now headquartered in a former glove factory perched on West Lafayette above the Lodge Freeway. *Donald Petersen*, the Ford Motor Co. chairman, has been seen rummaging in the stacks there. So has comedian Jay Leno.

Klugh, Earl—September 16, 1953; smooth pickin's.

He's the guitarist of choice among music fans who like a laid-back, silky, romantic sort of jazzy sound.

A graduate of Mumford High, he took up the guitar after hearing Chet Atkins on a television show. Both his father and grandfather played the instrument as a hobby. Earl was discovered at a tender age by jazz great Yusef Lateef playing in a Detroit music store. Before he was out of his teens, his playing could be heard with the likes of saxophonist Lateef, guitarist George Benson and pianist George Shearing.

Two partnerships with arranger Bob James have resulted in two Top 40 *Billboard* LPs. "One on One" (1979) sat on the charts for 13 weeks, and "Low Ride" (1983) was there for three. He even worked with Michael Jackson on a love ballad sung by Jennifer Holliday. These days he's not living on his guitar-playing abilities alone. He and impresario Clarence Baker opened a jazz club in Pontiac, and it seems to be doing well.

After going out on his own, Klugh elected to play acoustic guitar only. Some folks would like to hear what he sounds like plugged in.

Knight, Lester—June 6, 1958; urban cowboy.

A dozen of the town's best athletes weigh an average of 112 pounds, risk their lives as many as 10 times a day, compete from March to November, attract about 20,000 fans a week and almost never get their names in a newspaper story. They're jockeys. Lester Knight is the most exciting of the bunch, the kind you might go out to watch even if you couldn't bet.

Lester is the master at "rating" a horse—saving the animal's energies for a big stretch run. And he is unequaled in taking his mount through traffic to get there. The wise guys, and the percentages, favor front-runners. But the asphalt at Ladbroke DRC is strewn with trifecta tickets spoiled by 15–1 shots that Lester rallied to a share of the purse money.

One fine day in 1987 he was sitting on a horse called Strikemate, dead last entering the stretch of a *sprint* race. Lester saw a small opening near the rail and asked his horse to run. When the opening started to close, he went for it anyway. Strikemate crashed into one horse and almost went down. Lester jerked him forward, bumped his way through and made one of the more spectacular second-place finishes of the decade. The stewards disqualified the horse and suspended Lester for a week, but you can't say he didn't try.

He won the riding title that year, and in 1983, but suspensions have cost him top honors numerous times. Gene Guidi, the former *Free Press* racing writer who now covers baseball for the paper, has seen Lester throughout his career. "With Lester it's a kind of controlled aggression now," Guidi says. "He's evolved into a thinking rider. He's not just Boom Boom Knight. All things equal, he has the most horse left at the end of the race. And I think he is the most adept at figuring out the ever-changing DRC track bias."

When DRC closes for the winter, Lester abandons the racing circuit and returns to Panama, where he grew up, to fish and scuba dive. "I have a feeling he'd be pretty good elsewhere," Guidi says. But it looks like we'll never know.

Kocsis, Chuck—January 23, 1913; golfer for the generations.

Unarguably the most respected amateur golfer the state has ever produced. His record of six state amateur crowns (1930, '33, '34, '37, '48 and '51) still stands. Note that he won his first championship when he was 17—he was then in high school. By the time Kocsis ripened to age 18, he had beaten Tommy Armour (who was reigning British Open Champion at the time) in the Michigan Open. Although well into his 70s, Kocsis still commands great respect and strikes his shots with such machine-like precision and accuracy that last year he played and won a tournament in Scotland using the same ball for all 72 holes.

Growing up in the shadows of the Redford Golf Club, Kocsis began putting at the age of six. He had it all: technique, heart, and an ability to psych out his opponents. Years after he won the Michigan Open against Armour, he finally told how he played head games with his foe. Armour kept the young Kocsis waiting some 90 minutes for the big match. That gave Kocsis just enough time to lay a trap. When Armour came out of the lockeroom, Kocsis passed him without a sign of recognition and waited in the clubhouse for about a half an hour. Armour, who required a good deal more deference, was so steamed he wouldn't shake hands with Kocsis as they teed off. Armour stayed steamed—and lost the match.

During his decades-long golf career, he owned a tool distribution company. He went pro for less than two years, and reclaimed his amateur status because he wasn't all that nuts about the play-for-money game.

Given the size of today's purses, one wonders: How many millions could a Chuck Kocsis of the '90s win?

Kopcha, Steve—September 29, 1941; D'Arcy's creative engine.

This burly, bearded iconoclast is responsible for Pontiac's "We Build Excitement" campaign. He builds excitement himself around D'Arcy Masius Benton & Bowles's Bloomfield Hills offices. Kopcha rides a Harley Davidson motorcycle and plays rock saxophone in his spare time. To some of the suits at General Motors, this may seem like wacky behavior. But it dovetails with one of Kopcha's gospels. As he told a special meeting of the New York Ad Club at Little Darlin's Rock and Roll Palace in New York in late 1988: "Inexorably as sand through the hourglass, an historic fact is becoming apparent to me and that is this: Sometime in the next 10 or 12 years, we will have a president of the United States who was born and raised on rock and roll and television . . . the world as we know it is going to be significantly different 10 to 12 years from now because that's when the rock and roll generation becomes the 55-year-old power structure of the world . . . And one of the big differences will be in communications."

He joined D'Arcy's St. Louis office as a copywriter in 1968 and worked on the agency's Budweiser ads. He bounced between the St. Louis and New York offices a couple of times before landing in Detroit, where he is now deputy managing director/chief creative officer. He overseas the creative work on accounts such as Pontiac, Cadillac, GM Parts, Whirlpool and FTD. He is witty and irreverent, just what you want in a creative chief. Says a friend: "What you see is what you get with Steve. If he doesn't like something—or does—he'll tell you about it. He is absolutely fearless that way."

A telling Kopchaism involves employees working from home via computer: "We actually considered it, but rejected it when we realized: Where would people go to bitch and moan? An important human need."

Kughn, Richard—October 31, 1929; social omnipresence.

This Detroit millionaire can be found wherever two or more people are gathered in tuxedoes. Few in Detroit have enjoyed such spectacular business success. He owns the price-and trend-leading Whitney restaurant, which serves to magnify his social caché. Lionel Trains is his, too, but that's just for fun. He's a major investor in the Detroit Riverfront Apartments (along with partners *Al Taubman* and *Max Fisher*) and is a large contributor to *Mayor Young*'s superfluous campaign chest.

Kughn made most of his dough as an associate of zillionaire Taubman, hooking up with Big Al when the latter was a mere muddy-booted builder. Taubman had this idea that these new shopping centers might be the coming thing. Kughn, who joined Taubman's company in 1955, was around for the run-up. By the time Kughn punched out some 30 years later, both were stunningly rich.

Kughn wisely used his money to open doors for himself: He contributed heavily to charities (Michigan Cancer Foundation, Orchestra Hall restoration) and made plenty of four-figure donations to Young's campaign coffers. Possibly as a way of saying thanks, Young tapped Kughn as chairman of the Detroit Police Commission. His most prized possession may be his "Carail," a fairly nondescript building in northwest Detroit that houses his antique car and model train collection. Among the 175 or so autos are a million-dollar Duesenberg. He also owns Henry Ford I's private rail car, the Fair Lane, the finest coach that Pullman ever built. The car collection is said to make Tigers owner **Tom Monaghan** jealous.

When things get hot, Kughn and his wife, Linda, escape to the late G. Mennen "Soapy" Williams' home on Mackinac Island. Kughn owns that, too.

L

Laimbeer, Bill—May 19, 1957; tall talent.

The Detroit Pistons center is jokingly—and factually — known as the only player in the National Basketball Association who earns less than his father. His image is that of the blue-collar scrapper, a working-class hero. In fact, he's a well-heeled California boy who went to Notre Dame.

This 6'11" wonder graduated from high school in Palos Verdes and did three of his four years in college at Notre Dame. (He spent a year at Owens Technical College in Toledo, Ohio, but didn't play basketball.) Upon graduation in 1979, he played basketball in Italy, but returned to the states to join the Cleveland Cavaliers. He was there barely a year before the Cavs traded him to Detroit in 1982. The Cavs got a couple of guys nobody has heard of since, plus a couple of draft picks. In exchange, the Pistons got a centerpiece for their reconstruction—and the most effective elbows in town since Gordie Howe. They say certain kinds of birds shouldn't be able to fly. And a behemoth like Laimbeer, who can't jump as high as your obese Uncle Pete, shouldn't be able to rebound. But he does.

He has blossomed since arriving here. Laimbeer led the NBA in rebounding in 1986, and has made the All-Star team four times.

Lajoie, William—September 27, 1934; *this* is Detroit's finest dealer, Sparky.

The Tigers general manager has a way of spotting talent that mere mortal GMs have missed. He traded John Smoltz (that's correct) for journeyman pitcher Doyle Alexander in 1987. Suddenly, the Tigers were champions of a tough American League East.

It's been a long road to baseball eminence. A grad of Denby High School and Western Michigan University, he spent 10 years as a minor league player with the Baltimore Orioles system before a leg injury destroyed any major league prospects he had left. Lajoie turned to scouting, first with the Cincinnati Reds (1965-'68), then with the Tigers. The Detroit brass were impressed enough to bring him from Bristol, Virginia, where he managed the club's Rookie League franchise, to the front office as Michigan scout supervisor in 1970. A number of promotions brought him to the general manager's job in October 1983.

Some of his trades—notably John Wockenfuss and Glenn Wilson for Willie Hernandez and Dave Bergman—were thought to have been a major ingredient in the Tigers' 1984 World Championship. There was a small uproar in 1988 when Tigers owner *Tom Monaghan* decreed that nobody in the front office — including Bill Lajoie— should have a contract. The organization changed its mind when the Pittsburgh Pirates placed Lajoie on their short list for a new general manager.

Lawrence, David Jr.—March 5, 1942; general at the Mourning Friendly.

When the history of the *Detroit Free Press* is written, it may argue that Lawrence has had a bigger impact on the place than any executive except John Knight (who bought the paper in 1940) and Lee Hills (the publisher who led it into the modern era).

Although he had absolute power at Knight-Ridder's Detroit outpost, and commuted often to Miami headquarters, Lawrence seemed as shocked as staffers and the public when the company sought a Joint Operating Agreement with the *Detroit News* and Gannett. The "Great Newspaper War" had ended with the *Free Press* declaring itself to be a failing newspaper. Under JOA law, somebody had to throw up the white flag. Lawrence turned his attention from burying the *News* to marrying it. He led the propaganda campaign to assure Detroiters they wouldn't have their morning *Freep* without a JOA, or at least not a *Freep* owned by Knight-Ridder.

JOA aside, the newspaper became a far different animal under Lawrence. The graphics department grew from a cubbyhole to an empire, sports became front-page news, and—while the average hard-news story was capsulized—special project stories were given time and space previously unimagined. The public was invited to tell the paper what was on their minds, and staffers were ordered to listen.

Raised on a farm in upstate Florida and the son of a prominent Florida newspaperman, Lawrence made stops at the *St. Petersburg Times*, *Palm Beach Post* and *Washington Post*. After joining Knight-Ridder, he served as managing editor of the *Philadelphia Daily News* (1971-'75) and executive editor of the *Charlotte Observer* (1975-'78.) Then, already gray by the age of 36, he was named executive editor in Detroit.

The man is nothing if not energetic. It isn't unusual for a staffer to receive a reply to a memo hours after it hits Lawrence's mailbox. He's also quite serious about adding women and minorities to the newspaper's staff, and promoting them. Lawrence is probably the most talked-about exec when staffers gather for beers after work. Capable of incredible kindness, he has some boosters. He also has a terrible temper that has gained him some enemies.

Known as "Skippy" by his detractors, he has inspired both derision and intense loyalty among journalists who have worked under him. Listening to reviews from either camp, a stranger would wonder if both critics had seen the same movie.

Although he's a company man from his premature gray to his wingtips, nobody will ever know how hurt he was when Knight-Ridder went after a JOA. The cease-fire order came from headquarters, not from the field general.

LeFauve, Richard "Skip" — November 30, 1934; at the helm of GM's bold experiment.

He runs the company's Saturn division, GM's Brave New World. The first car division to be created in six decades, Saturn is to be on the cutting edge of labor/management relations, the prototype of how things will be done in the 21st Century. If the project runs as *Roger Smith* hopes it will run, Saturn will prove to America that the Japanese aren't the only ones who can make a cost-efficient car.

An Ohio native, LeFauve signed aboard GM as an industrial engineer in the Packard Electric division. A year later he ran away and joined the U.S. Navy, where he stayed for six years — rising to lieutenant commander. Upon retiring his sailor's legs, he returned to the fold and got serious. LeFauve took a series of increasingly important manufacturing jobs through the '60s and '70s. Immediately before joining Saturn as president in early 1986, he had been director of operations for GM's Buick-Oldsmobile-Cadillac group.

Saturn has had three presidents before building a single car. The first, Joseph Sanchez, died within a month of getting the job. The second, **William Hoglund**, was aboard little more than a year before getting a promotion to chief of the Buick-Oldsmobile-Cadillac group. The third's personal style is rather low-key. LeFauve wouldn't necessarily stand out in a Livonia bowling alley, but that may be a plus: The new Saturn system is supposed to break down barriers between GM's ruling class and its workers. The worst thing Roger Smith could have done is send a Yuppie to command the troops.

It is interesting that GM turned to a manufacturing guy for the top Saturn post. He is one of only two car division managers (the other being Cadillac's **John Grettenberger**) who have manufacturing responsibilities. The head of Pontiac, for instance, simply markets the cars built in Chevrolet-Pontiac-Canada group factories. GM may have been wily in choosing a man who knows how to tighten a bolt. When Saturn is offered to the public in the early '90s, the design may be outstanding, its advertising campaign breathtaking. But if it isn't put together properly, GM will never live it down.

Leonard, Elmore "Dutch" — October 11, 1925; Detroit's most famous literary export.

His books have been turned into movies for Paul Newman, Alan Alda, Roy Scheider, Glenn Ford and the two Burts — Lancaster and Reynolds—among others. He has graced the cover of *Newsweek*, been profiled in *Esquire* by the *New York Daily News*'s Mike Lupica and drooled on by *Chicago Tribune* columnist Bob Greene. He lives quietly in Birmingham with his wife, Joan, with no desire to move to Hollywood or New York.

A 1950 graduate of the University of Detroit, he wrote Chevy car and truck ads at the Campbell-Ewald ad agency (now Lintas: Campbell-Ewald). His literary exercises during his years in the advertising business were confined to the pre-dawn hours between 5 and 7. He quit in the early '60s to work full-time behind the typewriter. Check out "LaBrava" and "Stick" for examples of his special eye for south Florida. "Freaky Deaky" and "Unknown Man No. 89" find him training his telescope on Detroit. His "City Primeval" (1980) is a clever story which seems to pattern itself after disgraced pistol-packing Detroit Recorder's Court Judge James Del Rio, who was booted off the bench for a series of indiscretions in the mid 1970s.

Drinking is a big issue in Leonard's life. His battle with booze is portrayed well in *Dennis Wholey*'s "The Courage to Change": Leonard in the ad agency, drinking with the clients; Leonard hanging around Hollywood in the late '60s and early '70s, when he'd have 20 drinks or more in him by the time he got to his hotel bed; Leonard finally joining Alcoholics Anonymous. He had his last drink in 1977. "I am much more aware of things going on but in a very quiet way," he told Wholey. "I don't need excitement. I'm into my work now, all the way and I'm not straining. I stop at six o'clock, but I'm giving it a full shot every day. I see that I can continue to get better at it. That's an amazing thing after 32 years, to know I can get better . . . I'm sitting here all by myself, doing this story, getting all excited about it and getting paid for it—a lot of money. I'm not bending to a certain commercial way to fit a commercial need. I can't do that. I have to do it my way, and thank God, it's saleable."

Many readers think his latest, "Killshot," may be his greatest.

Lester, Harry—August 21, 1929; survivor of steel hard times.

There have been worse jobs than the one Harry Lester, boss of all the steelworkers in southeastern Michigan, held in the early '80s. Tailgunner on a B17 over Nazi Germany might be one. Tough times in the steel industry were eroding his union membership so quickly that United Steelworkers District 29 resembled an imploding star. Financially beleaguered McLouth Steel (Local 2659) was ready to turn off its blast furnaces for good. And downriver newspapers were dragging Lester through the muck. The heat of the McLouth plant, where Harry served time, looked cool by comparison. Harry and his members got out all right: McLouth was saved at the last minute, and the serious dip in union membership has been stemmed. As bad as it was, the McLouth episode was a vivid portrait of a Detroit labor boss's clout.

Bred in West Virginia, Lester came to the area as a young man looking for opportunity. He moved up the ranks of the McLouth local and into the union's district office, taking over in 1981 for Charlie Younglove, an immensely popular fellow who had run the local for two decades.

Younglove barely escaped with his gold watch before bad luck hit Lester so heavy he must have reached for his hard hat. McLouth Steel announced it was about to close up shop, taking a hunk of the downriver economy with it. Lester had to convince union members to take a pay cut. Members weren't wild about Harry's suggestion, but they liked the idea of losing their jobs even less.

Lester's moment in the sun was the "Save McLouth" march in Washington, D.C., which he coordinated with various civic and business officials. Ronald Reagan wasn't moved, but the march kept the McLouth problem in front of the news media. Bankers, though legendary for their hard hearts, didn't want to be turning out downriver's lights. Lester's kicking and screaming bought enough time for the steel company to find a new buyer, who ultimately sold to the steelworkers themselves.

Harry's name carries light weight in Oakland County's fern bars. In downriver towns like Southgate and Taylor, where liquor and the times have both been hard, Lester is not a man to be ignored.

Levin, Carl—June 28, 1934; Michigan's junior U.S. senator.

Levin graduated from Harvard Law School and worked as a lawyer for various governmental agencies (including a stint as an assistant attorney general throughout the 1960s) before getting into politics. In his first run for Detroit City Council in 1969, Levin outpaced well-known Detroit political names like Billy Rogell, Philip Van Antwerp and Anthony Wierzbicki with an impressive third-place finish. He vaulted to an even more impressive first-place finish four years later. His ability to speak to black and white voters with equal effectiveness helped him run the often-contentious (then, as now) City Council during those racially charged years.

He sat out politics for two years preparing for a Senate campaign. The preparation was the grease; incumbent Senator Robert Griffin's gaffes were the skid. Griffin said he'd retire, missed numerous roll-call votes, then decided to run. The voters said "not with my money you don't," and gave Griffin's job to Levin, 52 percent to 48 percent. (Griffin later was elected to a seat on the Michigan Supreme Court in 1986.)

Levin's run against Jack Lousma six years later netted him

roughly the same percentages. Now the third-ranking Democrat on the Armed Services Committee, he's in a position to do Michigan some good. He must run again in 1990. The early line is all Levin.

Levin, Sander—September 6, 1931; the Levin in the House.

Levin's congressional district includes the northern suburbs of Ferndale and Royal Oak, as well as Redford Township and, with the largest single bloc of voters, a hunk of northwest Detroit. Analyst Michael Barone describes Levin as "a natural legislator; a hard worker, a detail man, a strong partisan who is less interested in trumpeting his own opinions than he is in working out compromises and agreement among everyone involved in an issue—and who is willing to spend endless hours doing so."

A graduate of the University of Chicago, Columbia University and Harvard Law School, he spent six years in the state Senate, where he impressed his Democratic colleagues enough that they helped him run for governor against William Milliken in 1970. He lost, 51 percent to 49 percent. Four years later, the two ran squared off again. That time he lost 52 percent to 48 percent.

When the 17th Congressional District was carved out in 1982—and beckoned a newcomer because then-Congressman *James Blanchard* was running for governor and Congressman William Brodhead retired (at age 40) to practice law—Levin saw his chance and ran. He had a tough primary against former state Sen. Doug Ross and Detroit City Councilwoman *Maryann Mahaffey*, but finally savored the victory that had eluded him. He hasn't had trouble since.

There is a bit of a political dynasty in the making here. Brother *Carl*, younger by three years, is a U.S. Senator. Cousin Charles is a Michigan Supreme Court justice.

Lewand, Tom—July 24, 1946; in Democratic hot seat.

An old pal of *Gov. Blanchard*, he stepped into the No. 1 slot of the Democratic Party in early 1989. Unlike the old-style but effective Democratic politicians—highly charged, extraordinarily devoted and vicious on demand — Lewand is a rich bond lawyer who wears a suit, talks nice and goes to meetings.

A University of Detroit and Wayne State University Law School grad, he's a grass-roots sort of guy. Lewand was an Oakland County commissioner from Royal Oak (1978-'80) who left that job in 1980 to run for Oakland County exec against Republican vet *Dan Murphy*. Lewand lost, but his failure as a candidate was eclipsed two years later by success as a campaign manager. The candidate was Congressman James Blanchard, who very much wanted to be governor. Lewand ran Blanchard's campaign against Republican Richard Headlee, who committed some incredible foul-ups. Lewand's reward came when he was appointed Blanchard's chief of staff. Pleading devotion to home and hearth, Lewand quit that job after less than a year to rejoin the Detroit law firm of Jaffe, Snider, Raitt & Heuer. (Along the way, Lewand married Kathleen Sullivan, daughter of Michigan Court of Appeals Judge Joseph B. Sullivan, who is a major figure in Democratic politics.)

Lewand faces a panoply of problems in his new job as chief Democrat. They've been able to keep the governor's mansion since 1982 and both U.S. Senate seats since 1978, but Michigan Democrats haven't carried the state for a presidential candidate since 1968. The party has one of the most baroque presidential primaries imaginable. And there are other problems. "As long as you have *Coleman Young* as the big Democrat," mutters one local Dem, "what are your chances of carrying Bad Axe—or Ferndale?"

Lewand says he'll help solve these problems as a part-time chief. Good luck.

Lewis, Diana—(birthdate not available); seated beside the king.

Her return to the Channel 7 anchor desk in 1988 was front-page news, although sitting next to *Bill Bonds* is like feeding scenery to Don Rickles.

A native of Coatesville, Pennsylvania, she broke into television as a producer at Philadelphia's ABC affiliate. She eventually made the jump to an on-the-air job by total chance: When a talk-show host took ill one day, Lewis filled in and so impressed management that she was put in front of the cameras full-time. She performed so well that she landed at the much larger KABC-TV in Los Angeles. Her best-known appearance may not have been art, but it imitated TV life: She is the reporter in "Rocky" who interviews Sylvester Stallone as he punches out a side of meat.

Lewis didn't get her wish to become a weekday co-anchor until she joined Channel 7 in 1977. Her performance was creditable, but she left in 1985 when she and general manager Jeanne Findlater couldn't agree on a new contract. Lewis rejoined her husband,

Glenn, who was working at Universal Studios in California. During the next two years she spent time with her family (she has two daughters, Glenda and Donna) and did guest appearances on network TV (including a role as a reporter on NBC's "Hunter"). Channel 7 hired her back to replace *Dana Eubanks*.

Lezell, Maurice—November 29, 1921; Mr. Belvedere.

He stared into the television cameras and earnestly proclaimed: "We Do Good Work." No glitz. Just a deadpan proclamation of honest intentions from a shifty-eyed aluminum siding salesman. In Detroit, *he* is the original Tin Man, not Jack Haley. Those late-night television ads of the '60s were enough to make Lezell an honest-to-goodness local celebrity. Who else could fly a banner over Tiger Stadium reading simply: TY 8–7100?

By the early '70s, Mr. Belvedere fan clubs and T-shirts were a part of Detroit's camp cultural life. And they helped put Belvedere Construction Co. on the map.

Lezell started out after World War II selling screens and storms. He founded Belvedere in 1948, naming it after the '40s series of Clifton Webb movies. We don't see him on television that much anymore. The medium has gotten awfully expensive.

Linder, Mira—December 25, year not available; queen of the sauna.

Linder made a fortune pampering Oakland County's idle rich. Her clientele are the types who'll blow off a full day in the Jacuzzi and the sauna in between massages, facials, manicures, pedicures, hair styling, hair treatments and makeup.

Unlike some customers, whose toughest crisis is what to do when the gearbox on the Lamborghini blows, Linder has faced some truly difficult times. Born in Poland, she survived the Holocaust in a Russian concentration camp. While a young adult in Europe, she picked up seven languages (English, French, German, Hebrew, Polish, Russian and Yiddish) and a certain global outlook on things.

She arrived here in 1964 to be with her pregnant daughter. From giving facials in the late '60s in a Southfield office, she has massaged her way into three cities (Southfield, Palm Beach and Toronto). She also penned a book appropriately entitled "Beauty Begins at Sixty." She once said: "There are no ugly women, only lazy ones."

Linder makes the social scene, where she once told a startled male swell: "Dahlink, you most do something about your pooooors."

Lobenthal, Richard—July 29, 1934; antidote to hatred.

He has run the Michigan office of the Anti-Defamation League of B'nai B'rith since 1964. Visitors to his office can't help noticing the full-dress KKK outfit draped on a mannequin. If they miss that, there is a Nazi flag and a sign that says "Gentiles Only." They are constant reminders of Lobenthal's daily fight.

Lobenthal worked for the ADL in its Virginia/North Carolina office, then in Texas/Oklahoma before coming to Detroit. Bearded, tall, and possessing a booming voice, he is single-minded and very articulate.

Lobenthal took on the John Birchers in the late '60s when they exploited anti-sex education mania. He's on almost every hate group's mailing list.

Lopatin, Albert (October 26, 1929) and Miller, Sheldon "Shel" (April 19, 1936); personal injury law's gold dust twins.

If your neck has that whiplash feel, pay Albert Lopatin or Shel Miller a visit. Their idea of a good time is to terrorize some hapless insurance company lawyer into settling up, so their client can play wheelbarrow of fortune. Their specialty is personal injury work— auto accident cases, medical malpractice suits and such. They obtained millions for workers who were injured in the 1971 Port Huron tunnel explosion. Their work has not gone unnoticed nationally. Joseph Goulden led his "Million Dollar Lawyers" tome with a story about these two. Similarly, the *New York Law Journal* named Miller one of the "Bigs" of torts.

Miller's ancestors immigrated here to escape the pogroms in central Europe. A self-described thug as a teenager, he says he found salvation in law and retired his blackjacks and beer bottles as a result. Miller worked as an insurance company lawyer, a fact his colleagues regard with some amusement. Lopatin immigrated here from Canada.

Together, they are the Odd Couple of Detroit law. Miller's office looks like something out of "Animal House." He's brash, once greeting an accident victim with a boisterous "Howya doin', One Arm?"

Lopatin's office is disgustingly meticulous. He's a little more low-key, but no less effective.

Besides accident cases, the two vigorously pursue doctors in medical malpractice cases. In 1976, Miller even suggested that physicians become state employees, which would limit their income to $50,000 a year.

A Lopatin-Miller partner once visited a local hospital. He didn't announce that he sued doctors for a living, but he suspected the docs knew. Although he complained of double vision, the nurses were told to give him a rectal exam—which they did.

Loren, Barbara—April 23, 1935; insider with an outside point of view.

This high-flying marketing consultant is part of K mart chairman *Joe Antonini*'s brain trust. The K mart corporate culture tends to promote people who've worked their way up from the store floor, but Antonini keeps a few people nearby who aren't part of the system. That way, he gets fresh advice. The kind of advice advanced by Loren resulted in linking up high-style Martha Stewart with the retailer. "Nobody at K mart top management, except for one person, even knew who Martha Stewart was until I brought her to their attention," Loren recalls. She also recalls that Antonini took "about 20 minutes" to decide to go with the idea.

A native of Detroit, she learned marketing at Montgomery Ward (where she created the Wendy Ward concept) and Federal's Department stores—before Steven West took over. After a stop at Grey Advertising, she became general manager of the *Metro Detroit Shopping News*.

She had no intention of opening an ad agency until Hudson's president Edwin Roberts called her one day and said, "Why don't you open your own place, and we'll be your first account." Two years later she took a job with D'Arcy Masius Benton & Bowles and phased Hudson's into the agency, where the account was said to be worth some $2-million. Later, she worked for ABC-TV from an office at WXYZ.

Nowadays, she works from a small office at K mart headquarters in Troy and from her Loren-Snyder Marketing office in Birmingham. Her advice is said to be expensive—but very effective.

She is married to Murray Snyder, chairman of Brasscraft, a division of Masco Corp.

Losh, J. Michael—May 10, 1946; baby GM exec.

He has been newly tapped to run Oldsmobile, one of GM's most troubled divisions. When insiders talk about who might run the world's biggest corporation in the 1990s and into the 21st Century, Losh's name comes up. He wasn't even 40 at the time of his appointment to the general manager's chair at Pontiac in 1984, then landed the Olds job in June 1989. One wonders if such tender success might cause him to pull a John DeLorean and go gonzo. That isn't likely. To somebody younger, Losh seems like a successful but slightly hip older brother. To the graybeards at GM headquarters, he seems like the son they'd like to have.

A native of Dayton, Ohio, and the son of an engine test technician at Wright-Patterson Air Force Base, he developed entirely within the GM system. He picked up a mechanical engineering degree from General Motors Institute in 1970, so impressing GM that he was packed off for further training at Harvard Business School. Between graduation from Harvard in 1970 and landing his current job 14 years later, he spent only one year in the Motor City. Instead of devoting a year or two at a time detailing a chassis, he got the big picture. He spent a half-dozen years at the GM treasurer's office in New York, for instance. That gave him an overview of GM without getting lost in the belly of the bureaucracy. There were only four sections of people with eight to 10 analysts apiece. Later, he ran General Motors de Mexico, a microcosm of the General below the border. In that job, he did the payroll, paid the suppliers and negotiated contracts.

Pontiac already was on the rebound by the time he got there (see **Bill Hoglund**), but he hasn't messed it up, either. Former Pontiac general managers since 1960 include John DeLorean, three GM presidents (Elliott "Pete" Estes, **Robert Stempel** and James McDonald), one Ford Motor Co. president (Semon "Bunkie" Knudsen) plus one likely GM president (Hoglund).

Involved in many community activities, Losh saw the Charlie Gehringer Meadow Brook Golf Classic double in size during his three-year tenure as chairman. GM hopes he'll work the same magic at Olds.

Lucas, William—January 15, 1928; party-switching politician.

Blown out in his race for governor in 1986, William Lucas had to wait awhile for reward from the Republican Party. But when it arrived, it wasn't bad: a nomination by President George Bush for a post as assistant attorney general in charge of the Justice Department's civil rights division.

A native of New York, Lucas was raised by an aunt after his parents died when he was 12. He went to Manhattan College on a track scholarship and earned a law degree from Fordham University in 1962. He was appointed Wayne County undersheriff in 1968, after being posted here during his four years with the FBI. He stayed in the sheriff's job for 14 years, until he was elected to the newly created position of Wayne County executive. Chances are he could have stayed there, too. But he felt the Democratic Party establishment—particularly **Mayor Young**'s people—had taken him for granted. So he switched parties, ran for governor and was absolutely crushed by Gov. **James Blanchard**.

Civil rights groups questioned Lucas's lack of experience in civil rights enforcement when Bush called him to Washington.

Luedtke, Kurt—September 28, 1939; Birmingham screen bard.

Luedtke shot to the top in two careers before his 45th birthday: He was executive editor of the *Free Press* by the time he was 33, but quit five years later. On the beach for awhile, he tried his hand at writing movies. Good hand. He scored an Academy Award nomination for his debut script, 1981's "Absence of Malice." He won an Oscar in 1985 for figuring out how to transfer writer Isak Dinesen's "Out of Africa" to celluloid. Hollywood pillars such as John Huston and Orson Welles had been trying for years. "It took a smart aleck from Detroit like Kurt to do it," director Sydney Pollack said.

A Grand Rapids lumber broker's son, Luedtke left Brown University with thoughts of becoming a lawyer. But he quit the University of Michigan Law School after only one semester because he couldn't stomach the drudgery. He tried journalism, instead. His subsequent rise in the newspaper business was almost as phenomenal as his later rise in filmdom. From cub reporter at the *Grand Rapids Press*, he jumped to the *Miami Herald*, and arrived at the *Free Press* in 1965. In short order, he was named the first author of the paper's popular Action Line feature, and helped direct the *Freep*'s Pulitzer Prize-winning coverage of the 1967 riot.

He was practically running the *Freep* before he was 30, ostensibly as photo editor. His stewardship is remembered as a time of intense creativity—and also turbulence. "Nobody scared us as much before or since," recalls former *News* executive editor **Ben Burns**. "You never knew where he'd pop up." Many talented writers and editors rebelled at his management style. A top reporter put his fist through a wall (and his wrist in a cast) after one Luedtke editorial decision. Some went down the street (Joe Falls and George Cantor among them).

Five years into his executive editorship, Luedkte bailed out because he was bored—again. Against everybody's advice, he tried Hollywood. "Absence of Malice," starring Paul Newman and Sally Field, was in production within two years of his departure from the *Freep*. So much for advice.

While he makes screenwriting look easy, he's a perfectionist who sweats on each page. His work commands six-figure checks, although he doesn't seem much interested in money. Luedtke can be found hanging around Birmingham's Midtown Cafe in a sweater and jeans. If he feels really expansive, he might hunker down in the London Chop House.

Even though he hasn't had a newspaper job in more than a decade, he's still intensely interested in the business, and was one of the most eloquent foes of the Joint Operating Agreement between the *News* and the *Free Press*. His wife, Eleanor, shares the qualities of smart and tough. She has held several of the city's top public relations jobs, including Hudson's and the Detroit Symphony, and is mentor to many.

Lutz, Robert—February 12, 1932; No. 2 at No. 3?

Auto executives are a notoriously unsexy bunch. Chrysler Motors co-president Bob Lutz is an exception. A Marine fighter pilot (1954-'59), he has been known to ride a motorcycle to work, is popular with the town's automotive reporters because he doesn't treat them like dirt, and likes a good cigar. Standing around in a tuxedo at a charity event, he looks like something out of Dynasty, maybe Blake Carrington's slightly-mischievous brother.

It isn't unusual for top Ford or Chrysler executives to have worked at two of the Big Three, but Lutz has managed to complete the rounds. He started out at Adam Opel, a GM of Europe unit, before he was spotted by Ford. His career led him to the chairmanship of Ford of Europe on two separate occasions (both tours were deemed successes), and landed him a spot on the board. He was considered a candidate for the Ford presidency, and the public relations people were salivating at the thought of trotting Lutz around to the television networks. "He's got gas in his veins," one Ford PR man said.

Maybe the folks at Ford were jealous of a guy who seems to enjoy himself. (Indeed, according to one account in David Halberstam's "The Reckoning": "Henry Ford had become more and more hostile to Lutz and had said at one meeting when Lutz arrived a few minutes late, 'Well, here comes our movie star.' ") He was pulled back from the chairmanship of Ford of Europe in spring 1986 to run Ford's truck operations. The company insisted it wasn't a demotion, but Lutz had packed for a job at Chrysler within a few months.

M

Madonna (a.k.a. Madonna Louise Ciccone)—August 16, 1958; misunderstood Material Girl.

Her recordings and films should be placed in a time capsule to explain the '80s. From "Material Girl," a 1984 ode to crass consumption, to her 1987 film, "Who's That Girl?", she practically wrote the Me Generation's catechism on "Who cares if it's art, does it sell?" Artistic and spiritual questions aside, probably only Barbra Streisand has scored so big in LPs, Broadway and film.

Harry Crews wrote in a 1988 profile of Madonna that she'd take a wall down with her fingernails and teeth if it meant getting what she wanted. A review of how she got where she is — a millionairess who made it big in three media—seems to indicate that Crews understated the case. A graduate of Rochester Adams High School, Madonna moved to New York City in hopes of making herself famous. She labored in a Times Square doughnut shop, danced with the Alvin Ailey organization, even posed nude for photographers to make her rent. (Some of the nude photos showed up in 1985 issues of *Playboy* and *Penthouse*.)

Her 1984 LP "Madonna" stayed on the charts for 36 weeks. She followed up later in the year with "Like a Virgin," which scored a No. 1 slot on *Billboard*'s charts for three weeks, and hung in the Top 40 for one week short of a year. She's had a half-dozen No. 1 hits. There are singers who sing better, but she did them all one better with her appearance in "Desperately Seeking Susan," stealing the show from Roseanna Arquette. Subsequent film performances ("Shanghai Surprise" and "Who's That Girl?") didn't gross nearly as well. But just when the critics thought they had her nailed, she branched into yet another medium: Broadway, where she appeared in writer David Mamet's "Speed the Plow." The reviews were tepid, but box office sales were not.

She doesn't appear to enjoy her fame. Photographers get in her way, and her abortive 1985 marriage to actor Sean Penn has been a major source of embarrassment—and front-page grist for grocery store tabloids. Her fame apparently has been no fun for her family, either. Her younger brother's brushes with the law are forever being written up.

Into the '90s, goodness knows what she has planned. Whatever it is, it'll probably sell.

Mahaffey, Maryann—January 18, 1925; a voice for the hungry or homeless.

Mahaffey's big issues have always been hunger and the homeless— even before Hollywood made them fashionable. Mahaffey came to her social beliefs during World War II as a recreation director in an Arizona Japanese-American relocation camp. She never forgot. Mahaffey has always been insistent that government is here to aid the downtrodden. That kind of thinking may not get her elected in places like West Bloomfield, but it has kept her on the Detroit City Council.

An Iowan by birth, she earned degrees at Cornell College and the University of Southern California before arriving here in 1952 as a Girl Scout organizer. She had studied to be a librarian, but her experience in the internment camp persuaded her there were better rows to hoe. Mahaffey has been on Wayne State University's faculty for years and dabbled in Democratic politics before winning a council seat in 1973.

Her liberal credentials are impeccable: Mahaffey organized one of the first welfare rights organizations in the early '60s; was arrested at the South African embassy in Washington, D.C.; and screamed bloody murder when she was forced to enter the then all-male Detroit Athletic Club by the side door. A tireless campaigner, she placed no worse than third in the 1977, 1981 and 1985 elections.

After more than 15 years in a council chair, she'd like a shot at Congress. But that seems a distant hope. She ran in 1982, placing a poor third behind former state Sen. Doug Ross and two-time Democratic gubernatorial candidate *Sander Levin*. She married Herman

"Hy" Dooha, but kept her maiden name when few women were doing so. Having been mugged two times as of this writing, she knows firsthand about realities of life in the city of Detroit.

Mandel, Leon—July 31, 1928; master chronicler of the vroom vroom set.

Mandel is publisher of *AutoWeek*, a Crain Communications weekly for car enthusiasts. Filled with reviews, racing news and auto industry tidbits, it's designed for the person who suffers the bends waiting for his monthly *Car and Driver* to arrive.

He springs from old Chicago money. Mandel's ancestors founded Mandel Bros., a large Chicago department store, in 1849. Proceeds of the business were enough to allow Leon's Uncle Fred to buy the Detroit Lions in 1940. (A digression: As team owner, Fred persuaded Byron "Whizzer" White, now a U.S. Supreme Court justice, to try pro football, which White did in 1940-'41 before going into law.) Fred sold the Lions in 1948 for $250,000. "I guess if I'd kept it, all I'd've done was make money with it," Fred told the late Doc Greene. When the elder Mandel died in 1973, he had retired to Hawaii, where he operated a stamp and coin shop.

Nephew Leon didn't care much for dry goods. Intoxicated as he was by the smell of gasoline, he signed aboard *AutoWeek* in 1963, rising to editor before he left for *Car and Driver* in 1967. He lasted four years there, again rising to editor, before rejoining *AutoWeek* in 1971. That stay, which saw him rise to editorial director as well as publisher of *AutoWeek*'s Competition Press, lasted three years.

His nine-year free-lance career (1974-'83) produced a half-dozen books, including a critically acclaimed tome on Harrah's automobile collection. But *AutoWeek* called again in 1983. This time he joined as editor-in-chief, presiding over a remake from tabloid to glossy. Ever antsy, he quit the editor's slot in 1987, but returned as publisher after a 10-month respite to free lance again.

He's one of the true characters in automotive journalism. Bearded and irreverent, he looks like a refugee from the Beat era. He is said to have media magnate *Keith Crain*'s ear, so people tiptoe around Mandel when he roams the halls. As editor, he'd bellow, "The Visigoths are at the wall," when an ad rep would have the temerity to set foot on the writers' floor. Now, as publisher, he's the chief Goth. "I'm a Hun, not a Visigoth," is how he explains the transition.

Mandich, Donald—September 1, 1925; Comerica's leader.

He's chairman of Comerica, the state's second largest bank. As is the custom in the banking business, he got a job with his current employer a long time ago and stayed there. He joined Detroit Bank & Trust (since renamed Comerica) in 1950, rising slowly and making a name for himself in Comerica's international department.

Mandich has been at the helm since 1981. As *Business Week* put it, somewhat cryptically: "Mixed results from attempt to position company for long pull." While he thinned the company down a bit, Mandich couldn't pull off Comerica's hostile takeover bid for Michigan National Bank. The merger would have made the new combined operation bigger even than National Bank of Detroit, which is the reigning king in banking here. His heir apparent at Comerica is Eugene Miller, the company's president and chief executive officer.

Mandich's hobby is Russian heraldry, and he is translating a 10-volume set of Russian books.

Manoogian, Richard—July 30, 1936; millionaire master of the mundane.

The family fortune derives from the one-handled Delta faucet. Alex Manoogian, an Armenian immigrant, founded Taylor-based Masco Corp. almost 60 years ago. With Alex nearing 90, Yale-educated Richard runs the show. The now-common one-handled kitchen faucet, which the Manoogians sprang on the public in 1954, has been very, very good to them. *Forbes* magazine pegs son Richard's worth at about $625-million, dad Alex at a paltry $262-million.

Alex Manoogian came to the U.S. in 1920, two years after the Turks torched his hometown of Smyrna. The ambitious young Alex started a small screw manufacturing business which not only survived the Depression, but went public in 1936. But the Manoogian brass ring was the one-handled tap, which now pours about one-third of Masco's profits onto the balance sheet. Young people may find it hard to believe that Americans once coped with two handles—one for hot, another for cold — before the Manoogians found a better way. Golly, life was tough.

Richard has expanded the company's horizons a bit. He spun off Masco Industries from the main corporation, and has acquired some 100 smaller companies since the 1960s. The younger Manoogian, who looks rather like an elegant Mr. Belvedere, seems to enjoy the society circuit: He attended *Tom Monaghan*'s Drummond Island bacchanal, and is on Tom Schoenith's "A" list. His art collection is internationally known. Some of it rests in museums around the world, some of it hangs in Masco headquarters, which means you can win a bar bet by wagering there is fine art in Taylor.

The elder Alex, loyal to his roots, is heavy into Armenian causes. He once had a stock of books on the topic delivered via limo to *Free Press* columnist *Neal Shine*'s home. The "Manoogian" in Manoogian Mansion is Alex's old home. He donated his riverfront digs to the city in 1965.

Mark, Florine—February 21, year not available; weight loss czarina.

Florine Mark was unhappy as a young adult because she had a weight problem. She lost the weight and gained millions of bucks. Her calorie-counting franchise here is Weight Watchers International's largest. Untold multitudes plunk down $8 a meeting to get a little help losing fat.

For her, getting thin was tough. After numerous diets and gobs of pills, she commuted between Michigan and New York, where she completed a WW program. "Why not do it in Detroit?" she reasoned. "People are fat here, too." She did, starting in early 1966. The picture in her press kit says it all: On the left, we have a woman with authentic thunder thighs. The picture on the right is of a slim woman in a John T. Molloy "Dress for Success" suit. She was B'nai B'rith Woman of the Year in 1987.

If thinking thin isn't enough to pay Florine's MasterCard bill, her husband, Dr. William Ross, is an osteopathic physician.

Marlinga, Carl—January 9, 1947; Macomb upsetter.

He scored the Macomb County political upset of the decade by beating veteran prosecutor George Parris in the 1984 Democratic primary. Since then, Marlinga has been the voice of law and order in that county.

A University of Michigan Law School grad, Marlinga practiced law successfully throughout the '70s while unsuccessfully dabbling in politics. He ran failed campaigns for state Senate in 1970 and in a special election in 1977, and for county commissioner in 1982. But then he took a run at Parris, an abrasive politico who'd been ensconced since 1960. Parris, who was 63, had a reputation for spending more time on the golf course than in the office. He ignored the

37-year-old upstart, who made note of Parris's golfing expertise (gained on county time) by holding a press conference at a Warren miniature golf course. Marlinga also dumped $21,000 of his own money into the campaign, along with a $10,000 loan from his mother. The voters bought it in a big way. Parris was sent packing by a 2–1 margin.

No strong challengers to Marlinga have surfaced since then. He undoubtedly learned a lesson from Parris—that a politician who ignores voters and opponents will soon be an unemployed politician.

Marshall, Bella—March 11, 1950; Mayor Young's chancellor of the exchequer.

She's the person in the Young administration who writes the big checks, hassles with the New York bond traders, arranges financing on large projects and balances the books with budget chief *Walt Stecher*.

Coleman Young found her buried deep within the state bureaucracy. After picking up a law degree from the University of Michigan to go with her Wayne State BA, she joined the state government. She had climbed her way from administrative assistant to chief of the State Housing Development Authority's Detroit office to director of the agency's management and reinvestment unit. That job gave her plenty of practice massaging big numbers. After being named Young's finance director in 1982, she quickly worked her way into the mayor's inner circle. She's famous around city hall for calling meetings that resemble crowd scenes from "Ben Hur." The power behind the throne is said to be her No. 2 person, John Kanters, a lifelong bureaucrat who garners much respect in the City-County Building.

Possessor of beauty that could put her on magazine covers, she put an end to "most eligible bachelorette" status with her marriage to Detroit cable television czar *Don Barden* in May 1988. *News* columnist *Pete Waldmeir* had great fun reprinting her wedding wish list from Hudson's. Judging from that list, her tastes are expensive.

Martin, Fred—(birthdate not available); the mayor's top nuts-and-bolts guy.

As *Mayor Young*'s chief executive assistant, he's the day-to-day liaison with city department heads. Although a few (budget chief *Walter*

Stecher, finance boss *Bella Marshall*, DPW director Conley Abrams Jr., personnel's Joyce Garrett, and water/sewerage czar *Charlie Williams*) don't need permission to enter the inner sanctum, most city hall types humor Martin. "He says 'no' a lot," advises one fellow mayoral appointee. "If something big comes up, you call Fred. If it's something hot, he'll tell you not to do anything until he talks to the mayor. Fred might get back to you. Then again, he might not." This illustrates a key rule of existence on the 11th floor: Nobody there was ever fired for not doing something. Only when one forges ahead without the mayoral blessing does one risk one's neck.

Martin is hardly a city hall lifer. He spent 28 years with the Detroit public school system, where he worked with his brother-in-law, Dr. Arthur Jefferson. "Look," he told *News* reporter Howard Warren when Warren inquired about the relationship between the two after a major promotion, "if I read that Gov. Milliken had appointed his brother-in-law to some job I'd ask questions, too. But I just tell people now that Dr. Jefferson is the top man and I can't help him any more."

City hall beckoned in early 1981, and Martin rose quickly upon moving south from the School Center Building to Two Woodward Avenue. Martin joined the city's Personnel Department as the No. 2 man in January 1981. He jumped up one slot in personnel six months later, then moved into the chief executive assistant's slot in January 1982.

Martin isn't particularly tight with the mayor socially. There are few trips to Manoogian Mansion in a leisure capacity. But he's still the mayor's No. 1 guy, and he stands in for the mayor on public speaking appearances when Young can't make it.

Marx, Fred—March 23, 1942; ware wolf.

For some, it was a disaster when Minneapolis' Dayton Corp. combined operations of its Dayton and Hudson's stores in 1984 and moved the nerve center to the Twin Cities. Not for Fred Marx, who had been a senior vice-president at Hudson's from 1978-'85. Instead of moping, he opened up a Bloomfield Hills marketing/public relations shop, which has had no trouble attracting clients. His roster includes many Michigan-based retail operations, as well as hospitals, shopping centers and law firms.

Educated at the prestigious Wharton School of Finance, Marx added an MA in communications from the University of Pennsylvania before joining up with the Sharff's retail chain in Ohio. He served five years at Jacobson Stores Inc. as v.p./advertising, did two years at Lazarus in Dayton, and another year at Macy's in Atlanta before hiring on at Hudson's as a senior v.p./marketing.

Prematurely gray and veddy dignified, he's one of the most charming guys in the retail trade.

Marx, Sue and Conn, Pam (birthdates not available); the envelope pleased.

Three words made this duo heroes from Ishpeming to Monroe. Accepting an Oscar for their film, "Young at Heart," Marx yelled: "Hooray For Michigan." While their prices have swelled since then, their heads have not. They've landed some fairly interesting gigs, such as a chance to produce the film that celebrated the reopening of the Fox Theatre. But the next big break—such as a feature-length film—has yet to happen.

"Young at Heart" was the story of Marx's father, Louis Gothelf, and her stepmother, Reva Shwayder, and how they fell in love in their 80s. Critics at the Telluride, Colorado, film festival were utterly charmed. So was the rest of America. And so were the Hollywood voters for best short documentary of 1988.

Marx and Conn co-wrote, produced and directed. Among the fetes for the dynamic duo to celebrate bringing their Oscar back to Michigan, was a bash hosted by *Jim Blanchard* at the Governor's residence in Lansing.

Mason, John—June 18, 1957; big voice in the morning.

A lot of ego-obsessed idiots in morning drive-time radio can't touch the ratings that WJLB-FM's John Mason brings. In some ratings books, "Mason and Company" runs second only to WJR-AM kingpin *J.P. McCarthy*. This is the truest cross-over story in Detroit radio. Mason and 'JLB are black. But you don't get those kinds of numbers with a monochromatic audience.

Mason came to 'JLB in 1983 as a production director after a short stop in St. Louis. His specialty is the character: Granny (an elderly woman with a bit of cunning); the Old Man (Shug), who is stuck back in time; and Doosey, who has a hangup about Whitney Houston's wigs.

Ask him to do his Michael Jackson impression. It's deadly.

McCabe, Robert—November 24, 1923; image maker.

McCabe had a lot to do with the Grand Prix's success in Detroit. Now that the *tres* continental racers have been replaced by Indy cars, McCabe is in charge of that, too.

A native of Depression-era Michigan, he grew up in Detroit, Flint, Traverse City, Mt. Pleasant and tiny Empire. Educated at Central Michigan University and the University of Chicago, he hopscotched through a variety of urban development jobs around the country before returning here as Detroit Renaissance Inc.'s first full-time president in 1971.

One stop was as deputy assistant secretary in the U.S. Department of Housing and Urban Development from 1967 to 1969, a post he left the day Richard Nixon was sworn in. He was cooling his heels as general manager of New York State's Urban Development Corporation—a job he got through the late Nelson Rockefeller—when *Max Fisher* tracked him down. "There I was sitting in my office on the 44th floor of the Burlington House, happy as a clam," McCabe recalled. "I thought I had the second best job in New York State. My secretary buzzed me and said Mr. Max Fisher of Detroit was on the phone. She put Mr. Fisher on. He said he was from Detroit, that he was chairman of a business leadership group, and he wondered if I might have breakfast with him in his suite at the Waldorf. To this day, I don't know why I accepted that breakfast invitation. I hate breakfast."

He rejected the job at first, but Fisher, Henry Ford II and NBD's Robert Surdham put the arm on him to return home. Says McCabe: "We're at the cutting edge of America's future. The success of Detroit is fundamental to the survival and progress of America. Here I am 18 years later. I'm not sorry I came." Now, McCabe spends most of his time polishing the city's image. Since Detroit Renaissance's board is a Who's Who of Detroit corporate heavies, he may be one of the best-connected guys in town.

The "Champagne Bob" nickname derives not from his drinking habits, but from his predilection for doing things in style.

McCarthy, J.P.—(birthdate not available); Detroit's radio king.

His morning show on WJR-AM has been No. 1 since at least 1965. And the guest list at his annual St. Patrick's Day party shows his clout. Among the luminaries who made stops on their way to work one such morning were GM chairman *Roger Smith*, *Freep* executive editor *Heath Meriwether*, then-Oakland County prosecutor L. Brooks Patterson and about half the people in this book. "If you're looking for impact, forget about begging for an interview with the *Wall Street Journal* or the *New York Times*," observes Justin Moran of the Michigan Bankers' Association. "This (J.P.'s show) is it." J.P. and his producers have the best phone list in town. When Henry Ford II died, McCarthy had *Automotive News* publisher *Keith Crain* on the horn to recall the Deuce's life. Of course, Tigers skipper *Sparky Anderson* is on during baseball season, as is whichever Lions coach is in power at the moment. Sparky, *Jacques Demers* and the Lion *du jour* are paid big bucks to call in. More amazing is the range: from *Governor Blanchard* to psychiatrist Emanuel Tanay to crimebuster Patterson.

J.P. is authentic Detroit. He grew up on the east side and graduated from DeLaSalle Collegiate High School, famous for taking the sons of the working class and teaching them with methods that are part Rome, part Athens and part Parris Island. He attended the University of Detroit, where he studied mechanical engineering.

Uncle Sam got J.P. into his current line of work. He landed a spot on Armed Forces Radio in Alaska, avoiding a transfer to some place worse. He liked the microphone, and goodness knows the microphone liked him. Except for some air time in Fairbanks and Flint before his 1958 arrival at WJR, and a short two-year stint in San Francisco between 1963 and 1965, he has spent his entire career at 'JR.

If J.P. ever were to fly his Fisher Building coop, his bosses at Cap Cities would require immediate treatment down the block at Henry Ford Hospital.

McCarthy, Walter Jr.—April 25, 1925; high-voltage chairman.

He's a key player in the town's corporate/civic ecosystem. Not only does McCarthy run Detroit Edison, which supplies electricity to some 1.8 million customers, but he held two other key civic chairmanships of lasting impact. He co-chaired *Mayor Young*'s Detroit Strategic Planning Commission, which gathered ideas from the town's corporate shooters on how to save a decaying Detroit. And he chaired the Detroit Symphony Orchestra in one of its most difficult passages. For his efforts, he collected an impressive number of detractors.

A New York native, McCarthy graduated from Cornell University

in 1949, then spent the next decade and a half with the Public Service Electric and Gas Co. in Newark, New Jersey. His forté was
nuclear energy, which got him in the door at Edison. The job was to
be a temporary one, but he stayed on to become a leading light at
the company. McCarthy was named president in 1979. Two years
later he became chairman and chief executive officer. In 1989 he was
elected chairman of the Institute of Nuclear Power Operations.

The DSO post earned him headlines, but not the right kind.
Brought in as chairman in 1982 to help a fiscally starved orchestra,
he was a short-term hero. But the late 1980s saw the rapid disintegration of the band amid escalating money problems and a musicians'
strike. By late 1987, the DSO was in absolute turmoil. Perhaps the
symphony would have reached that point no matter who sat in the
chairman's office. But McCarthy and DSO president Oleg Lobanov
took the rap. Lobanov left, eventually to run a ballet organization in
Chicago. McCarthy stepped down in October 1988 for the relative
calm of Edison's executive offices.

McCloskey, Jack—September 19, 1925; "Trader Jack."

The Detroit Pistons were nothing when he arrived in December
1979. But they're something now, partially because of this tennis-
playing, white-haired hoops wizard. While Pistons chief exec *Tom
Wilson* handles the books and the business operations, McCloskey
handles the basketball. Coach *Chuck Daly* reports to him.

McCloskey grew up in Pennsylvania coal-mining country, where
his father ultimately died of black lung disease. Faced with the un-
pleasant prospect of life in the mines, McCloskey worked that much
harder at sports. He coached at Pennsylvania and Wake Forest before going pro with the Portland Trail Blazers. It wasn't pleasant. He
and star Sidney Wicks didn't hit it off, and the team's won-lost
record was miserable: 48–116 in two years. McCloskey was fired,
and he took it hard. He didn't attend a basketball game for two
years, and didn't expect to return. But he bucked himself up, spent
three years as an assistant coach with the L.A. Lakers, then spent a
short stint as an assistant coach of the Indiana Pacers before Pistons
managing partner *Bill Davidson* hired him. It's unusual for someone
to jump from assistant coach to general manager, but Davidson was
desperate.

McCloskey has drafted and traded smart. He picked up *Isiah
Thomas* when Thomas was a sophomore at Indiana University. Kelly

Tripucka was drafted from Notre Dame the same year, 1981. He got *Bill Laimbeer* from Cleveland, then was smart enough to unload a troubled Tripucka to the Utah Jazz for Adrian Dantley.

How well is McCloskey regarded around the league? The New York Knicks offered him $2-million to move east. He said no, then proceeded to pick up an NBA championship ring in 1989.

McCulloch, John—December 1, 1945; radio talkmeister.

He's the morning drive host on WXYT-AM, the all-talk radio station. A bit more diverse and unpredictable in his opinions than some talk show hosts, he took over from Roy Fox, who flamed out after less than a year on the station.

McCulloch started in radio, not as talent, but in sales. While in Cleveland, he had been called upon to emcee and speak at various social functions. Noticing he was good at that, he made the on-air switch at WWWE, the 50,000-watt biggie in Cleveland. McCulloch joined WXYT in 1986 as the afternoon drive personality. He got his current job in spring 1989.

McDonald, Alonzo Jr.—August 5, 1928; his future is now.

This Troy businessman was a key figure in Jimmy Carter's White House and William Agee's Bendix Corp. These days he's chairman and CEO of Avenir Group Inc., which buys interests in small and medium-sized companies. Avenir is a group of small corporate cats and dogs that—when added together—makes a pretty impressive money-making menagerie.

A native of Atlanta, McDonald originally set out to be a journalist. He had been a reporter at the *Atlanta Journal* before ditching his notebooks for Harvard Business School. He later worked at Westinghouse and McKinsey & Co., the international consulting firm, where he rose to chief exec and managing partner. Jimmy Carter snared him in 1979 to become White House point man. When McDonald was through serving his country, he signed on as William Agee's heir apparent at Bendix. But when Agee lost Bendix after a botched merger attempt, McDonald left. He was pulling in about $740,000 per year when he got the ziggy.

Ah, but all is not lost. McDonald and associates started Avenir, which means "time to come." McDonald's future is apparently right here in Troy.

McGehee, Bishop Coleman Jr.—July 7, 1923; the L-word in the pulpit.

One might describe the leader of 58,000 Episcopals in eastern Michigan as the flip side of the Pat Robertson coin. Bishop Coleman McGehee Jr. has spoken against the death penalty and for corporate disinvesting in South Africa, and has written that prayer in public schools is unnecessary and unconstitutional. He has led public gatherings for prayer against Williams International Corp., the Commerce Township concern that builds Cruise missile engines, and was an early proponent of women priests. If there were such a thing as a card-carrying liberal, McGehee might qualify for a gold card.

McGehee grew up in Depression-era Virginia with no thought of becoming a priest. Educated as a mechanical engineer, he switched career paths and received a degree from the University of Richmond Law School, class of '47. He had advanced to a post as Virginia's assistant attorney general (1951-'54), when his career suddenly looked heavenward. A sermon by English priest Bryan Greene made torts and depositions seem unimportant. He traded his law books for prayer books and signed up at Virginia Theological Seminary in 1957.

Appointed as rector of Immanuel-on-the-Hill Church in Alexandria, Virginia, he found himself shepherding a passel of Pentagon types and then-Congressman Gerald Ford. They didn't like it much when McGehee housed a group of civil rights types during the Poor People's March on Washington in 1968. When church clergy held an election to find a successor for retiring Bishop Richard Emrich in 1971, McGehee's tweedy elegance impressed all. He officially became bishop in 1973.

Although some of his conservative flock don't care much for his politics (*W. Clark Durant III* once wrote a letter to the *News* complaining about one of McGehee's sermons), he remains very effective. Says the Rev. Harry Cook, a close friend: "He'll just wear you down with sheer logic." He'll retire on January 1, 1990, but will remain active in local affairs.

McGuane, Thomas—December 11, 1939; literary heavyweight and ex-downriverite.

Some say McGuane is the best writer of his generation. He grew up in Wyandotte and Grosse Ile, though he was boarded away from the smokestack suburbs from grades six through 12 at Cranbrook. Now, he lives on a ranch near Livingston, Montana, with money he made selling his literary output to Hollywood. Upon seeing his photograph, one newspaper editor remarked that he looked like "an intellectual Marlboro man."

The son of a Harvard-educated industrialist, McGuane kicked around Cranbrook, Michigan State University and Yale before he hit big with "The Sporting Club" (1969). The book is a delicious tale of mayhem at a northern Michigan businessmen's retreat—not unlike the Huron Mountain Club, an exclusive hideout for many Detroit pashas. The book also features a wonderful scene at the dedication of the Mackinac Bridge. A wise-guy protagonist hijacks a bus during the bash, leaving the assembled dignitaries suspended somewhere in the middle of the original Bic Mac. "A version of that outrage really did happen," McGuane later told the *Miami Herald*, "but on a much smaller scale. A friend and I were at the opening of the bridge, and it was very boring, so we got on the bus and ate lots of box lunches, but then we walked home."

He used the cash he made from the screen options on "Sporting Club" to grab a place in Key West and put a $2,500 down payment on a Montana ranch. Next came "The Bushwacked Piano" (1971) and "92 in the Shade" (1973), which was filmed two years later starring Peter Fonda and Warren Oates—with McGuane directing. "Rancho Deluxe" with Jeff Bridges and Slim Pickens, released the same year, became a cult favorite. Friends worried in the mid-'70s that his substance-induced tailspin might snuff out one of the country's best writers. After punching a Texas deputy sheriff in a bar, he realized he was on the wrong track and changed direction.

He and his wife, Laurie (singer Jimmy Buffett's sister), are peacefully married. He has abandoned Hollywood because — as he told reporter Gregory Skwira (then *Free Press*, now *News*) — he didn't want to spend his few remaining years doing business with "scheming liars." His father's business — McGuane Industries—was sold to *Richard Manoogian*'s Masco Corp., which just about removes any reason for McGuane returning to town.

McInerney, Hoot—January 23, 1929; *the* dealer.

He plays golf and pals around with WJR's *J.P. McCarthy*. He has a great laugh and a hearty handshake. McInerney possesses the bonhomie auto dealers had before the Japanese invasion. He is, in fact, the quintessential Detroit auto dealer. McInerney peddles GM, Ford and Chrysler products at nine dealerships. Most dealers would kill for a Toyota or Honda franchise, but McInerney won't have any part of imports. Has it hurt McInerney's checkbook? The answer: *Crain's Detroit Business* ranks McInerney's dynasty as the largest dealership collection in town. With some $301-million in sales in 1987, McInerney's revenues were half again as large as his nearest competitor's.

A native of the Dickerson-Warren area of Detroit's east side, he graduated from Southeastern High School. While at Southeastern, he worked part-time at—where else?—a car dealership. He served in the Marine Corps twice (1945-'47, 1950-'51) before plunging head-long into the car business. "It's the only business I know. The reason I did well is because I liked it."

Now, about his philosophy on imported cars. "I think it's un-American . . . I think that anybody who buys a Japanese or German car ought to realize he's putting his neighbor out of work," McInerney says. He thought about signing up for a Japanese deal-ership only once. "It felt like surrender."

He's a big donor to the Roman Catholic Church, and sees to it that *Cardinal Szoka* rides in style. With two sons, three daughters, two brothers and five nephews in the business, there are plenty of McInerneys around. "I've got four grandsons coming up, too," he said. "I have plenty of firepower."

McMasters, Robert—January 29, 1935; from caddyshack to directorshack.

His life illustrates why it pays to be nice to your caddy. McMasters once carried bags for 10 years at Royal Oak's Red Run Golf Club, where he later served as a member of the board of directors. His most impressive achievement, however, was the way he raised some $1.3-million for a new Evans Scholars House at Michigan State University. The home provides a roof over the heads of kids who've won Evans Scholarships. The scholarships are named after the late Chick Evans, a crack amateur golfer who made recordings titled: "How to Teach Golf to Your Kids." Evans set up a scholarship fund and sent kids to school rather than collect royalties and blow his amateur status. That fund has sent 5,800 kids to school, including McMasters. The fact that McMasters, a 1956 University of Michigan grad and captain of the U-M golf team, overlooked his school alle-giances to raise money for MSU students speaks volumes.

Although he didn't join a country club until the age of 39, he has earned plenty of respect on the upscale links. He persuaded more than two dozen country clubs to loosen their wallets for $12,500 apiece. Some of the wealthier clubs anted up twice that. He's also a governor of the Golf Association of Michigan, and a director of the Western Golf Association.

McNamara, Ed—September 21, 1926; count of the county.

Wayne County is more populous than 22 of the 50 states, and McNamara runs its government. The measure of his success is that Wayne County government isn't in the news much any more. At one time, it was on the front pages because of managerial incompetence and consistent insolvency. McNamara can claim much of the credit for the no-news good news.

Unlike the normal pol who likes to shake hands and schmooze with the constituents, McNamara seems slightly ill-at-ease with the public side of politics. He is most at home with the tedious, colorless minutiae of running a bureaucracy.

He spent a decade and a half in the trenches before moving up to higher command. He served 16 years as mayor of Livonia and was Democratic gubernatorial candidate *Sander Levin*'s running mate in 1970. McNamara must have wondered if he'd ever escape the pleasant-but-dull life out I-96.

The early '80s saw Wayne County government falling apart. The county's 27 bickering, blustering commissioners had become commonly known as "the county clowns." (The nickname has been traced to WJR reporter Bill Black, who first used it when he penned a column in the *Michigan Chronicle*.) McNamara figured his high suburban profile would carry some weight on the other side of the county, in the Grosse Pointes. And he figured that *Coleman Young* liked him, so maybe he could pick up some votes in Detroit. Thus, in 1982, he made his first run for county executive.

What McNamara hadn't counted on were the vicissitudes of racial politics. Young couldn't get away with backing a white suburban mayor against a fellow black politician (Sheriff *William Lucas*). And even if Young did back McNamara, that probably would have meant more harm than good in the burbs. Lucas skated to an easy victory, and McNamara looked like he'd be trapped in Livonia forever. Lucas, who felt an urge to convert to the Republican Party and run for governor, bowed out in 1986. Suddenly, the man from Livonia didn't look so bad, after all. He waltzed downtown, with 29 percent of the Democratic vote in a race against three strong opponents.

Meriwether, Heath—January 20, 1944; calm in the eye of the storm.

Heath J Meriwether (that's right, no period after his middle initial), executive editor of the *Detroit Free Press*, calmed the troops considerably during the confusing pendency of the Joint Operating Agreement between the *News* and the *Freep*. The fact that no journalists jumped from the *Free Press* tower during that period, when it looked like the paper might go out of business, was an accomplishment. The fact that the paper managed to turn out some impressive journalism is even more astonishing. (For the record, the JOA is still pending as this book is written.)

With his wire-rim glasses and tossled blond hair, Meriwether looks like an aging Harvard frat boy. In fact, he earned a master's degree in teaching from Harvard, after picking up degrees in history and journalism from the University of Missouri. He joined the *Miami Herald* as an education reporter, rising to the executive editorship in 1983. The *Herald* staff won three Pulitzer Prizes in two years while Meriwether ran the place. The *Herald* is not the *New York Times*, but it has long been ranked among the nation's top 10 newspapers by *Time* magazine. In a sweet irony, the *Herald* beat the *Times* and *Washington Post* for a Pulitzer on the Iran-Contra story. His last act at the *Herald* before vacating his office was explaining to the country why the *Herald* had camped outside Gary Hart's townhouse, making Donna Rice a household name, however briefly. Meriwether joined the *Freep* in July 1987.

Merz, Charles—see Schervish, David

Middlebrook, John—January 26, 1941; on the move at GM.

He runs Pontiac, GM's "We Build Excitement" division. Before that, he was v.p. in charge of General Motors' marketing and product planning staff, where he was ultimate overseer of GM's billion-dollar-plus ad budget. Among agency types, he *is* the General, and gets five-star treatment.

A graduate of General Motors Institute (BA in engineering) and Michigan State University (master's in marketing) he signed on at

Oldsmobile when he was barely 18. He joined Pontiac in 1969, spending a dozen years there in various sales and marketing capacities before joining GM's worldwide product planning group.

Beginning in 1983, the promotions came about every two years. Middlebrook spent two years acquiring a global perspective with worldwide planning, another two years back at Pontiac, then signed on as a v.p. of the Saturn Corp. subsidiary. He was there another two years before moving to marketing in 1987. Two years later, he landed his current job at Pontiac.

Milgrom, Steve—November 19, 1952; the impresario of hip Ferndale.

Before Milgrom opened his Sam's Jams record/tape/compact disc store, "shopping in Ferndale" was considered an oxymoron. Now Milgrom's Jams is the anchor store of metro Detroit hipdom, retail division. His store has created an army of foot traffic. Music lovers, especially jazz fans, beat a path from across town. Where else could they purchase an entire collection of Mothers of Invention compact discs?

Milgrom started his shop as a tiny used record store in a 20-foot-by-20-foot space that is now an insurance agency. But one thing led to another, and he's operating in 9,000 square feet down the block on Nine Mile near Woodward. Between Sam's Jams and Paperbacks Unlimited (maybe our best bookstore), one could argue that Ferndale has become a cultural center. Milgrom once predicted that Ferndale "could be a cheap Birmingham." His wish apparently has come true. For some, the ambiance is more comfortable and more, uh, real.

Miller, Sheldon—see Lopatin, Albert

Miller, Steve Jr.—November 4, 1941; Chrysler's top money man.

Steve Miller Jr., vice-chairman of Chrysler Corp. and the guy in charge of the company's financial arm, remembers how he got into the car business: It had something to do with a box of Cheerios.

As a young man who had just completed a pretty rigorous intellectual marathon (Stanford University undergrad, Harvard Law School, Stanford MBA) Miller interviewed at General Mills. It was an attractive offer, Miller recalls, but a box of Cheerios sitting on a credenza behind an executive's desk just . . . bugged him. "I didn't want to devote my life to Cheerios," Miller said. He opted, instead, for the automobile business as a finance man at Ford in the late '60s.

He was having a great time at Ford, and probably could have kept going. But *Lee Iacocca* did a fan dance and talked Miller into leaving in 1970. "Once Lee's been through with you, it's all over," he said later. After Iacocca's pep talk, Miller remembers that he "went out in the hallway here. Nobody ever said what I'm going to get paid . . . You had to have a big leap of faith that it was all going to work out."

During what Chrysler folks call "the dark days," Miller had the toughest job of all: He dealt with some 400 hungry banks, all of whom wanted a piece of Chrysler's heavily mortgaged hide. Miller later described it as "hard, grueling work. The roof was falling in on all sides . . . the hard part was waking up 5 a.m. every morning in a cold sweat. If you screwed up that day, you could put half a million people out of work."

One widely circulated story was his announcement to a group of bickering bankers that Chrysler had filed for protection from its creditors under federal bankruptcy laws. It was April 1, but the money men were not amused—though it did bring the bankers face-to-face with the possible consequences of their intransigence.

Miller's style has brought him some friends. "It's not that guys here are stuffy," says one insider, "but Miller's the guy who is most likely to be spotted outside of Chrysler headquarters in a softball uniform."

The Detroit Symphony Orchestra, struggling through its own financial dark days, named him board chairman in 1988. Maybe he'll work some sweet music there, too.

Milner, Ron—May 29, 1938; what the playwright sells.

One of the country's best playwrights lives right here in Detroit. Among his biggies, which have been performed both in New York and L.A. are "Don't Get God Started" and "What the Wine-Sellers Buy." A native Detroiter, Milner worked in a variety of jobs (mail clerk, construction worker, orderly) before a grant from the Rockefeller Foundation helped him develop his talents.

His eulogy at attorney Ken Cockrel's funeral was especially touching. Milner is also a strong and effective voice against greed and materialism—which makes him rare for the 1980s.

Monaghan, Tom—March 25, 1937; Tigers owner/pizza czar/enigma.

He has risen from the pepperoni and mushrooms to own one of baseball's most lucrative franchises, the Detroit Tigers. *Forbes* says he's worth $480-million. With that, he's able to indulge his passion for Frank Lloyd Wright architecture and antique cars. So why isn't he having a better time?

A Michigan native who spent time in an orphanage, he got his start in pizza in Ypsilanti with one shop he bought into on a $500 loan. After a few expensive lessons, he finally got out on his own and compulsively built a $2-billion-a-year empire. Domino's was well-known when Monaghan bought the Tigers from octogenarian millionaire broadcaster John Fetzer for $45- to $50-million in 1983, but Monaghan was not. *People* magazine sent out a reporter to capture his gee-whiz style. Even greater luck fell upon Monaghan when the Tigers won the World Series during his first year of ownership.

But his public image has changed, mostly as a result of his ill-fated Drummond Island party in the fall of 1987. The bash, attended by 75 or so of Monaghan's friends, all of whom happened to be famous, was played out on the front pages of both Detroit newspapers. Nobody could figure it out. Was Monaghan trying to break into society? He owns the Detroit Tigers. Society people come to him. Was he looking for good press? He said as much in stories about the bash. But a lunch-bucket town like Detroit was mortified by such blatant consumption. An operative theory is that the only thing that went wrong on Drummond Island was that the press was invited. Millionaires throw lavish parties all the time. But they don't jet reporters in to record the follies. Sniffed one employee during the event: "He forgot how to have a good time—if he ever knew in the first place. So he hired people to have a good time for him."

A telling comment, perhaps a road map to Monaghan's mind, happened at the end of a film that was prepared especially for the Drummond Island occasion. "I'd like the Tigers to win more games than anybody," he said. "I'd like to sell more pizza than anybody. And I'd like to go to heaven when I die."

Muer, Chuck—April 23, 1937; from bytes to bites to megabites.

While brother Joe tended to downtown *Joe Muer*'s (see below for a Muer family history), Chuck built his own suburban restaurant empire. Chuck, who usually sports a trademark bow tie and cigar, now has 19 restaurants in five states. Always dignified, he was once photographed in a tuxedo eating a lobster, just to prove it could be done.

A graduate of University of Detroit High School, Chuck swept floors and bused tables at the family restaurant, though at first he wasn't crazy about entering the business. Chuck graduated from Cleveland's John Carroll University, where he majored in accounting, then joined IBM. He says his five-year stay there taught him discipline, although he bucked at corporate rules. (His bow tie, for instance, was not appreciated much by company brass.)

He traded his floppy disks for forks and spoons when he took over as the Pontchartrain Hotel's food maven in 1965. He was 27 at the time, and his C.A. Muer Corp. was one year old. His chain restaurants are considered very good, as in not necessarily great. Decades after abandoning IBM, he still has a computer bug. He created a software division, which sells computer programs for restaurant managements.

Muer, Joe—March 3, 1936; Muer-to-Muer-to-Muer.

Who says fish doesn't age well? Joe Muer operates the seafood restaurant founded by his grandfather six decades ago, making it even more venerable than the London Chop House. Even into the '90s, it remains a restaurant of choice for high rollers. A local official, audio-taped by federal investigators while allegedly asking for a bribe, requested lunch at Joe Muer's. The official could have picked the Whitney or the Chop. What greater salute to a restaurant?

A word on the Muer name in Detroit: Grandfather Joe founded the restaurant that now bears his name in 1929, one day before Wall Street crashed. Grandfather Joe opened the place with seven seats and an oyster bar. It was a hedge against his slumping cigar business. He had seven employees. Soon, the elder Muer was out of the cigar business. Grandfather Joe died at age 74 in 1958, handing it off to son Joe W., who died in 1979 at age 70. Which brings us to the current generation. Grandson Joe carried on the family business; brother *Chuck* took the expansive route.

Joe Muer's is one of the best power-lunching joints in town. At night, a lot of Grosse Pointe's old money still hangs out with the lobsters and the swordfish.

Murphy, Daniel—August 9, 1923; a dynasty north of Eight Mile.

One way or another, he has been an important figure in Oakland County government since the mid-'50s. He was elected as Oakland County's first chief executive in 1974. So far, he has been the county's only exec, and voters show no inclination to kick him out.

Murphy's career began, humbly enough, in the county clerk's office. From 1955 to 1963, he ran the county clerk/register of deeds operation. Snooooze. His next job was anything but boring. He was elected chairman of the county's three-man board of auditors in 1963, and found himself with real power in the bureaucracy. Even the county commissioners, who ostensibly were in charge, had to rely on Murphy for scraps of information. When the county elected its first CE, Murphy became top dog by title, too.

His further political aspirations thus far have been frustrated. Oakland County is key to Republican success in Michigan, but Murphy mistakenly thought the adulation he received in Pontiac translated to adulation in Grand Rapids and Wyandotte. He hoped to land the Republican gubernatorial nomination in 1986, but finished a distant fourth in the primary won by *William Lucas*. Maybe the voters did Murphy a favor, because Lucas was beaten by *James Blanchard* in one of the biggest landslides in Michigan political history.

Mutchler, E. Michael—March 13, 1935; GM position player.

He had been running GM's truck and bus group for just over seven months when company brass chose him to run the Chevrolet-Pontiac-Cadillac group in February 1989. Talk about upward mobility: The C-P-C post is Mutchler's fourth job switch in as many years. He was named head of the company's electric components group in 1986; group exec in charge of body and engine components group in 1987; then vice-president at truck and bus in 1988.

An Ohio native, he joined GM as a co-op student at General Motors Institute in 1953. He snaked around manufacturing jobs through the '60s and '70s before things started happening in very quick order. His current mission: design and build the best Chevies and Pontiacs he can, plus watch the Great White North, where GM sold 559,000 cars and trucks in 1988.

Mylod, Robert—November 21, 1938; Michigan National Bank's main man.

He runs Michigan National Corp., the state's third-biggest bank holding company. Immediately before Mylod arrived, the place took a media battering when its former chairman was accused of having done some strange things with bank assets. The only kind of headlines Mylod generated were the kind proclaiming increased earnings. Wrote *Crain's Detroit Business*: "To those schooled in the Stoddard style (that's Stanford "Bud" Stoddard, the former chairman), Mylod—a product of the U.S. Navy and giant Citicorp—is building a cold, efficient machine." Sweet words to a banker.

Rather confused as a youth about what he'd like to do when he grew up, Mylod majored in English at St. John's University in New York. Finally settling on a career as a mortgage banker, he spent eight years with Citicorp, and a couple more as president of Advance Mortgage Corp. in Southfield. When Advance was purchased by a Dallas firm, Mylod signed on as president of Federal National Mortgage Association rather than move to Texas. Just two years later, Michigan National's board asked him for help. Bud Stoddard, had been caught in a number of financial improprieties and had to go away in 1984. (Eventually, Stoddard was convicted in U.S. District Court. The conviction was later voided on appeal.) The Stoddard episode rocked the bank because nobody could imagine Michigan National without a Stoddard in charge. Stoddard's father founded the bank in 1941.

On the day Mylod started, Comerica launched a hostile takeover bid—not the kind of welcome wagon Mylod expected. He warded off Comerica and set to work. Now all the place does is make money.

N

The Nederlanders—Jimmy (March 31, 1922), Joey (June 1, 1927), Harry (September 15, 1917), Fred (December 29, year not available), Robert (April 10, 1933); *those* Nederlanders.

This nationally known theatrical family has been around Detroit since before the Civil War, but it was David Nederlander, known as "D.T." before he died in 1967, who got the clan into show business back in 1914. D.T.'s obituary in the *Free Press* described him as having "a voice like a sputtering of a shorted high-voltage power line. When he came in peace, he was gentle and polite, but when he came in war, as he sometimes did, he was something to tiptoe around."

His five sons enlarged on D.T's theatrical interests and are now into television production, movie houses, Broadway and the law. Jimmy, Joey and Harry are the show-biz arm of the current generation. Locally, they own the Fisher and Birmingham theaters, along with an interest in Pine Knob. Joey fell into the cookie jar as an early investor in Broadway's "Annie." Fred is an auto supplier. Robert is a lawyer active in local Democratic politics. He was Michigan treasurer of Jimmy Carter's presidential campaign in 1976, and served as a University of Michigan regent for 20 years until 1984.

Newman, David—November 6, 1940; we talk, he listens.

This WXYT-AM talk show host has been a New York cabbie, a newsman, a disc jockey, and a truck driver. For the last 15 years, however, he has listened to Detroiters spout off on everything from abortion to tax cuts.

Newman's first job was as the afternoon deejay in Coatesville, Pennsylvania. "The format was middle of the road," recalls Newman, "so middle of the road that the Beatles and the Bee Gees were banned. We played the stuff by the Letterman and the New Christy Minstrels." From here, he went on to cover the Chicago Seven Trial for Westinghouse, then joined CBS in Boston. He signed on with what was then WXYZ in 1974.

Nugent, Ted—December 13, 1948; Motor City Madman.

His guitar playing has all the subtlety of a Rouge Plant blast furnace. Sensitive, haunting ballads such as "Cat Scratch Fever" and "Wang Dang Sweet Poontang" have made him the main man among the heavy metal set. For extra effect, he was lowered from the ceiling of Cobo Arena during his New Year's Eve (1987-'88) Whiplash Bash. He plays his instrument at ear-splitting levels, drives fast and hunts bear in northern Michigan. His personal life is something else, entirely. He lives peacefully on a farm near Jackson, eschews alcohol and drugs, and dotes on his two children.

A Redford native, he blasted his way into the ears of Detroit rock fans during the mid-1960s as the lead guitar player for the Amboy

Dukes. His solo on "Journey to the Center of Your Mind" (1967) is a rock classic. "You Talk Sunshine, I Breathe Fire" was another hit. He outgrew his fellow members musically, however, and went solo during the mid-1970s. LSD-wrecked fans would hurl oranges on stage during his early solo gigs, on the theory that an acid casualty like Nugent needed Vitamin C to replenish his body. (In fact, Nugent has never taken drugs—which explains why he's still healthy and working 20 years after his first hit.) Both he and Epic records made a bundle with "Weekend Warriors" and "Double Live Gonzo," both of which went platinum. In all, he had seven LPs on *Billboard* magazine's top 40 charts in 1976-'80.

Nugent can do things besides strum his guitar. He is so articulate that WLLZ-FM often gives him the microphone when morning personalities *Jim Johnson* and *George Baier* vacation. He once played a woman-beating drug dealer on NBC-TV's "Miami Vice." Like most bad guys on that show, he died at the end. Nugent preached against the dangers of drugs and alcohol before hardly anybody thought of saying no. Early in the psychedelic era, he noticed that some of his colleagues were fading away in drug-induced stupors. His booze consumption tops out at one pina colada annually.

Most of the time, he plays Mr. Mom to his two children, Sasha and Toby. His estranged wife died in a traffic accident in 1982. So impressive are his child-rearing capabilities that he once was named "Father of the Year" by his kids' school.

O

O'Connell, Robert—July 7, 1938; GM's head money stacker.

This imposing figure guards the world's largest privately owned checking account. Somebody with an idea that'll cost more than $1.98 must, sooner or later, go hat in hand and face O'Connell, who is said to be a hard sell. The *Wall Street Journal* revealed that O'Connell is known as "Roto Rooter" around GM headquarters, because his initials are "RTO" and because of his aggressive nature.

O'Connell has a bachelor's from Yale and a master's from Harvard, which must make it confusing for him on the egghead version of Buckeyes-Wolverine day. He joined the GM treasurer's office in 1965, was immediately recognized as a bright light and hasn't stopped rising.

As executive v.p./finance, he is speculated to be future chairman twice removed. When *Alan Smith* (a possible *Roger Smith* successor) reaches the mandatory retirement age of 65 in April 1996, O'Connell will be only a month or so from his 58th birthday. When current president *Robert Stempel* (also rumored to be a Smith successor) hits retirement age, O'Connell will have just turned 60. What an amazing coincidence: The average age of the last seven GM chairmen on their ascendancy to office has been 59.

O'Connor, Richard (December 29, 1931) and Dow, Peter (October 7, 1933); ruling duo at Lintas: Campbell-Ewald.

They are, respectively, the chairman and president of Lintas: Campbell-Ewald, Michigan's biggest ad agency. That means keeping the Chevrolet account at the agency's Warren headquarters, where it has been since 1922. Just how important is the Chevy account? O'Connor once wrote a staff memo wagging his finger at the troops for driving (gasp!!!) foreign cars.

O'Connor joined Campbell-Ewald in 1956 as a trainee on the Chevy account. He has never strayed far from the car division's familiar bow tie. A protege of C-E legend/former chairman *Tom Adams*, O'Connor landed the presidency in 1976, and was named vice-chairman/chief executive officer upon Adams' retirement three years later. O'Connor's status here in Detroit gives him clout with the Interpublic Group of Companies Inc., the agency's New York corporate father. O'Connor is a director of the corporation, and banks one of the group's top five paychecks. In 1987, that was $475,274.

Dow, a Detroit native, joined C-E only two years after O'Connor. Unlike O'Connor, he moved around a bit: He left C-E for Young & Rubicam in 1966, then went to Chrysler in 1968 for an 11-year stay. He returned to C-E in 1979.

O'Hair, John—September 29, 1929; reserved, respected lawman.

As Wayne County prosecutor, he's charged with putting an army of felons behind bars. As a Presbyterian elder and experienced jurist, he has more integrity and knowledge than you'll find in most any two practitioners of public service these days. The only criticism anybody has of him is that he's not very exciting. But who wants Geraldo Rivera in the prosecutor's office, anyhow?

A graduate of DePauw University and Detroit College of Law, O'Hair spent nine years in the Detroit corporation counsel's office (1956-'65). He left when he was elected to the Common Pleas bench (now 36th District Court). Three years later, he ascended to a seat on the Wayne County circuit bench, where he made his reputation.

There, he was a model judge: scholarly, contemplative, serious and a wee bit dull. Legal types were shocked in May 1983 when O'Hair retired from the bench after 15 years to be then-Wayne County exec *William Lucas*'s top lawyer. O'Hair pleaded boredom. But the move was as if Walter Cronkite had renounced his allegiance to CBS News and joined the staff of "Entertainment Tonight." Later that fall, prosecutor William Cahalan announced he was giving up his job after 16 years to enter private practice. O'Hair's old friends on the circuit bench, after five ballots, gave their former colleague the prosecutor's job over 13 other candidates.

Some back-room Democrats reacted as if Richard Nixon had been appointed. O'Hair hadn't done much time on the rubber-chicken circuit and was totally inactive in party affairs. Gov. *George Romney*, a Republican, had appointed him to the circuit bench in 1968.

O'Hair isn't a politician, but he isn't stupid. He appointed lawyer Elliott Hall, who had close connections to *Mayor Young*, to the No. 2 position in the prosecutor's office. That co-opted one wing of the party. He breezed through his next primary, and had no opposition in 1988.

He is married to *Free Press* reporter Barbara Stanton, who had been an associate editor of the *Freep* and was a major contributor to the newspaper's Pulitzer Prize-winning coverage of the 1967 riot.

O'Hara, John—July 15, 1929; keeper of the world's largest address book.

He's the first non-family chief exec at R.L. Polk & Co., one of Detroit's oldest companies. Polk, which was founded in 1870 by Ralph Polk, puts out city directories and keeps motor vehicle stats. Newspaper reporters, for instance, need books with phone numbers for various addresses around the city. Ford Motor Co., for instance, may wish to know how many Volkswagens are on the road in Oregon. Polk has all that info —and charges plenty for it.

A grad of the University of Virginia (BA 1951) and its law school (where he graduated seventh in a class of 180), O'Hara spent a decade as a lawyer in New York before joining Polk in 1968. A series of promotions vaulted O'Hara into the president's chair in 1985, then the chairmanship two years later. Associates describe him as patrician and very serious.

Polk has been a family affair for most of its history. It began with 21-year-old Ralph Polk publishing a guide to towns along the Detroit and Milwaukee railroad. With a little help from *Detroit News* editor James Scripps, Polk expanded into city directories.

These days the operation is high-tech. However, some things never change. There are still family members hanging around more than a century later. Stephen Polk, great-grandson of founder Ralph, is an executive vice-president.

Ovshinsky, Harvey—April 9, 1948; a real producer.

He has made his mark in three media: as publisher of the *Fifth Estate* underground newspaper in the '60s, as a WABX-FM radio commentator and news director in the early '70s, and as a television producer at Channels 4, 7 and 56 in the '70s and '80s. Going into the '90s, he hopes to make it as a screenwriter.

The son of inventor Stanford Ovshinsky, he published the *Fifth Estate* (1965-'68) fresh out of Mumford High School. Those who recall the hippie era in Detroit remember the weekly as a counter-culture beacon. He might have become a left-wing Rupert Murdoch had not Uncle Sam ruined his plans. Instead of reporting to Vietnam, he became a conscientious objector and worked in Detroit's Lafayette Clinic. After that tour of duty, he signed up as news director on WABX-FM. Unlike some of his rip-and-read counterparts around the radio dial, he didn't merely rewrite the *Free Press* every day. But radio newscasting remained one-dimensional to Harvey, so he moved on to Channel 7 as a producer.

He did his best work in later stops at Channels 4 and 56, where he picked up a crate of Emmys and other awards. Local commercial television hasn't popped with anything as dramatic since Ovshinsky produced "A Gift for Serena" and "City Nights" for Channel 4. But, once again feeling constrained, he moved on to Channel 56. He has received a total of seven Emmys at Channels 4 and 7, and supervised countless more award-winners at Channel 56.

Never content, Ovshinsky began writing a screenplay between 5:30 a.m. and 9 a.m. every day. At this writing, his work has been making the rounds of Hollywood, but he hasn't had any luck—yet.

His track record suggests he'll beat the very long odds of La-La Land.

P

Pailen, Donald—(birthdate not available); Mayor Young's chief attorney.

Coleman Young used to have a lot of trouble filling the city's top legal job. The pay, well under six figures, eliminated most top lawyers. At one point, there were eight Law Department directors in eight years. One lawyer spent a full year as acting director, then left in frustration. Another problem: Despite the fact that Young had two lawyers as roommates during his Lansing days, he never liked attorneys much. He seems to have solved his problem with Donald Pailen, who has run the department since 1982, which makes him—by far—the longest-serving chief lawyer under Young.

Pailen spent 11 years in the U.S. Justice Department's Civil Rights Division before coming to Detroit. Serving under Presidents Nixon and Ford, he left when he became convinced that Reagan was about to dismantle the department. If Pailen ever had questions about job security, they were solved in the fall of 1988 when Young called him a "hero." Pailen refused to give the *Detroit News* documents regarding a city land deal. Wayne County Circuit Judge James Rashid wasn't amused, so Pailen went to the pokey. This pushed a lot of buttons with Young, who always has been sensitive about grand jury leaks and has regarded grand jury "secrecy" clauses as a sham. Pailen did four days in an executive cell at the Wayne County jail, then was sprung when he coughed up the documents.

Pais, Donald—October 23, 1935; the source for outsources.

Auto suppliers genuflect when Pais enters the room. He's General Motors' v.p. in charge of materials management. That means he buys all the billions of gaskets, bolts and plastic widgets it takes to make GM cars. To countless widgetmakers, gasketmakers and boltmakers, he's a very important man.

A Detroit native, Pais signed with Chevy in 1957—the same year he earned a BS degree from Michigan State University. After going through Carnegie-Mellon University's executive program in 1975, he made several important stops. In 1978, he became Delco Morain's director of production control and purchasing; then Pontiac's material management director in 1980; then director of materials management at the Chevrolet-Pontiac-Cadillac group in 1984. He landed in his current job the following year.

Penhallow, Arthur—December 20, year not available; Baby!!!

In his prime, he was a walking definition of a rock 'n' roll hedonist. With his distinctive growl, six-figure income and wild life-style, Penhallow was the envy of the rock generation. But his beard has gone gray, and a heart problem — probably brought on by non-stop hearty partying—forced him to curtail the booze intake. Time hasn't dimmed his familiar growl, however, and he still makes big bucks spinning discs on WRIF-FM, where he's been since 1970 (when it was WXYZ-FM).

A native of Hawaii, he landed in Detroit when ABC decided to make WRIF-FM the top "underground" station in town. With Arthur doing his drive-time schtick, it worked. Some wonder if he's getting a little long in the tooth to rock 'n' roll. But his ratings are still good. And he's still WRIF's signature during drive time. Penhallow continually threatens to move back to Hawaii, but comes to his senses when he realizes there is no money to be had spinning discs there.

Penske, Roger—February 20, 1937; gasoline alley guru/corporate turnaround artist.

Penske gives new meaning to the phrase "hard-driving businessman." A former race car driver, he has a habit of succeeding where hidebound *Fortune* 500 corporations have failed. Penske bought a piece of Hertz's sputtering truck leasing unit in 1982 and turned it into a winner; he purchased 80 percent of General Motors' troubled Detroit Diesel Corp. in 1987 and 1988 and had it turning a profit within a year. And those are only two pieces of Penske's $2-billion transportation principality. He owns the country's biggest auto dealership (Longo Toyota near Los Angeles) and mega-dealerships in New York City. Even his hobby brings him astonishing success. Penske-managed cars have won the Indianapolis 500 seven times.

A graduate of Lehigh University (**Lee Iacocca's** alma mater), he was well on the road to auto racing fame when he made a permanent pit stop for a business career. A Grand Prix driver during the early 1960s, Penske was crowned "driver of the year" by *Sports Illustrated* in 1961, with the *New York Times* weighing in with a similar honor a year later. He hung up his goggles two years later to run a Philadelphia Chevy dealership when he decided he couldn't afford the pricey insurance premiums of a race driver. Judging from the zeal with which he has attacked business, it's safe to say he doesn't miss racing much.

He took on Hertz's truck leasing venture, which lost $40-million the year before Penske got involved. It made $1.2-million the first year Penske was in the driver's seat. He's on the same track with Detroit Diesel, which everyone at GM and Wall Street thought was a dog. Detroit Diesel went from losing $60-million in 1987 to a tidy $15-million profit in 1988 with Penske in charge. He once threw a bash for 9,000 Detroit Diesel employees as a way of saying thanks. Pal **Leon Mandel**, *AutoWeek* magazine publisher, attributes Penske's achievements to "sheer force of will."

A nut for detail, Penske even insists that his race drivers' uniforms are pressed regularly. He spends about half his time in Detroit, the other half in his mansion near Red Bank, New Jersey. Published reports put his net worth at $100-million, but he doesn't talk much about that.

Peoples, John—December 4, 1934; independent voice on City Council.

Although John Peoples got his City Council job with **Mayor Young**'s blessing, he hasn't exactly been a Manoogian Mansion martinet. He was out front in the fight against the mayor's beloved gambling casinos and voted twice against the Mayor's Office on a tax break for General Motors' Detroit-Hamtramck "Poletown" plant. Peoples thought GM had sampled enough of the city's charity.

An Oklahoma City native, Peoples arrived here on a Greyhound bus in the mid-1950s knowing no one. He worked the midnight shift on a Ford line. Peoples became a tool and die maker—the elite in the plant—and later ran his own west-side gas station and repair shop. Merely making money became hollow after awhile, so he left it behind to become a Baptist minister in the early 1960s. He took over as pastor of the east side's Calvary Baptist in 1976. Amid the preaching and the politicking, he found time to complete a doctorate in education from Wayne State University in 1988.

If he owes his political career to any group, it's the powerful Baptist clergy. The ministers pushed hard for his election in 1981, as did Young. Peoples' margin of victory in his first race was just 1,500 votes, barely one vote per precinct. He once again rounded out the bottom of the nine-member pack four years later, but his margin was a substantial 30,000 votes.

He resigned the pastorate of Calvary Baptist in 1986 to devote full time to politics. Blunt-spoken, he's become more confident as an incumbent. He was one of the few people brave enough to call the Joe Louis fist "ugly," and he tried to have it moved from Detroit's riverfront to the Detroit Institute of Arts where the snobs could enjoy it. He was one of only two council members to call for a freeze on the sale of handguns, and he takes a law-and-order stance on crime. "I guarantee you that if police start going out there and start cracking some heads there will be some lawsuits, but so what?" he once said. In a city that has a terrible crime problem, that kind of talk will take him a long way.

Perkins, J.C.—March 7, 1935; GM's GM Jim.

Perkins, general manager of General Motors' Chevrolet division, has done something that few have ever done at GM: He left the General and was accepted back. More important, nobody can remember a prodigal son becoming the chief of the company's biggest division. If anything, Perkins' return is an indication of how times have changed.

Perkins had been with GM almost a quarter of a century before he left for Toyota in 1984. At GM, he ran the gamut of Chevy zone offices (San Diego and Dallas among those stops) before bolting for Toyota. There, Perkins became a major part of the brain trust that introduced the Japanese automakers' new Lexus division. GM got Perkins back in early '89 to replace veteran Chevy chief Robert Burger, who was getting ready to retire.

Perles, George—August 16, 1934; trying to build a mean green machine.

University of Michigan fans would like to think otherwise, but *Bo Schembechler* isn't the only football coach in the state. This guy Perles won a Rose Bowl in 1988 with the *other* team. And MSU fans were delighted that their man was able to win the one that Bo's boys traditionally botch. (The laughter lasted only a year, however, as U-M redeemed itself with roses in 1989.)

Born in Detroit, he played for MSU in the '50s, then broke in as a coach at St. Ambrose High in Grosse Pointe Park. Later he served as an assistant to MSU legend Duffy Daugherty, then joined the Pittsburgh Steelers as defensive coordinator. He was there for 10 straight years (and four straight Super Bowls, 1974-'77), finishing up as assistant head coach. Although Perles had a dream job and a collection of Super Bowl rings, he never lost his passion for MSU.

The Spartan football program had languished in the early '80s under Muddy Waters, and Perles was happy to respond to entreaties that he return and resurrect the glory days when the Wolverines were the team that people felt sorry for. When he arrived in 1983, there were doubters. And when he went 4-6-1, 6-6, 7-5 and 6-5 in his first four seasons, MSU supporters saw improvement but remained nervous. The '88 Rose Bowl triumph over Southern Cal settled the nerves, but it remains to be seen whether Perles has brought the program back or only brought it a moment in the sun.

Pestillo, Peter—March 22, 1938; liaison with the line.

Pete Pestillo, who ultimately oversees Ford Motor Co.'s labor negotiations, certainly can't determine how much the company will offer its hourly workers at contract time. But he is the company's eyes and ears at the bargaining table. There, he apparently has earned the respect of the UAW. Doug Fraser and Donald Ephlin, both of whom sat across from Pestillo, give him high marks for at least understanding the union and its politics.

Pestillo grew up in Connecticut, where his father was a lathe hand. He earned a degree from Georgetown Law School, gave guided tours at the Jefferson Memorial and wrote a newsletter for the National Restaurant Association before going into labor relations.

Unlike most car people in this book, Pestillo is not a life-long employee of an auto company. He worked as a labor expert at General Electric and B.F. Goodrich Co., enduring 100-day strikes at both before joining Ford in 1980. Nobody blamed Pestillo for the messes. Despite being one of the few who have suffered through major work stoppages in two different industries, he hasn't seen a national strike in his eight years at Ford.

In January 1986, Ford made him vice-president for employee and external affairs, giving him the added responsibilities of running the company's public affairs and governmental affairs departments. The move made sense. He is unusually comfortable around reporters, even inviting them to Detroit Lions football games for an afternoon of drinks and story-swapping.

Petersen, Donald—September 4, 1926; low profile, high profits.

Everyone would notice if *Lee Iacocca* walked into a room. No one might notice Donald Petersen, Ford Motor Co.'s chairman. He is maker of few waves, but maker of many bucks for Ford. Since he assumed his present position in 1985, Ford has become the most profitable automotive company in history. A native of Minnesota, he earned a BA from the University of Washington and a master's degree from Stanford before joining the company in 1949. Although he had been trained in the art of management, he became a product planner with Ford. That allied him with the "car guys" — the people who are more interested in snazzy machinery than impressive profits. During those years, he did what successful Washington politicians do: made few enemies, kept his own counsel, and thus avoided corporate fire fights. Somehow, he also avoided the cliques. For instance, he never allied himself with Iacocca, nor did he aim any obscene gestures toward the man as he was fired. Even when he had conflicts—as he did with former chairman Philip Caldwell—he kept it to himself. So when Henry Ford II was looking for a new chairman, Petersen was knighted.

He listens to jazz, and seems to have set himself an orderly transition when he retires in the early 1990s. That's something that even Henry Ford II couldn't arrange properly. The only fire he's had to ward off is the friendly fire sent his way by Ford scions *Edsel Ford II* and *William Clay Ford Jr.*, who wanted committee assignments on the board of directors.

Poling, Harold—October 14, 1925; No. 2 at No. 2.

As a top Ford exec, he was integral to Ford's turnaround from a company that lost $3.26-billion in 1980-'82, to one that made $5.3-billion in 1988—outstripping General Motors in earnings in 1986, '87 and '88.

A graduate of Monmouth (Ill.) College and Indiana University, he joined Ford in 1950 and rose up the company's finance side. He was a protege of J. Edward Lundy, the pre-eminent money man at Ford, who for decades had such an impact on how the company operated. Poling spent the '70s in Ford's all-important European operation, as the unit's finance man (1972), later as president (1975) and then chairman (1977). He was tapped for a company executive vice-presidency in 1979, in time for some of Ford's darkest hours. When the company lost billions in the '80s, it was Poling's job to stop the bleeding. As chief executioner he cut $2.5-billion out of fixed costs in 1980-'81. Factories were closed, thousands of mid-level managers were pink-slipped. For all the pain, there is evidence that such major surgery was necessary.

Poling's reward: He became president and chief operating officer under chairman **Donald Petersen** in 1985, then got the vice-chairman's job in 1987.

"Red," as he's called, speaks with a flat, good-ole-boy Indiana accent.

Portnoy, Lynn—June 13, 1938; clothier to Detroit's working women elite.

While most clothing stores were moving out of downtown in 1980, Lynn Portnoy went the other way. Figuring that somebody had to dress downtown's professional women, she decided she was the person to fill the void. Five banks thought she was crazy, but the banks were wrong. She hung her shingle on Congress, doing well dressing judges, lawyers, city hall types and countless other female power brokers who would otherwise be stuck shopping in the sterile suburban wilderness.

Portnoy bought for Claire Pearone, the woman who brought *haute couture* to Detroit, for some 16 years before going out on her own. She's forever jetting off to Paris in search of the latest.

Power, Philip—June 3, 1938; press baron of the burbs.

While the *News* and *Free Press* lost tons of money battling each other throughout the 1980s, Power watched from the suburbs and made money with his *Observer-Eccentric* newspaper group. He has also enjoyed several flings with politics, and may yet be a candidate again.

The family's wealth comes from Power's father, Eugene, who founded University Microfilms west of Ann Arbor in 1938. The young Power earned degrees from the University of Michigan and Oxford University, got into journalism as a newsman in Fairbanks, Alaska, where he was acting city editor of the *Daily News-Mirror*. He returned to Michigan as an administrative assistant to Congressman Paul Todd Jr. of Kalamazoo. Power dumped politics, however, when—at age 28 — he bought the *Observer* chain in 1966.

As successful as the newspapers were, Power couldn't leave politics alone, spending some $800,000 in a run at the Democratic nomination for U.S. Senate in 1978. But his ambitions cooled when he was beaten 2–1 by *Carl Levin,* who went on to Washington.

His wife, Sarah Goddard Power, much admired for her own political and humanitarian efforts, died tragically in 1987 — an apparent suicide in a fall from U-M's Burton Tower. Power was appointed to her seat on the U-M Board of Regents.

Prechter, Heinz—January 19, 1942; Duke of Downriver.

Is there anything southwest of Detroit this guy won't own soon? Prechter's portfolio includes downriver's Heritage Newspapers chain; Southgate's Presidential Inn; a bevy of auto dealerships; and a five percent chunk of Security Bancorp Inc. The bulk of his fortune, however, comes from ASC Inc., which puts sunroofs or special components in some 350,000 cars a year. In 1988 he organized a deal to pick another bagatelle off the pastry cart: the London Chop House, Detroit's most revered eatery. Maybe elephants will fly and one day downriver will become chic.

Like most great entrepreneurs, Prechter made his money by being five minutes ahead of his time. He helped popularize the sunroof, which became commonplace in the United States in the '70s but was unheard of when Prechter began hacking away in the 1960s. A native of West Germany, Prechter got his start in L.A., which has always been receptive to automotive innovation. Some of his early Lotusland customers included George Burns, James Garner and Steve McQueen. L.A. is a nice place, but the big money is in volume, and that is in Detroit. His baptism with the big-time Detroit automotive community happened when Lincoln-Mercury sent Prechter 300 Cougars for surgery in 1967. Henry Ford II even had Heinz hack a hole in the roof of a Lincoln for President Lyndon Johnson. Prechter told *Detroit Monthly* senior editor Lowell Cauffiel: "He (Johnson) wanted it for rabbit hunting in the prairie."

Prechter certainly has entrée to Detroit society. He hosted a $1,000-a-head fund raiser for George Bush in 1986 — when the odds were short that Bush would come up wimp rather than White House. When *Tom Monaghan* threw his infamous bash on Drummond Island in 1987, Prechter was put up in a stateroom on Monaghan's yacht. Interestingly, Prechter spent the Sunday morning after Monaghan's black-tie dinner jawing away with crew members and press photographers instead of rubbing elbows with the swells.

Prechter and his family—wife, Wally, and two children — live on Grosse Ile, putting their mouths where their money is: downriver.

Psarouthakis, Dr. John—June 29, 1932; mining gold in the rust belt.

This Ann Arbor-based industrialist thinks positive and makes money. His philosophy, laid out in a 100-page volume entitled "Better Makes Us Best," involves a strong belief that we should try to improve a little each day. His company's earnings statement emphasizes making lots of money each year. His philosophy will go national when the book appears in a commercial edition in late 1989.

As a young immigrant from Crete in 1951, Psarouthakis was held for a week by customs officers who couldn't believe he had been admitted to the Massachusetts Institute of Technology. Now that Ellis Island is closed, we hope the customs officers are doing all right, because Psarouthakis certainly is. His company, JP Industries, sold $383-million worth of unrelated objects such as bidets, transmission bearings and acrylic tubes in 1987. *Forbes* magazine named JP Industries one of the best 200 small companies in America. But JP isn't so small anymore. It made the *Fortune* 500 within 10 years of its founding.

After graduating from MIT, Psarouthakis worked for a variety of companies, including Masco Industries. He took two months off and emerged with a six-page blueprint that eventually made him king of JP Industries.

JP certainly has swum upstream. While everyone else has gone high-tech, Psarouthakis is making things like replacement engine bearings for M60 tanks. And while everyone else is going to the Sun Belt, he sticks around in places like Ohio, Minnesota and Iowa.

It works. Sales have increased at least $100-million each year since 1984.

Pulte, William—(birthdate not available); homebuilder.

Pulte was on *Forbes'* list of the country's 400 richest people in 1982, but fell off the list in 1984 when a depressed housing market sent the value of his stock tumbling by about half. Undoubtedly he has enough left to cover his MasterCard payments. Although his family is the biggest stockholder of PHM Corp. (he owns 19.8 percent of the firm), he has stepped back a bit from the company he founded in 1956. James Grosfeld, who owns 13.4 percent, is now chairman and chief executive officer. Approaching 60, Pulte is content to chair the company's executive committee.

During the '50s and early '60s, he was just another builder. An article about homes in the Washington area caught his eye. "Those houses looked a lot like the ones I was building in the suburbs of Detroit," Pulte told *News* reporter Jack Woerpel. "They were selling very well in the hot Washington market. I figured I could do as well (in Washington), so I started operations there. We've been doing fine there ever since." He later expanded into the Sunbelt, though economic problems in Texas and Colorado have caused him headaches.

Pursell, Carl—December 19, 1932; right at home in a mixed-bag district.

Quick: What do Ann Arbor and Livonia have in common? When you realize that Carl Pursell is the only possible answer, you see just how schizophrenic this congressman's district is. The sprawling tract of west exurbia has done well by Pursell, nonetheless.

Pursell rose from the muck of the Wayne County Board of Commissioners, where he served in 1969 and 1970, to the state Senate (1971-'76), then on to Congress in 1977. His first election, against Ann Arbor's Ed Pierce in 1976, sent him to Washington by the slimmest of margins—344 votes out of more than 190,000, with his Plymouth/Livonia base carrying the day. Since then he has breezed with at least 55 percent of the vote.

He's rather moderate by Republican standards, and was part of the "Gypsy Moth" brigade of GOP legislators who fought President Reagan on budget cuts. Instead of spouting ideology, he works quietly with attention to the details that get the state federal bucks.

Democrats thought they had a chance against Pursell with state Sen. Lana Pollock in 1988. She was energetic, bright, had collected a bag full of chits from five years in the state Senate and had raised a considerable amount of money. But she, too, went the way of Pursell's last half-dozen opponents. Pursell's victory was at least partly assured by his rather shrill series of radio advertisements.

Purtan, Dick—(birthdate not available); veteran funnyman/WCZY-FM's franchise player.

Detroit's longest-running comic act, he's able to skewer people and situations without being obnoxious about it. And how popular has his brand of comedy made him here? A series of promotional ads had only to show his trademark mustache and glasses. Nobody was confused.

Purtan was Ted Koppel's boss at the campus radio station of his alma mater, Syracuse University. Like most disc jockeys, he made the rounds of smaller radio stations hoping for a crack at the big time. Among his stops were Syracuse, Buffalo (his hometown), Jacksonville and Cincinnati. It was in Cincinnati in 1964 that he brought in the Beatles for southern Ohio's entertainment pleasure. "The deal was $12,500 down and $12,500 before they went on stage," he recalls. "Since I didn't have that kind of money, I went in with four other jocks at $2,500 apiece. As I recall, we made $2,200 each." His first stop in a Top 10 market—Detroit—happened in 1965. He's been here ever since, except for five weeks and one day in Baltimore in 1968. (A little known fact: "I still have some of the tar and feathers on me. The governor of Maryland at the time was one Spiro T. Agnew—this was just before Nixon picked him up. I made a joke about him, calling him Spiral Tax Agnew. I was told I shouldn't do that again. So I did it again. I got a call from the governor's office and summoned to lunch. There, I was told I shouldn't do that again. So I did it again. I wasn't around much longer. This is a free country, but Maryland isn't a free state.")

From there it was to WXYZ-AM for a 10-year stay (1968–1978), then on to CKLW (1978–1983), then to WCZY-FM. When Gannett sold the station so it could buy the *Detroit News*, the new owners—nervous that Dick might bolt and walk away with their listeners—arranged for Purtan to have a small piece of the action.

Sure, he's wealthy and can afford his toys. But an anecdote illustrates how smart he is about handling the perks of success. (Pay attention, *Tom Monaghan*.) When Purtan's attorney negotiated a contract for him at CKLW, the station threw in a limo and a helicopter for Purtan's daily transportation pleasure. Dick refused. "This is a working class town," Purtan observed, "and I figure people wouldn't appreciate their friendly neighborhood disc jockey coming to work in a limo." Thinking like that will keep him on the air in Motown for a long time.

Q

Quick, William—May 20, 1933; southern preacher at home in the North.

Quick, pastor of Detroit's Metropolitan United Methodist Church, was a leading foe of *Mayor Young*'s casino gambling proposal. He explained to his congregation: "The dice of God are always loaded." Since arriving here in 1974 from Durham, North Carolina, he has been up to his collar in matters civic.

Raised on the border of the Carolinas and a graduate of Duke University Divinity School, Quick did religious duty in Virginia and North Carolina before receiving an invitation to preach here. His first act was to sandblast and tuck-point Metropolitan United Methodist, an impressive 80-room edifice that had fallen into disrepair on Woodward Avenue in the New Center. He told *News* reporter Al Stark: "I have always believed that church buildings preach just as men preach; they are a witness to the community."

There have been chances to return to the Sunbelt, but Quick has refused. Most recently, he turned down a job with a 6,000-member church in Dallas. Detroit is now his hometown. Like many other mortals, he fights a never-ending battle with his waistline.

R

Ravitz, Justin—August 29, 1940; from radical activist to jurist to successful attorney.

When Ravitz was elected to a Detroit Recorder's Court judgeship in 1972, conservatives screamed "The Commies are Coming, the Commies are Coming." Ravitz was an avowed Marxist who once refused to rise for the Pledge of Allegiance. Within a year, he was presiding over what was called the "10th Precinct conspiracy" case, which involved more than two dozen people (a dozen of them cops) accused of running a drug ring. The trial ran 210 days, said to be the longest criminal trial ever held in the state.

By the time Ravitz went into private practice in 1986 with the Southfield law firm of Sommers, Schwartz, Silver & Schwartz, he had been described as one of the state's best legal minds. He was particularly tough on drug pushers. About the only time he let his political beliefs show through was the time he called right-wing activist Donald Lobsinger a "worm" during an encounter on Detroit's streets.

Over at Sommers-Schwartz, he dinged the city of Detroit for a couple of million for not being particularly helpful in providing the town's handicapped citizens access to DOT buses. Ravitz will undoubtedly ring the cash registers for his clients again.

Ravitz, Mel—January 7, 1924; City Council's resident intellectual.

Ravitz is probably the most genuine egghead ever to occupy a City Council seat. Possessor of a Ph.D in sociology from the University of Michigan and a Wayne State University instructor since 1949, he is easily the most educated. Except for an eight-year hiatus from 1974 to 1981, he's been a councilman since 1961—making him the senior guest at the table of nine. He never catered to the worst instincts of the city's white yahoos, earning him a tag as the council's designated "liberal." So what has it gained him? The mayor doesn't like him, since Ravitz has the temerity to speak against *Coleman Young* on casino gambling, pension increases for elected officials and other matters. With a failed mayoral candidacy in 1973 and another busted run for Wayne County executive in 1982, Ravitz probably isn't slated for another office. If his hard work is to be rewarded, it may be in another life.

Sick of theorizing about social problems, he took a swipe at a council seat in the Camelot year of 1961 and landed the job with a ninth-place finish. He bettered himself with a fifth-place showing in 1965, and then became the council's top vote-getter in 1969. His mayoral run in 1973 looked good on paper: He would get the liberal white vote from those who might be nervous about a law-and-order candidate like top cop John Nichols. There were voters who didn't care for then-State Sen. Young. Ravitz had the UAW, Teamsters and AFL-CIO endorsements. Pundits figured he had a free trip to Manoogian Mansion. But the Ravitz candidacy fell right through the cracks: The white yahoos voted for Nichols; John Mogk took a piece of the white liberal bloc, and blacks voted for Young, so Ravitz was out of work. Timing is all in politics. The numbers suggest he should have ridden the crest of his popularity in 1969 and run against Roman Gribbs and Richard Austin. He returned to City Council in 1981 with a sixth-place finish, which he scored again four years later.

Ravitz spoke eloquently against pension increases for Young and his colleagues. "I don't believe public officials should set their own pension benefits," he wrote, explaining his dissenting vote. (*Jack Kelley* and *Maryann Mahaffey* voted with him.) "I don't accept the argument that Detroit elected officials require a more generous pension plan because their tenure is more at risk than other city employees. Incumbent defeat has not been the history in Detroit for either mayors, city clerks or council members."

That includes Ravitz.

Reuss, Lloyd—September 22, 1936; would-be General Motors president.

His turf is the General's North American automotive operations, which is the largest chunk of the company's business: 3.8 million cars and 1.7 million trucks in 1988.

Reuss (pronounced Royce) joined GM as an engineer in 1959. Chief engineer on the 1970 Camaro (a hit) and Chevy Vega (a bomb), he bounced around increasingly important engineering posts at Buick and Chevy in the 1970s. When GM announced its massive restructuring in early 1984, he was named chief of the Chevrolet-Pontiac-Canada group. An appointment to the GM board and stewardship of GM's North American automotive operations was only two years behind.

That put him in line for the presidency of GM, in lock step with *Bob Stempel*. Stempel got the job. For a while thereafter, Reuss was mentioned as a possibility in practically every ranking automotive post that opened up outside GM. One rumor had him going to Honda, another to Nissan, yet another to TRW, which supplies seat belts to most automakers. But Reuss has stayed put thus far.

Richardson, Dean—December 27, 1927; Manufacturers—that's his bank.

He runs Manufacturers National Corp., the area's third-largest bank holding company. The outfit's assets are just above the $9-billion mark, trailing the competitors at Comerica by only $1-billion.

A native of West Branch, he picked up a bachelor's degree from Michigan State and a law degree from the University of Michigan before beginning his career that same year with Industrial National Bank—Detroit. Richardson stayed put when Manufacturers bought out Industrial two years later. He made a quick rise during the '60s, with four promotions in as many years from 1966 to 1969. That last bump made him president. Four years later he became chairman of the board.

Riegle, Donald—February 4, 1938; losing youth and gaining power.

As a young man, Donald Riegle thought he'd be president one day, and some took him seriously. He's older now. If he has national political ambitions, he keeps them to himself. But as a U.S. senator beginning his third term, he is no less fiery. And as chairman of the U.S. Senate Banking-Housing and Urban Affairs Committee, he's somebody to deal with in the Senate. Riegle pushed hard for Chrysler's loan guarantees in the early '80s, and has done yeoman's work gathering federal grants for Michigan cities. He also has scored three victories against Republican challengers, which would seem to indicate his seat is safe.

A graduate of the University of Michigan (BA, 1960) and Michigan State University (MBA, 1961), he was elected to Congress as a Republican from Flint in 1966. His liberal views (liberal, at least, in comparison to most Republicans) made him a little uncomfortable. So he became a Democrat in 1973. He won the party's Senate nomination three years later against two long-established Democrats, Secretary of State Richard Austin and Congressman James O'Hara.

A wildly ideological *Detroit News* launched an attack on Riegle when he ran in the general election later that year. Some romantic talk between Riegle and a lover had been captured on tape, and the *News* reprinted transcripts. The articles disgusted people, all right—disgusted them about the *News'* ridiculously partisan attack.

At one time, Riegle himself was considered something of an ideologue on the liberal side. The *Washington Post* reported that his speeches could empty a Senate chamber. That reputation has been tempered somewhat. He now is seen as a hard-driving Democratic stalwart with plenty of accomplishments to point to.

Robinson, Jack—February 26, 1930—biggest link in Perry chain.

Robinson started Perry Drugs in 1957 with $200 of his own money and help from relatives and suppliers. (His first store, at the corner of Perry and East Boulevard in Pontiac, was named after the street. "Perry" was $225 cheaper in neon than "Robinson.") Now the company is the leading player in the country's fourth biggest chain drugstore market.

The company's biggest shareholder with some 15 percent of the stock, Robinson had some cranky investors to deal with in the late '80s. The company lost $7.9-million in 1987, its first loss ever. He mollified shareholders somewhat when he sold Perry's auto parts subsidiary for $51-million. The company lost $29.9-million in 1988, and *Eugene Applebaum*'s Arbor Drugs Inc. is yapping at Robinson's feet.

Big in Oakland County society circles, Robinson has other board meetings to attend when he's not running the store: He was named chairman of the 1984 Allied Jewish Campaign, and was named "Entrepreneur of the Year" in 1983 by the Harvard Business School Club of Detroit. He's also on the board of Highland Appliance.

Robinson, William "Smokey" — February 19, 1940; Motown stalwart.

After *Berry Gordy Jr.*, he's probably the second most important reason for Motown's success. Besides his own wildly successful singing career (five Top 40 albums on his own in 1975-'82, five with the Miracles in 1965-'69), he also wrote many of Motown's biggest hits. Among them: "My Girl," "Don't Mess with Bill," "The Way You Do The Things You Do," and "It's Growing."

A graduate of Detroit Northern High School, Robinson joined up with Berry Gordy in 1958. He was named a v.p. of Motown in 1963, and he remains one of Gordy's biggest defenders.

Romney, George—January 8, 1907; clean-living maverick.

He went from chairman of a second-tier auto company to governor of Michigan to serious presidential candidate in six years.

Romney was considered a bit of a maverick in both the automotive and political fields. For one thing, as a Mormon, he didn't smoke or drink—in an era when filtered cigarets were new and light beer hadn't been invented. As top man at American Motors Corp., he gave America one of its first successful small cars: the 1950 Rambler. Later, he offered a Washington congressional committee a formula for breaking up General Motors. As chairman of Citizens for Michigan in the late 1950s, he pushed for reform of Michigan's antiquated constitution. He said he was entirely non-partisan—which raised eyebrows in both parties. Republicans didn't know what to make of him, and Democrats were suspicious. When he was elected as a delegate to the constitutional convention—a gathering that launched not only Romney's career, but that of an east-side Detroit politician named *Coleman Young*—he finally declared himself a Republican.

Romney's first gubernatorial victory in 1962, over incumbent Democratic Gov. John Swainson, came with barely 51 percent of the votes. His victories over Neil Stabler and Zolton Ferency in 1964 and 1966, respectively, yielded booming 56 percent and 61 percent margins.

That gave him national political ambitions. But a throwaway line on television gadfly Lou Gordon's show (Romney saying he had been "brainwashed" about Vietnam by the military establishment) put the lid on his ambitions. Gordon saw to it that the "brainwash" tape made it to the local *New York Times* correspondent in time for Sunday editions. And that was that.

Nowadays, he dotes on his grandkids in Bloomfield Hills and issues an occasional political pronouncement.

Roselle, June (April 1, 1930) and Robert (August 18, 1925); City Hall clout, past and present.

June Roselle is one of *Mayor Young*'s top appointees/fund-raisers. Robert was a top gun at city hall under mayors Jerome Cavanagh and Roman Gribbs, highly regarded and nicknamed "The Silver Fox." These days, he's the top financial man at the Lintas: Campbell-Ewald ad agency.

June Roselle is a rarity: a Gribbs staffer who held on after Young took office. She began dabbling in politics as a housewife, helping Gribbs on a couple of campaigns. When the kids left home, she took Gribbs up on his offer of a job in the City Assessor's Office.

Some three years later, Gribbs was gone. But there's always room for someone who is well-organized and adept at picking the pockets of potential campaign contributors. Young liked what he saw. She was good on follow-through, in an administration that notoriously lacks that trait. And she's expert at throwing the elegant little party that can make contributors feel like they got something for their money.

While June Roselle was walking into City Hall, husband-to-be Bob Roselle was walking out. He started as a payroll clerk in the Department of Transportation after World War II. Roselle catapulted into top budget jobs when mayors Cavanagh and Gribbs realized what they had. He quit in 1973 for a job at Campbell-Ewald the same year Young was elected, but before anybody had guessed who might become mayor.

The two married after their respective spouses died. They are loyal to their friends, they know everybody, and they know where the money is. In a large small town such as Detroit, this makes them invaluable to their employers.

Ross, Diana—March 26, 1944; the glamour girl from the projects.

Consider Diana Ross's success: As a Supreme, she and her two colleagues had 19 Top 40 *Billboard* LPs, including three that hit No. 1. After going solo in 1970, Ross recorded another 17 Top 40 LPs. The way *Billboard* calculates it, using a complicated mathematical system that involves numbers of LPs and their relative position on the charts, the Supremes have been more successful than Ray Charles, and Diana Ross as a soloist has had more clout than John Denver.

Ross grew up in the Brewster Projects, auditioning for Berry Gordy as a member of the Primettes in 1960. Gordy changed the group's name to the Supremes. Within four years, the group had recorded three No. 1 singles ("Where Did Our Love Go," "Baby Love" and "Come See About Me"). It was inevitable that the star of the show would go out on her own — which she did in 1970. She also did some screen work, getting an Academy Award nomination for "Lady Sings the Blues," in which she played singer Billie Holiday. (Liza Minnelli got the Oscar for "Cabaret.") She appeared in two other films, including "Mahogany" and "The Wiz." Berry Gordy wasn't doing her any favors by having Ross—then sliding into middle age—play a teenager in "The Wiz." She hasn't done another movie since.

Her switch to RCA wasn't particularly successful. She had only three Top 40 *Billboard* LPs there, one apiece in the years between 1982 thru 1984. She returned to Motown in 1989 as both a recording artist and a key stockholder. She now lives in a Connecticut mansion with her three daughters, and two sons by her latest marriage to a Danish millionaire.

Ross, Lou—March 23, 1932; Ford globalist.

Lou Ross's turf at Ford is intercontinental. As executive v.p. in charge of the company's international automotive operations, he's in charge of everything automotive beyond our shores. He is famous at Ford for his early hours, reportedly arriving at his twelfth-floor Glass House office as early as 4 a.m. Colleagues describe him as decent, very bright, shy and a bit of a technoid.

Ross, a Wayne State grad with an MBA from Michigan State, joined the company in 1955 as a research engineer. He worked his way through the technical ranks, laboring on the Thunderbird in the early '60s. He stretched his resumé a bit with stops in Ford's parts division and Brazil before settling in at North American operations in 1979.

In the late '70s, when most people barely knew his name, word got out that Ross was a riser. The prediction was true. He was tapped for a seat on the board in 1985, the same year he got his current job, started his fourth decade at the company, and joined the ranks of the five highest-paid execs at Ford.

In the fall of 1985, when there were difficulties at the Atlanta plant where the Taurus and Sable were to be produced, it was Ross who decided not to force the manufacturing people. The ads were ready. The dealers were ready. Everybody was ready but the factory people, the people who count the most. In a different era, Ford would have pushed the cars out the factory gate, ready or not. Ross didn't do that with Taurus/Sable. Job One rolled out in December instead of September, but consumers got a prize-winning car that didn't lose parts every time it hit a bump. It made the automotive history books, partly because of Ross's courage.

The guy who preceded Ross in his job was *Allan Gilmour*. Those two will move up another rung—together.

Ryan, Tom—July 28, 1942; WOMC-FM deejay/Count Scary.

Ryan added the phrase "oooooh, that's scary" to the Detroit lexicon. As the joke-cracking vampire Count Scary, he brought sky-high ratings to both Channels 4 and 50. His soothing, guy-next-door style brings decent numbers to WOMC-FM in the morning.

Ryan grew up in the Herman Gardens projects alongside the Southfield Freeway and was a member of the University of Detroit's basketball squad in the early '60s. "I played guard and left out," he jokes. Realizing that his 6'2" frame wouldn't earn him a living in the National Basketball Association, he chose radio instead. Deejay *Dick Purtan*, who worked the 10 p.m.—1 a.m. shift at WKNR-AM in the mid-'60s, was vastly entertained by the young mailboy who could do voices when he wasn't doing his job—sweeping the floor and answering the phone. Ryan would call in with different voices when things got slow. The Purtan/Ryan combo turned into one of the more successful partnerships in modern Detroit radio. With Purtan talking and Ryan producing and providing occasional voices, the two cooked up some wonderfully perceptive local humor. That partnership lasted through two of Purtan's subsequent station switches—to WXYZ-AM and CKLW-AM. The two parted ways when Purtan quit CKLW to join WCZY-FM.

Ryan struck out on his own and got canned by CKLW after doing a year of mornings sans Purtan, but was rescued from the scrap heap by WOMC-FM in 1984. Ryan's Count Scary, seen in a series of local TV specials, was a Detroit humor classic. He transported himself about town in the Scarymobile—a pink 1955 Chrysler Imperial. He was forever fighting with his crew, and always had problems with his evil, preppie brother—Val Scary, the Vampire with the foot-long alligator on his cape. When things got too tough for the Count, he'd yell: "The heck with this scary stuff. Let's dance." The ratings for Channel 4 and 50 were wonderful.

Ryan will have to place his vampire duds in mothballs for awhile. Channel 4 officials threatened to sue Channel 50 if they trotted out the Count for some Halloween shows. It's preposterous to think that Channel 4 could stop anybody from marching around in a vampire outfit. But weak-kneed Channel 50 execs took the threat seriously. So it's down for The Count.

Ryder, Mitch—born 1947, date not available; grandfather of blue-eyed soul.

Before Hall and Oates, Bruce Springsteen or even *Bob Seger*, there was Mitch Ryder. He translated black rhythm and blues into an idiom that was acceptable for white greasers, particularly on Detroit's east side between 1965 and 1967, until his fans went psychedelic and put him out of work. Now that the former hippies are into materialism, they still remember his work. They'll even buy his CDs from time to time.

Ryder performed as though in mid-seizure. His scream would boil the skin off a Teamster's neck, though it was never quite as blood-curdling as Wilson Pickett's. With the pointy-toed shoes, the greased-back hair, the tough-guy attitude and high-voltage performance, Ryder had it all. The schtick gave him an impressive string of hits between 1965 and 1967: "Jenny Take a Ride," "Little Latin Lupe Lu," "Devil with a Blue Dress On" and "Sock It to Me Baby." His decline coincided with the Summer of Love in 1967. He simply didn't ride with the times when his fans found flower power.

The Warren native still gets respect: Springsteen does Ryder when he does Detroit, and *Was (Not Was)* brought Ryder on stage for a rendition of "Bow Wow Wow" at Was (Not Was)'s triumphant return to Detroit in 1988.

S

Sachs, Sam II—November 30, 1935; minister of art.

The bickering at the Detroit Institute of Arts stopped about the time Sam Sachs walked in the door in September 1985. Fred Cummings, the previous director, had gotten into snits with the folks at city hall (who pay part of the DIA's budget), his staff and just about anybody else who came near him. Cummings' reign had more the texture of a hockey game than a still life. So Cummings had to go. Sachs' reign has resembled a genteel tennis match, which is as it should be. A few art snobs moan from time to time about some of Sachs' popular tastes, but one just can't please some people.

He started out at Harvard as, of all things, a chemistry major. But, as he told *News* staffer Joy Hakanson Colby: "I didn't want to continue in that field. I took some art history courses because they interested me. When I graduated from college (in 1957) I took a job at the Minneapolis Institute as a general assistant selling postcards in the museum shop. It was serendipitous. I made the decision at that time to stay in museum work."

After further study at New York University and the University of Michigan, where he worked as an art history prof, Sachs landed back in Minneapolis in 1964, rising to director in 1973—a post he held until Detroit called in 1985. Only the DIA's ninth director, his forté is 19th and 20th Century European and American Art. A few things have changed since he got here. The brass on the door gleams, and there are few of those intramural clashes that marked Cummings' tenure.

Oh, the grousing. Some people didn't like Andrew Wyeth's "Helga" paintings. So what if the art snobs don't like Wyeth much. Helga drew 91,000 people.

Sales, Soupy (a.k.a. Milton Supman)—January 8, 1926; pie-throwing Picasso.

Some of us assemble cars for a living. Some of us write newspaper stories. And some of us get hit in the face with pies. Nobody has done it as successfully as Soupy Sales. Soupy, with his cohorts White Fang (the Meaneast Dog in all of Deee-troit) and Black Tooth (the town's sweetest pooch) sewed a manic stitch in the fabric of every Baby Boomer's childhood.

Sales began his show at Channel 7 in 1953. The advice he gave kiddies ranged from the goofy ("Be true to your teeth and they won't be false to you.") to the practical ("When you are in the car with Daddy, don't shout or climb all over him."). By 1955, he had gotten so big that the fledgling ABC-TV network used Sales' show as a summer replacement for "Kukla, Fran and Ollie" from 7 p.m.-7:15 p.m. Monday through Friday. His punishing schedule in those early days included a 45-minute kids' show at 11:45 a.m. and a half-hour gig for adults at 11 p.m. At night he'd play Charles Vichyssoise, a berserk French crooner who was always fighting with his piano player. The network also used him on Saturday afternoons in "Lunch with Soupy Sales." By the time he left Detroit in 1960, it appeared Soupy would, indeed, make a big splash.

Somehow, it never quite happened. He did a quick stint as host of the "Tonight Show" in 1962 between the Paar and Carson eras. He also worked as a regular on Sha Na Na's musical variety show (1978-

'81) and syndicated his kiddy stuff from time to time. Numerous endeavors started out successfully, but fell like, well, a meringue.

For the record, the first person to be hit by a Soupy-propelled pie was Sonny Eliot. Frank Sinatra was hit, too. Today's Soupy, working the fringes of Hollywood and New York, doesn't look all that different from the one who worked Channel 7 in 1953.

Schembechler, Glenn "Bo"—April 1, 1929; maize and blue demigod.

The worst crack freak's addiction pales in comparison to the average University of Michigan football fan. At last count, more than 100,000 crazed football hounds had packed themselves into U-M Stadium for 85 consecutive games. Orchestrating the spectacle, like a Caesar in headphones, is Glenn "Bo" Schembechler.

"There are fans who have been eating breakfast at the same place, parking in the same spot, sitting in the same seat, and having dinner in the same place since they've been undergrads," says Keith Molin, U-M director of communications. "It's the thing to do." The fans give thumbs down on occasion, but that doesn't happen usually until the Rose Bowl. In 20 years of coaching, Bo has won 89 percent of U-M's home games, and 79 percent overall.

Part of Bo's power is tradition. In the 1989 season he'll go against his third Ohio State coach and his fifth field general at Michigan State University. Some students who were born when Bo assumed the helm are seniors now. "Continuity leads to stability," says Molin, "and stability leads to tradition." (All of this, of course, is in the U-M mold. In 91 years, it has had only 11 presidents and six athletic directors—the latest, of course, being Bo.)

Schembechler joined U-M from Miami of Ohio in January 1969, which makes him the senior coach in Big Ten football. He apprenticed under Ara Parseghian at Northwestern and Woody Hayes (twice) at Ohio State. "Bo is one of the most intense people I have ever known," Parseghian told *News* sports columnist Joe Falls. "He is always striving for perfection." Falls on Bo: "Bo Schembechler is almost scary. You can see his intensity, and you can feel it. You can feel it burning inside him like a white-hot flame and you ask yourself: 'Is this what it takes to be a great football coach anymore?' " He has paid a price. There have been two heart bypass operations and one heart attack.

He is not always popular. U-M fans are forever excoriating him for losing in the Rose Bowl, as he has done seven out of nine times, and for playing a dull hand. Entering his third decade at the helm, the dullness has been diminishing. Either way—by air or by ground—he wins.

Oh yes, he's also athletic director of arguably the most successful college program in history, courtesy of Don Canham. How important is that new hat to Coach Bo? Well, he turned it down at first when a string attached said he'd have to step down as football coach after a season. Nobody tells General George Patton Schembechler to pack it in when he's not ready.

Schervish, David (April 1, 1945); Vogel, Steven (December 24, 1940); Merz, Charles (March 16, 1945); architects on the rise.

These three University of Detroit grads have, in one short decade, become major players in Detroit architecture. Incredibly well connected, they seem to be city hall's firm of choice, plucking the few plums the city fathers hang out on the development tree these days. The Schervish Vogel Merz firm designed Chene Park and the Detroit Zoo's chimpanzee exhibit, and has a number of other things on the drawing boards.

Schervish handles the company books, Vogel does overall office administration and Merz develops new business. They work out of a refurbished carriage house not far from the eastern edge of downtown Detroit.

Schmidt, Chuck—January 22, 1947; dollars and cents, not x's and o's.

Agents looking for big bucks for Lions players must deal with Chuck Schmidt, the team's v.p./finance. The official bio on Schmidt says he "is charged with the crucial, yet often thankless task of signing the Lions' draft choices." *Often* thankless? Name one thank. Nonetheless, the Lions were the only NFL team to have all their draftees signed before training camp in 1987 and '88.

A Detroit native, he earned three letters at the University of Michigan in—of all things—baseball. While there, he majored in business, then picked up an additional sheepskin in finance from Wayne State University. The Lions picked him up after he spent five years at the Ernst and Whinney accounting firm.

Discussions of who might be *Russ Thomas'* successor often involve two names: *Jerry Vainisi*, the v.p./player personnel, and Schmidt. Vainisi has some impressive football credentials, but Schmidt knows the team's books. In modern corporate sports, that counts for something.

Schmidt, Jimmy—February 11, 1955; kitchen whiz kid.

This slight, blond, bearded chef/businessman is the Rattlesnake Club's engine. He slaves away in his trademark baseball cap at his establishment in Stroh River Place. For a while, his horizons extended far beyond the Detroit River. He was also the founding force behind the Denver Rattlesnake Club and the Adirondacks in Washington, D.C. In 1989 he gave up interest in those foreign outposts to concentrate his energies on the Detroit operation. Not yet 35, he has been profiled in the *New York Times* and is expanding his entrepreneurial realm.

He didn't start out as a "foodie." He studied electrical engineering in his home state at the University of Illinois and fooled with fast cars. Eager to get a look at France, he chanced upon a magazine article that fortuitously suggested a chef's school in Avignon. Until then, he had no thoughts of becoming a chef. But it turned out he had more talent behind a wheel of cheese than behind the wheel of a Ferrari. He learned. As he told the *Times*' Craig Claiborne: "The greatest thing I learned was the sense of taste, how to harmonize flavors, and the search for quality."

Schmidt returned to the United States in 1975 as a protegé of Madeleine Kamman, a cookbook author and teacher. Cooking on weekends at Kamman's Boston restaurant, he attended her chef's school and graduated at the top of his class. The late Lester Gruber named Schmidt executive chef of the London Chop House in 1977. Schmidt was all of 22.

There is no telling how long the relationship would have lasted if Gruber, who was into his 70s, hadn't sold the Chop to Max and Lanie Pincus. Schmidt left in 1985 to create his own restaurant in Denver. The first Rattlesnake Club did exceedingly well. So Schmidt returned to transplant the magic in his adopted hometown. He opened Detroit's Rattlesnake Club in June 1988 amid as much publicity as any restaurant here has seen.

Not content with two places, he opened a third in Washington, D.C., in January 1989. Only months later, he and his partners decided on an amicable divorce. Which means Jimmy's frequent-flier mileage went down and close attention to the Detroit eatery went up.

Schultz, Robert—May 22, 1930; plugged in at GM.

As an executive v.p. at General Motors, he monitors much of GM's non-automotive efforts. Electronic Data Systems (EDS), GM Hughes Electronic Corp. and Delco Electronic Corp. are all on his watch.

Michigan State University-educated Schultz went a couple miles up the road to join Oldsmobile as a college grad-in-training in 1955, two years after earning his BS in mechanical engineering. He patiently camped out at Olds through the '60s and '70s (adding an MBA from MSU to his wall in 1969) before he got a call from GM headquarters to become chief massager of emission controls in 1977. He got the chief engineer's job at Buick a year later, making stops at three other tech jobs before getting the biggest promotion of his career—chief of the Chevrolet-Pontiac-Canada group. He got his latest boost in early 1989.

Schwartz, Alan E.—December 21, 1925; boardroom habitué.

This legal patriarch has the best Rol-o-dex in town. He sits on all the right boards (Comerica, Michigan Bell, Detroit Edison, etc.), is a force with the Detroit Symphony Orchestra and headed *Mayor Young*'s Strategic Planning Commission. Put it this way: when Schwartz steps in for lunch at the Detroit Club, he gets a wide berth.

Schwartz earned it himself. The son of a Russian immigrant, he attended Cranbrook, the exclusive Bloomfield Hills institution that later gave us such disparate products as writer *Tom McGuane* and All-World jock Pete Dawkins. Schwartz went on to the University of Michigan and Harvard Law School. He walked away with all imaginable kudos, including a magna cum laude key and editorship of Harvard's law review. Arriving back in Detroit in 1952, he helped build the Honigman, Miller, Schwartz & Cohn law firm, the most prestigious Detroit legal shop begun in the last 40 years. The firm, which now has about 225 lawyers, boasts a very nice list of clients that includes the *Free Press* and Arbor Drugs.

Schwartz seems to know everybody, but he would never be mistaken for a glad-handing Babbit. He is the consummate behind-the-scenes operator who tells no tales—especially to reporters. He's important to the Republican money machine, and is a large presence in Jewish philanthropic circles. To have a phone call returned from Alan Schwartz more or less means you've made it. He rarely appears in court, preferring to leave that to the litigation experts at Honigman-Miller. His advice, which is said to be very expensive, is given quietly in the confines of the boardroom.

Schweitzer, Peter—August 31, 1939; shepherd of the Ford ad account.

He's J. Walter Thompson's man in Detroit, which means keeping JWT's sacred Ford account in the fold. This hasn't been easy. Following Britain's WPP Group takeover of JWT in 1987, pieces of the Ford account fell off. Nine of the automaker's European accounts drifted to Ogilvy & Mather, while Young & Rubicam got Canada. The $300-million domestic account stayed with JWT, where it has been since 1943. Which meant Schweitzer didn't have to hurl himself from atop the Renaissance Center.

The son of a Battle Creek construction company president, he hooked up with General Foods Corp. in marketing management upon graduation from the University of Michigan in 1961. Like many peripatetic marketers, he kept moving. He prepped himself for the ad biz with an MBA from Western Michigan University in 1967, and joined Grey Advertising two years later. Next came a stop at Kenyon and Eckhardt, from where he jumped ship to JWT in 1975. Schweitzer was watching the agency's Eastman Kodak account in New York when he was packed off to Detroit in 1986.

A Big Promotion came in the summer of '88: JWT's vice-chairmanship, making him No. 2 at the agency worldwide. That means watching JWT's 184 offices in 37 countries from his Ren Cen office overlooking the Detroit River. But the main thing—maybe the only thing—is keeping Ford execs smiling. He spends maybe 60 percent of his time here. The rest he splits between New York City and JWT outposts.

Leisure time is spent on his 30-foot sailboat, the Nonsuch, Bodacious. His office is filled with sailing memorabilia, and he has done the Newport-to-Bermuda race. He sports a beard, as do many JWT types. As the *New York Times* once observed, "So many top Thompson executives have beards that they resemble a 19th-Century baseball team."

Scott, George C.—Oct. 18, 1927; raucous Redford High School grad.

Although born in Virginia, Scott's father (later an Ex-Cello-O vice-president) moved the family to Detroit when George was a youngster. Scott joined the Marines, did a little acting, but mostly drank too much and fought in bars during his 20s. By age 30 he had brought himself around enough to act in Shakespeare's "Richard III," a Joseph Papp production that brought him national attention. The moviegoing public got an eyeful with his portrayal of a flinty-eyed, cynical gambler in "The Hustler" (1961).

Several years later into stardom, he tried to repay a debt to his hometown by forming the Theatre of Michigan (TOM) in the early '60s. Figuring that Broadway needed a shot of fresh blood, he came up with a scheme: He'd cast and rehearse his plays here in Detroit, then move them to New York City. Broadway didn't want the transfusion, so TOM went bust. Scott personally repaid the debt.

His work speaks for itself. Hired to portray General George S. Patton, he had caps made for his teeth to match Patton's tobacco-stained choppers. He read everything available on the man, and practically wore out the film documentaries that were given to him for study. Scott received an Academy Award for his trouble, but he refused the honor. He called the awards "an orgy of self-adulation." Others roles include another general, Buck Turgidson in "Dr. Strangelove," and leads in "Hardcore," "Day of the Dolphin" and "The New Centurions."

Although he is considered an artist, he's not averse to doing a job or two for the loot. American Motors Corp. once paid him $1-million to appear in an ad campaign. Although long gone from Detroit, he's a Detroit Tigers fanatic of considerable seniority over *Tom Selleck*.

Scott's fifth marriage, this one in 1972 to actress Trish Van Devere, finally took, and his life is said to be much more peaceful, thank you.

Scribner, Edgar—April 1, 1932; Teamster on the rise.

This Teamster was named to replace Tom Turner as chief of the metro Detroit AFL-CIO. That means keeping peace among the various labor organizations in town.

A native of Oakland City, Indiana, he spent most of his early career (1951-'71) as a *Free Press* circulation district manager. He picked up a degree from Wayne State University's Institute of Labor and Industrial Relations along the way and got himself very involved with Teamsters Local 372, which represents drivers at the newspaper. (As any reporter will tell you, Local 372 is the only union that can stop a Detroit newspaper from publishing.) Scribner was local president for eight years (1972-'80) before going full-time with Teamsters Joint Council 43, which represents just about all truck drivers in the area.

Seger, Bob—May 6, 1945; working class hero.

The Motor City can't get enough of this rock star. Seger filled Cobo Hall for seven consecutive nights in 1987. Detroiters in their early 40s remember Seger as the guy who played "East Side Story" on Robin Seymour's "Swingin' Time" television show, or the guy who played the Hideout in the mid-1960s, or who played a free concert on Belle Isle as late as 1972. Fans in their 30s might recall him as the "Nutbush City Limit" man. Those in their 20s and teens think he's the guy who began singing songs for movies like "Risky Business" and "Beverly Hills Cop II."

His popularity was generally confined to the Midwest in the mid-1960s. But his first album, "Ramblin' Gamblin' Man," took him national, going to number 17 on the *Billboard* Top 20 chart in early 1969. There were times in the early 1970s when he looked like he might become a mere regional star again, or an answer on a Motor City rock trivia quiz. But he got hot again with 1976's "Live Bullet." "Against the Wind" (1980) held the No. 1 spot on *Billboard*'s LP chart, and spent 43 weeks in all in a Top 40 slot. Seven LPs in 11 years (1976-'86) isn't bad.

Briefly married twice (once for less than a year in 1968, another time for a year to actress Annette Sinclair in 1987-'88), he likes to pal around with road manager Bill Blackwell, or Eagle *Glenn Frey*. When he isn't in the Detroit area, he's commuting to either northern Michigan (summer) or L.A. (winter). Although the society mavens would love to have him on the charity circuit, he's not interested. Seger showed up at *Tom Monaghan*'s Drummond Island extravaganza in fall 1987. He even dressed in a tuxedo and had dinner with Tigers pitcher Jack Morris. But the sight of all those swells made him nervous, so he helicoptered back home before the rest of the crowd.

Selleck, Tom—January 29, 1945; east-side hunk.

Five-0 is gone. Now, so is Magnum. But Tom Selleck, the ex-Grosse Pointer, remains Hawaii's most famous detective. Where Jack Lord, in "Hawaii Five-O," never cracked a smile, the better-looking Selleck had a self-effacing sense of humor that sat well with viewers. That helped take him out of the realm of hunkdom and near the superstar category.

Selleck, the son of an investment banker, grew up in Grosse Pointe. The family moved to the West Coast, and Selleck played basketball at the University of Southern California while moonlighting as a model. He turned down Harrison Ford's role in "Raiders of the Lost Ark." It's hard to decide if that was a good move or not. "Raiders" was good cinema, but "Magnum" provided continuous and lucrative years of employment between 1980 and '88.

"Magnum" ran out its string, finally, leaving Selleck to wonder what he'd do next. Critics were having doubts about his viability on the large screen after "High Road to China" (1982) and "Runaway" (1984). But after the success of "Three Men and a Baby," Hollywood doubts no more.

Seneker, Stan—May 10, 1931; keeper of Ford's checkbook.

As Ford's chief financial officer, he has the enviable job of sitting on $10-billion in cash and marketable securities. What to do?

A native of Bristol, Tennessee (Tennessee Ernie Ford's hometown), a burg on the Virginia border, he went west to school and swam competitively at Santa Clara (California) University. After landing a master's degree in industrial management from the University of Pennsylvania's renowned Wharton School, he signed with Ford as a cost analyst in 1957. He labored in a variety of financial jobs and rose to president of Ford's credit and finance subsidiaries in 1984. Two years later he was named treasurer, then got his current job (executive v.p./chief financial officer) on October 19, 1987. If the date sounds familiar, it should: That was the day Wall Street crashed, with the New York Stock Exchange dropping 508 points. He made lemonade out of lemons by buying back some of Ford's stock at rock-bottom prices.

These days, Seneker is such a hero that the *New York Times* made him a cover boy on one of its magazines. The headline read: "SUPERSTARS. Chief financial officers command power and status.

Ford's Stanley Seneker rides herd on $10 billion in cash." Some PR guy undoubtedly got a bonus for that one.

The best detectors of fraud in any corporation are low-level clerks and secretaries. They are savvy judges of character, and know who is up and who is down before the principals themselves figure it out. Seneker's biggest fans are the low-level folks. That tells you the man has character.

Shine, Neal—September 14, 1930; soul of the *Free Press*.

Shine is the keeper of the institutional flame at 321 W. Lafayette. In a highly transient business, he has chosen to stay at one newspaper for his entire four-decade career. Longevity and impressive recall of Detroit lore give the paper a sense of history and heart that few news institutions have. He remembers Bill Bonds as a punk radio reporter, knows what it's like to work for a living (his dad was a streetcar conductor in Detroit) and has a feel for Motor City life that many highly paid newspaper editors don't possess. He is no less than the paper's heart and soul. That, along with the weekly public television talk show he hosts, give Shine "local hero" status.

Although he has chosen to teach at Oakland University and write one less column a week, his thumbprint will remain for decades.

The son of Irish immigrants, Shine is a product of Detroit's east side. He joined the *Freep* as a copyboy in 1950, though his goal at the time was not necessarily to become senior managing editor and columnist at a large newspaper. Mostly, as a University of Detroit student, he was looking for beer money. His finely honed Irish wit and impeccable news instincts guided him up through about every city desk job and into the paper's executive ranks by the mid-'60s. As city editor, he guided the *Freep* to a Pulitzer Prize for its coverage of the 1967 riots. In 1971 he succeeded Frank Angelo as managing editor, which gave Shine a chuckle because Angelo once told him to forget about a future in newspapers.

Job offers came Shine's way often, but he is a loyalist. Knight-Ridder, which sends an ever-changing train of execs here with a Fodor's guide to Detroit, should feel lucky to have had him.

Simon, Howard—August 11, 1943; defender of everybody's rights.

He's executive director of the American Civil Liberties Union of Michigan. That means fighting for human rights, even when it means running smack against the grain of popular opinion. Simon's group opposed drug testing and sobriety check lanes on grounds people have a basic right to be left alone unless they're suspected by officials of breaking the law. He also fought to have a Nativity scene removed from in front of Dearborn City Hall. Somehow, the fact that Simon was trying to get government out of the religion business was lost in the translation.

A native of New York, Simon earned a Ph.D. in philosophy from the University of Minnesota. Before coming to Detroit he taught at Minnesota and at DePauw University, one month after Dan Quayle departed the Indiana school. He was pondering law school when he came to Michigan in 1974 to take over as chief of the state's ACLU chapter. He never got his law degree, but the ACLU got the man it needed. Contributions went up in the Simon years, which meant the ACLU could finance a few more court fights.

Simon is branded a troublemaker, but he sees that as his job. "I think we are the most authentic conservative organization around," he once told a reporter. "If conservatism means anything, it's trying to defend traditional principles, and I don't know of any other organization trying to preserve basic 19th Century American principles."

Sinclair, John—October 2, 1941; faded flower of the '60s.

Sinclair organized the 1967 "Love In" at Belle Isle, managed the MC5 rock band and got under parents' skin by allowing high schoolers to hang around his Artists Workshop at John Lodge and Warren. There, they could read volumes on Eastern religion or poetry. "It's good for these kids to be reading poetry and literature and discussing life," he observed at the time. "It's better than riding around in cars or watching television." You can't argue with the logic, although it probably wasn't the poetic part of the hippie lifestyle that bothered the parents.

Sinclair truly became a counter-culture symbol after his arrest in early 1967 for giving two joints to undercover cops three days before Christmas in 1966. Being his third conviction, Sinclair was hit with the maximum 10-year prison term by Detroit Recorder's Court Judge Robert Colombo. The late John Lennon showed up for an all-star Free John Sinclair benefit that included *Bob Seger*, *Stevie Wonder* and Commander Cody and his Lost Planet Airmen. Sinclair eventually spent 29 months in prison. The Michigan Supreme Court voided the conviction in 1972. A couple of the judges ruled that the jail term was "cruel and unusual" punishment, a third believed Sinclair had been entrapped.

The '70s and '80s found him running the now-defunct *Detroit Sun* newspaper, promoting jazz concerts, dabbling in radio and writing poetry.

Slade, Roy—July 14, 1933; Cranbrook arts czar.

This fiery Wales native is president of the Cranbrook Academy of Arts. He injected life into the place, which had settled into a bit of torpor when he got there in 1977. Energetic, patriarchal and possessing a head of wavy gray hair, he would stand out in any crowd.

A graduate of the University of Wales and Cardiff College of Art, he ran the Corcoran Gallery of Art in Washington, D.C., from 1969-'77. He had decided that he simply wasn't having fun any more when Cranbrook offered, as he put it, "money, security and an academic schedule." So he signed up to run the troubled academy. It had begun to fade somewhat since Eliel Saarinen's death in 1950. By Cranbrook's 60th anniversary in 1983, enough luster had returned that a retrospective ("Design in America: The Cranbrook Vision 1925–1950") impressed the arts crowds in New York, Paris, London and Helsinki. One overwrought Washington writer dubbed the 360-acre Cranbrook complex "the most enchanted and enchanting setting in America."

Slade lives in a five-bedroom house designed by Saarinen. Every night, Slade falls asleep realizing he is a very lucky man.

Smith, Alan—April 21, 1931; chairman Smith redux?

This Smith is related to the current General Motors chairman only by history and proximity, which may be enough. He is always mentioned as a candidate for the top job when chairman *Roger Smith* steps aside in 1990. Ever since Alfred P. Sloan Jr. sculpted the modern GM in 1937, the chairmanship has been the province of financial types. Alan Smith, who is quite handy with an abacus, certainly qualifies on that count.

A product of Dartmouth's prestigious Amos Tuck School (class of '52), Smith joined GM after mustering out of the Navy in 1956. By his mid-30s he was receiving promotions every two or three years, spiraling into a seat on the board of directors in 1981. Except for two years as chief bigwig with the company's Canadian subsidiary (November 1978-January 1981), he never strayed far from his abacus. The Smith-to-Smith succession already has occurred once: Alan Smith replaced Roger in the executive v.p./finance slot. And when Alan Smith was given additional responsibilities of running the public affairs and operating staffs in June 1988, analysts raised their eyebrows: Nothing like a little non-finance experience to broaden a guy's resumé, eh? This Smith drew GM's fourth highest paycheck, $506,000, in 1987.

Normalcy at GM means an engineer in the president's office and an accountant in the biggest suite, reining in the product people. But these aren't normal times at GM. Whether Smith will rise another notch is truly a guess.

Smith, David— February 7, 1931; the warden at *Ward's*.

He's considered the dean of Detroit's auto writers. Smith, editor-in-chief of *Ward's Auto World* and editorial director of all six Ward's publications, delivers a monthly mix of analysis, profiles, technical information and industry gossip.

Ward's Auto World was one of the perches from which corporate maverick H. Ross Perot chose to fire at General Motors chairman *Roger Smith*. Perot knew full well that a message delivered through *Ward's* would be heard. Everybody in the Industry reads *Ward's*. And Perot, who gave the interview to Jon Lowell (an ex-*Newsweek* bureau man here) knew that Dave Smith wouldn't send over a rookie who'd miss the message.

A University of Michigan grad, Smith worked at the *Detroit Times*, *Toledo Blade*, the *Wall Street Journal* and as business editor at the *Free Press* before jumping into the editor's slot at *Ward's* in 1970.

An ace recruiter, Smith is somehow able to divine when talented journalists have fallen out of favor with their management, or vice-versa. Then he hires them. His staff includes two ex-*Detroit News* reporters, one ex-*Newsweek* Detroit bureau reporter and an ex-*Free Press* art director.

Smith, Gail—November 9, 1917; ad guru emeritus.

There is a little-known codicil to the state constitution that says no more than four advertising types may gather without Gail Smith being present. Readers of this book may not take that sentence seriously, but those who work in the ad industry will testify to its veracity. This retired General Motors advertising chief is every-where. He hits most of the Detroit Club Adcraft lunches, and all major industry functions.

A native of Kansas City, Smith worked in radio and with Procter & Gamble's ad department before signing up with GM in 1959. Most of the next two decades were spent as GM's general director of advertising and merchandising. That meant most of the ad agency chiefs here would gladly shine his shoes if he asked them. Smith finally retired in 1981. D'Arcy Masius Benton & Bowles, which has the Pontiac and Cadillac accounts, put him on the payroll as a consul-tant in 1981, a relationship which lasted some five years.

A longer-lasting relationship—and a harmonious one—is his mar-riage to Barbara Whiting, of the musical Whitings. Her father was a famous orchestra leader and she and sister Margaret were nationally popular singers.

Smith, John Jr.—April 6, 1938; GM's global man.

His fourth promotion in as many years made him GM's executive vice-president in charge of international operations in 1988. Figure this: GM's European operations earned more for the company in 1988—$1.8 billion—than the company's U.S. operations, which brought home $1.7 billion. With the auto business becoming more global, Smith's job will become even more important.

He signed on with the General in 1961 at the company's Framing-ham plant in his native Massachusetts. Spotted as a comer, Smith joined the company's New York financial office in 1966, then bounced around in a series of financial jobs for a decade and a half. The '80s were good to him: six promotions between 1980 and 1988, four of them between 1984 and 1988.

Barely into his 50s, you can bet this isn't his last assignment.

Smith, Otis—February 20, 1922; pioneer.

He was the first black person on the Michigan Supreme Court, then finished his career as GM's top lawyer in the '80s.

A native of Tennessee, Smith peddled newspapers and worked as a porter in the state's capitol. After earning a law degree from the Catholic University of America (1950), he landed in Flint as an assis-tant Genesee County prosecutor. His career throughout the late

1950s and '60s was marked by a series of firsts: he was appointed state auditor general by Governor G. Mennen Williams in 1959, which made Smith the first black to be named to a full-time statewide elective office since Reconstruction. Williams later appointed Smith to the Michigan Supreme Court in 1960, which also made him Michigan's first black Supreme Court justice. (There has been only one other since: Justice **Dennis Archer** who was appointed by Governor **James Blanchard** in 1986.) Smith was defeated for re-election in 1966, but wasn't on the beach long. GM hired him as a member of its legal staff. Smith also did a four-year stint on the University of Michigan Board of Regents (1967–'71), courtesy of Governor **George Romney** a Republican. That made Smith one of only a few politicians who've received appointments from opposite parties.

As an Associated Press profile put it, Smith is "a composed, mild-mannered man, [who] has an inner intensity that belies his tranquil exterior and brought him ulcers in his 20s."

Smith, Patti—December 31, 1946; punk rock priestess (retired).

She abandoned a blazing rock 'n' roll career in 1979 to settle quietly on Detroit's east side with husband Fred "Sonic" Smith, the former MC5 rhythm guitarist. There, she told writer Lisa Robinson, she works on a novel and studies 16th Century Japanese literature while raising a son and daughter.

A native of New Jersey, she broke through the New York scene of the early and mid-'70s with a single, charmingly titled "Piss Factory." With her Rimbaud-inspired poetry, she became (it seems strange to say it now) the grandmother of the punk rock scene. Her stage manner was once described as "watching a head-on collision between Dondi and Machine Gun Kelly." Smith once did a two-screen slide show which she insisted was the story of cartoon character George Jetson. One 1978 description of an Ann Arbor concert said she "strutted around smoking a joint, talking in foul language and making noise on her guitar."

While stunts like that gained her fans, they scared most record company executives—with the exception of Arista's Clive Davis. Her LP "Horses," with the single "Gloria" (1975), enjoyed moderate success. "Radio Ethiopia" did moderately well. "Easter" (with its single "Because the Night," which was written by Bruce Springsteen) was on the charts for eight weeks in 1978. Her LP "Wave," released the next year, was there for seven.

About that time, she adopted Detroit as her home. She dropped by in her usual bizarre clothing one day at the Detroit Symphony Orchestra offices and said: "Hi, I'm Pat Smith and I have a rock band." The DSO received $4,200 from two benefit concerts.

She stepped out of the house long enough to go into the studio for a 1988 album, "Dream of Life." Rock critic Ben Edmonds wrote that the record "exhibits a grace and generosity of spirit that could only have come out of the environment she constructed with husband Fred Smith."

Smith, Roger—July 12, 1925; radical in accountant's clothing.

By the time he retires from General Motors in 1990, he will have been the longest-running GM chairman since Alfred P. Sloan Jr. retired in 1956 after nearly 19 years. Whether one likes the radical change Smith wrought since taking over in 1981 or not, one must admit the place won't be the same again. Either Smith has prepared GM for the 1990s and beyond — which would make him a hero long after he retires to the hunting and fishing he loves so much; or he has reduced market share and created a less impressive GM, a Paradise Lost GM.

An Ohio native and son of a businessman, Smith went to work for the automaker just out of the University of Michigan Business School. After a tedious crawl through the corporate hierarchy, mostly in bookkeeping jobs, he took over as the company's 10th chairman.

Nobody, apparently, recognized the corporate maverick that lurked inside the bean counter. He reorganized the company's North American auto operations into two big units, Buick-Oldsmobile-Cadillac and Chevrolet-Pontiac-Canada, jolting the company to its boots. He launched Saturn Corp., the company's sixth nameplate; bought Electronic Data Systems from entrepreneur H. Ross Perot; gobbled up Hughes Aircraft Co.; and announced plans to shutter 11 U.S. assembly plants.

In the auto industry, one can't judge a chieftain's actions as wise or foolish until years after the fact. And that's certainly true of Smith. The negative side of the ledger shows that the company had 44.5 percent of the market in 1980. By the end of 1988, that number stood at 35.9. *The Gallagher Report* named him one of the 10 worst business executives of 1983, one of the 10 best of 1985, and—yes—one of the 10 worst of 1986.

Subordinates find him to be caring or infuriatingly curt — depending on the situation.

Sokol, Dr. Robert—December 18, 1941; Wayne State University's med head.

He runs Wayne State University's Medical School, which is the largest single-campus med school in the country. A native of Rochester, New York, he picked up his medical and undergraduate degrees from the University of Rochester before earning his spurs at Barnes Hospital/Washington University in St. Louis. He later made stops at Rochester and Cleveland.

Sokol's forté is research in the area of alcohol-related birth defects. He's also considered a wizard in the area of applying computer-based methodology to his field.

Sosnick, Robert—January 23, 1934; the strong silent type.

Sosnick is probably Oakland County's biggest land developer. He built the Palace of Auburn Hills, the Travelers Tower office complex and the Top of Troy office tower, among other things. He and his wife, SuSu, are major league arts patrons and members in good standing of the society crowd.

Oh so quiet with his wealth, he built the Palace without public money because having taxpayers' help meant taxpayers would pry into his business. Sosnick didn't want that.

Spina, Tony—(birthdate not available); keeps the Pope in focus.

The *Free Press*'s Tony Spina may be the most decorated press photographer in America. At last count, he had almost 500 national awards in his collection. Spina was part of the team that snared the Pulitzer Prize for the *Freep* in 1968, and his work has been exhibited in such places as the Vatican and New York City's Nikon House. Especially notable are his photographs of popes. Pope John Paul VI was so impressed with Spina's work that he conferred the title of Knight of St. Gregory the Great upon him in 1965. So it's technically correct to address the subject of this profile as Sir Tony Spina.

A Detroit native, Spina worked as chief photographer for the U.S. Navy during World War II. When the U.S. finished with the

Axis powers, Spina returned home to shoot for the *Freep* in 1946. He was named chief lensman five years later, and began collecting his honors. He won the top photo award from the Detroit Press Club for 10 consecutive years until he quit to give others a chance.

Colleagues say Spina is so effective because he works so hard. Even shooting mug shots of reporters for their press cards becomes a big deal when Spina does the job.

The biggest tribute of all is what has happened to people he has taught: Two of his charges (Taro Yamasaki and Manny Crisostomo) have won Pulitzer Prizes.

Stecher, Walter—(birthdate not available); city hall's money man.

Walter Stecher was at City Hall when Albert Cobo ran the place. He's lived through the regimes of Louis Miriani, Jerry Cavanagh, and Roman Gribbs, and he'll be there certainly when *Mayor Young* leaves office. That's all anybody needs to know about Stecher, who tells Mayor Young where the money comes from and where it goes. Probably nobody has a better handle on goings-on in city government.

He got to city hall in 1956, when Albert Cobo was in charge. Always working in the Budget Department, he caught Mayor Jerome Cavanagh's attention and rose to budget director. He switched to the city controller's job under Roman Gribbs, but was back in the budget post when Young took office in 1974. That means he knows where every nickel went since Young was elected. How does he survive? He's probably the most competent man in the building, according to insiders. He doesn't talk much, and his eyes take in more than they give out. Insiders say he has a well-concealed sense of humor, too. And that always helps.

Stella, Frank—January 21, 1919; man with fingers in a lot of civic pots.

He has co-chaired *Mayor Young*'s Casino Gaming Study Commission, raised enormous amounts of money for the Republican Party and helped Orchestra Hall come alive. That's Stella's spare time. In daylight hours, he's the man to see if you're opening a restaurant. His company, F.D. Stella Products Co., designs and distributes food-service and dining-room equipment.

The son of Italian immigrants, he graduated from the University of Detroit in 1941. During World War II he drew duty supplying everything from grub to boots to the troops. He showed so much talent at it that he decided to stay with it stateside once the Germans and Japanese were properly disposed of.

The local arts community owes him a debt for his work at Orchestra Hall. The modern history of the listening post can be written in two chapters: pre-Stella and post-Stella. Pre-Stella was largely an interesting architectural reclamation project. After Stella became involved, the joint turned into a full-fledged arts organization. He pumped some energy into the effort and corporate money followed.

He's a shooter in the Roman Catholic Church, which is at the receiving end of his generosity.

Stempel, Robert—July 15, 1933; No. 2 at No. 1.

He has the toughest job in Detroit. With General Motors' market share dipping, analysts are beginning to wonder: Will GM recover, as *Roger Smith* says it will? Or is there no bottom to GM's slide? Smith will retire in 1990, leaving Stempel to deal with the answer. And it may be an answer the gang on GM's 14th floor won't like. Probably none of Stempel's 16 predecessors have lived in such an exciting time. But then again, "May You Live in Interesting Times" is also an ancient curse.

Stempel came from the company's engineering ranks, beginning his career as a chassis detailer at Oldsmobile. He made his mark on the 1966 Olds Toronado, an early front-wheel drive car that included some engineering advances. Ed Cole, the late GM president, took a liking to Stempel and made him his surrogate in the early 1970s. "It was obvious by then that he (Stempel) was on a fast track," says one insider. Cole became heavily dependent on his protegé.

Stempel's engineering talent would have brought him somewhere near the top in any case, but Cole's assistance lubricated the upward slide. It took Stempel in turns to the top of Pontiac, then Adam Opel (GM's German arm), then Chevy, then the Buick-Oldsmobile-Cadillac group, then trucks and international operations.

His management style is described as collegial, which inspired loyalty along the way. As former GM president F. James Mc-Donald's retirement date neared, it became clear that one of two men would get McDonald's job: either Stempel or *Lloyd Reuss*, who had risen at about the same speed. The "Will it be Stempel or

Reuss" question became a favorite parlor game in mid-'80s Bloomfield Hills. Stempel, the engineer with a lot of friends, prevailed.

All eyes are on the Chrome Colossus. The company that once
sold one of every two domestic cars in any given year isn't what it
used to be. Ford Motor Co. made more money in 1986, '87 and '88.
But there is one comforting thought. "He likes automobiles," says
one GM insider. "You can't say that about some of the guys at the
top."

**Steward, Emanuel—July 7, 1944; the brains behind Kronk's head-
bashers.**

As a teenager making his first foray out of Michigan, Emanuel
Steward got a taste of the good life. While boxing at the National
Tournament of Champions, he stayed at Chicago's Conrad Hilton. It
changed his life. After perfumed soaps and linens, the grit and funk
of Detroit's east side didn't look so good. Now, as boxer *Thomas
Hearns*'s manager and king of the Kronk Gym dynasty, Steward has
all the perfumed soap and linens he needs. He has a knock-em-dead
home on Detroit's west side and a fleet of cars that would have
embarrassed the Shah of Iran. He dines at the London Chop House
with his old pal *Coleman Young*, and he counts numerous other
major politicians among his friends.

The son of a West Virginia coal miner, Steward began boxing in
Detroit at age eight. Always the hustler, he sold newspapers and ice
cream, crated groceries, and worked as a landscaper. He bought his
own car at the age of 16. He won the National Golden Gloves ban-
tamweight title in 1963, but got out of boxing the following year after
failing to find an honest, competent manager. He got into electronics,
instead, and began working his way up at Detroit Edison in 1966. He
stayed there six years, when he worked with junior boxers (age 10–
15). He later left Edison to sell insurance and cosmetics.

Hilmer Kenty, who held the lightweight title in 1980 and '81,
helped put Steward into the national arena. A number of Kronk
teammates have held titles and rankings in the byzantine world of
boxing in the '80s, but it was the Motor City Hit Man, Hearns, who
rang the big-time bell for Steward.

It's not hard to spot the Kronk, which is at the corner of McGraw
and Junction: That's the gym with the expensive cars out front.

Stroh, Peter W.—December 18, 1927; Detroit's braumeister.

The Strohs, like many old-money families in Grosse Pointe, lead quiet lives among the stately mansions. Peter Stroh, the elegant Princeton grad who took over as chief of the country's No. 3 brewery in 1980, pops up at a press conference now and then. But that's how a powerful old-money guy is supposed to act: somewhat aloof, obviously in control. He chairs Stroh Brewery Co., the state's largest privately held corporation. And if it's breeding you want, his family has been a force here since the mid-19th Century.

As a young adult, Stroh thought about becoming a CIA mole. But a runaway truck clipped him at the corner of M Street and 31st in Washington, ruining not only his legs, but any chance of becoming a spy. Oh well. He packed himself off to the family business, starting off at the brewery in 1950 as a plumber's helper on the same day his father died of lung cancer. Stroh was so good with a pipe wrench that he was promoted to president in 1968, chief exec in 1980, then chairman in 1982 when his 88-year-old uncle John died.

The fact that the Stroh company is still up and running almost a century and a half after its birth is no small feat, given the number of breweries that have fizzled out. The fact that Stroh has managed to keep the company in the family is even a bigger feat. Its sales approached $1.5-billion in 1986. The last time *Forbes* estimated the family fortune, it was said to be worth $300-million, though nobody really knows. Peter and his wife, Nicole, show at an occasional society bash, but not often. They were married in 1964 in an Episcopal church in France.

Less than a decade away from retirement, he must begin pondering weighty dynastic decisions. Perhaps he should look among the plumbers' helpers for his successor.

Sullivan, Brian—December 31, 1924; No. 1 at Law Shop No. 1.

With some 296 ornery, irascible lawyers stumbling around Dykema Gossett's 10 offices, somebody has to keep them from bumping into each other. That somebody is Brian Sullivan, who was elected as executive partner in 1981. He monitors everything from the size of the offices (which is easy—all Dykema partners have equal office space) to salaries.

A graduate of Amherst College and Harvard Law School, he joined the firm as a corporate securities specialist. Since Sullivan took over, the firm has almost tripled its roster of lawyers. Some of that growth has come from aggressive merging with other firms. It picked up some 67 lawyers by joining forces with legal shops in Detroit, Lansing, Grand Rapids, Sarasota, Ft. Lauderdale and Tampa. These days, Sullivan spends as much time thinking about marketing, the future legal needs of his clients, and how he'll grub more business for the firm in Florida (a priority these days) as he does practicing law. With that many hungry lawyers in one shop, somebody has to do it.

Szoka, Edmund Cardinal—September 14, 1927; administering to his flock.

The area's 1.5-million Roman Catholics have been taking their spiritual cues from Szoka since 1981, which makes him the most powerful clergyman in Detroit. With one quick heft of the ax, however, he has caused more controversy in his short stint as Cardinal than his predecessor, John Cardinal Dearden, did in 22 years at the helm of the archdiocese. For whatever his accomplishments have been, Szoka's flock can't seem to stop talking about his 1988 order to close city churches deemed unviable by the archdiocese.

Szoka's boosters say he is whip smart and doesn't shrink from the tough decisions. Among priests he has a reputation as aloof and imperial. *William Kienzle*, a priest-turned-mystery-novelist, called him "a thinking machine encased in skin."

Szoka graduated from Detroit's Sacred Heart Seminary and was ordained in 1954. He spent most of the next 17 years in the Upper Peninsula outback, with stops in Manistique, Marquette and Ishpeming. Two paths usually are open to a priest not long after ordination: parish priest or administrator. Szoka chose the latter. His savvy with the books apparently caught his superiors' attention. He was installed bishop of Gaylord—a job created for him—in 1971. He put together an organization there, no small task.

His forté is money—raising it, counting it and figuring how to spend it. He has served on numerous finance and administration committees for the National Conference of Catholic Bishops. His detractors—and there are many—argued that Szoka shouldn't run the archdiocese the same way General Motors runs a plant, where cost effectiveness is pre-eminent and non-performing entities are dumped. Szoka argued that death is part of life, too, and that some parishes simply needed pruning. Even with the pruning, there is a Catholic church roughly every mile in metro Detroit. Nevertheless, the cutbacks kicked up a lot of dust and headlines. It remained to be seen how much dust would be kicked up by suburban pruning, due next.

All the controversy obscures Szoka's 1987 coup: Pope John Paul II's visit to Detroit.

T

Talbert, Bob—May 28, 1936; the *Free Press*'s Captain Outrageous.

He's the guy readers love to hate. His daily mash of trivia, gossip and observations make him one of the most-read, most-recognized newspaper columnists in Detroit. And he is paid handsomely for it.

Talbert got his start in Columbia, South Carolina, where he worked as a reporter, feature writer, feature editor, sports editor, state editor and, finally, Sunday editor and columnist. The mother of a '60s *Free Press* executive spotted Talbert's folksy meandering in the South Carolina newspapers, so she sent clips north to her son in Detroit. Mort Persky, the executive in question, liked Talbert's style, too. Persky hired Bob during the newspaper strike of 1967-'68.

Since then, Talbert's life has been an open book for Detroiters. He chronicled the breakup of his first marriage, and the joys of beginning a second. He has written—time and time and time again—about his adolescent bout with alcohol. He has even written about what it's like to shave off his beard, as if it were something that has never been done before.

Freep staffers are often asked, "What's Bob Talbert really like?" The answer is that there is little discernible difference between Talbert and his column. The columns that have been running seven days a week for two decades are probably an accurate reflection of the man. Besides that, he is unassuming and straight-ahead.

Talbert doesn't spend much time in his office, preferring instead to travel about town and work from a home computer. He considers his office to be anywhere in Detroit or Michigan he feels like heading when he steps out.

Taubman, Al—January 31, 1924; malling the jack/Detroit's richest man.

Forbes magazine says he's worth $1.85-billion. None of it, however, was inherited, which is how many rich folks in town balance their checkbooks. Taubman made it the old-fashioned way: through a good idea and savvy investing.

He controls some 20 shopping centers with about 24 million square feet of retail space. That's enough for 555 simultaneous football games. Various business deals, such as the Irvine Ranch investment (a large chunk of southern California which he purchased with *Max Fisher* and Henry Ford II and sold six years later), made him somewhere between $100 million and $150 million. He's the largest stockholder (5.4 percent) in Manufacturers National Corp. and has a majority ownership in Sotheby's, the auction house. When he's not in Bloomfield Hills, he's in New York City, where he sits on the board of the Whitney Museum and is said to be a power in society.

So what does Big Al think of all this? "Every year *Forbes* calls and every year he tells 'em the same thing—it's not important," says an aide, Chris Tennyson. "And I'm not sure even he knows what he's worth."

Teeter, Bob—February 5, 1939; truth through numbers.

This Ann Arbor-based pollster/political strategist was a key player in President George Bush's win in 1988. But when the time came to collect the spoils of victory in Washington, Teeter stayed put in Ann Arbor. Lots of power brokers say they are family-oriented because it plays well in print. With his steadfast refusal to uproot to D.C., Teeter proved it.

A native of Coldwater, where his father was mayor, he picked up his education at Michigan State University and Albion College. *Frederick Currier,* chairman of Market Opinion Research, discovered Teeter when the latter worked as gofer in *George Romney*'s 1966 gubernatorial campaign. Currier added Teeter to the MOR roster that year and eventually made him the firm's No. 2 man.

Soon, however, the student outgrew the teacher. Teeter surveyed the U.S. for Gerald Ford in 1976, and was said to be a key factor in giving advice that saw Ford rebound from 30 points behind Jimmy Carter. He also played similar roles in Ronald Reagan's 1980 and 1984 campaigns, and was one of two key strategists (the other being campaign manager Lee Atwater) who steered Bush to victory.

Democratic pollster Peter Hart once told the *New York Times:* "He's confident without being arrogant, and he knows how to say 'no' when something's not right." The *Times* also pointed out that Peter had "no discernible enemies" waiting to do him in—very unusual in a place like Washington.

Telnack, Jack—April 1, 1937; Ford's foremost designer.

As the 1980s dawned, Ford needed—as the Monty Python comedy group would say—"something completely different." On its way to a $1.5-billion-loss in 1980, Ford's corporate fathers asked its designers to push the edge of the envelope. The results from Telnack's easels and clay models were the curvaceous Ford Taurus and Mercury Sable.

Growing up in Dearborn, Telnack would drive his bicycle to Ford's test tracks for a peek. He took that early bent to the Art Center College in Pasadena, one of the country's top automotive design schools. He joined Ford in 1958, rose through a series of design jobs here and in Europe before being named chief design executive for Ford's North American automotive operations.

Designers are allowed to talk and act differently than, say, the folks on the financial staff. And Telnack dresses in a way that might even get him in the front door of Bill Blass's shop. With the success of the Taurus/Sable, he seems to be enjoying himself immensely.

Did Telnack create the "aero" look? Well, not exactly. The 1934 Chrysler Airflow beat him by about five decades. But it was the correct design for the moment. And who cares about such trifles, when Taurus/Sable took about five minutes to outsell the Airflow? When the short version of the company history is written, Telnack's design will certainly rate a chapter.

Temptations, the—Eddie Kendricks (December 17, 1939), David Ruffin (January 18, 1941), Paul Williams (died August 17, 1973), Melvin Franklin (birthdate not available), Otis Williams (October 30, 1941) and later, Dennis Edwards (birthdate not available) and others; the most magical doo-wop sound of all.

What the Beatles were to rock groups, the Temptations were to rhythm and blues groups. They had the fantastic choreography. They had two of the world's best soul singers in the persons of David Ruffin and Eddie Kendricks. The group's success in its field was unparalleled. And like the Beatles, recordings and program directors refuse to let them slip into the past tense.

Formed in 1960, the group hit big with "My Girl" (1965), a tune that *Smokey Robinson* (a co-writer) had planned to record with his own group, the Miracles. Smokey let the Tempts have it, and it became their ticket to the *Billboard* charts. They had three more No. 1 hits with "I Can't Get Next to You" (1969), "Just My Imagination (Running Away with Me)" (1971) and "Papa Was a Rollin' Stone" (1972). Another 11 singles hit the *Billboard* Top 10, and 28 Tempts albums hit *Billboard's* Top 40 charts from 1965 through 1982.

Success eventually cut the group to pieces. Paul Williams, who formed the Tempts with Kendricks, ran into a wall of personal problems—some brought on by alcohol. In 1973, police found Williams in the street near West Grand Boulevard and Fourteenth, dead from an apparently self-inflicted gunshot wound. His funeral was attended by some 2,500 fans and friends. (According to Otis Williams, Paul Williams paid a return visit to several of the band members after the funeral. "I'm all right where I am, Otis, I just want you to know," Otis quotes Paul as saying.)

Ruffin was more or less asked to leave the group in 1968, according to Williams. One account says Ruffin decided it was more important to catch Dean Martin's daughter's act one night than it was to make his own gig, so he had to go. Ruffin was unable to regain the fame or artistry he enjoyed with the Temptations. He did score two Top 10 hits with "My Whole World Ended (The Moment You Left Me)" (1969) and "Walk Away from Love" (1976).

Kendricks, who left in 1971, followed a similar career path. He did record the No. 1 hit "Keep On Truckin' " (1973). Ruffin and Kendricks later regrouped as a duo, including one performance on the "Live Aid" program. But they, too, were unable to perform with the intensity of the original Temptations.

Some musical organizations are more than the sum of their parts.

Thomas, Isiah—April 30, 1961; premier Piston.

Thomas is the only Detroit personality who can sponsor a "No Crime Day" and not get laughed out of town. The engine of the Pistons basketball franchise, he's also the highest-paid athlete in Detroit, raking in comfortable millions, plus commercials and endorsements.

The 6'1" Chicago native served time under Bobby Knight at Indiana University. As a sophomore in 1981 he boosted the Hoosiers to the summit of college basketball—an NCAA championship. According to John Feinstein's "A Season on the Brink," the Knight-Thomas relationship was extraordinarily tempestuous. "You know there were times," Feinstein quotes Thomas, "when if I had a gun, I think I would have shot him. And there were other times when I wanted to put my arms around him, hug him, and tell him that I loved him." Presumably there was more of the former than the latter, because Thomas went pro after his championship season.

Of course, the Pistons began doing something after signing Thomas that they seldom did before: winning games and a championship. In the four seasons before his arrival there were two fourth-place and two sixth-place finishes. The last two pre-Thomas seasons were particularly awful: The Pistons' 21–61 record in 1980–'81 was only a mild improvement on their 16–66 showing the previous year. Shrewd trades, clever drafts and sharp coaching brought the team to the verge of an NBA title. But Thomas clearly is the star of a very talented team which motored to a 63–19 mark in 1988–'89, the fifth-best record ever in the NBA.

He lives in Bloomfield Hills with his wife, Lynn, and son Joshua. He seems to have an eye for life after hoops: In 1988 he hired a Dallas-based PR woman to trumpet his off-the-court persona. Oh, Isiah!

Thomas, Russ—July 24, 1924; Lion tamer under the whip.

No figure in Detroit sports has been so maligned so harshly for so long. Every yobbo who called in to local sports talk shows during the '70s and '80s would say the same thing about the boys in Honolulu blue: "The Lions ain't gonna do nuffin'—hear?—unless they get rid of Russ Thomas." It's a suffering fan's mantra.

An All-Big Ten and All-America player at Ohio State University, Thomas joined the Lions in 1946 as a tackle. He was All-Pro his rookie season, but within three years a knee injury had ended his career. In 1952, Lions coach Buddy Parker hired Thomas as an assistant coach. Thomas has been here ever since, rising to general manager in 1967 and executive vice-president in 1972.

The gig may be just about up. Team owner *William Clay Ford* told reporters in late 1987 that Thomas would be retiring soon. Thomas said he hadn't heard anything about that. But insiders took it as a hint.

The Lions haven't won a championship since 1957. The only constant during those long decades, with the exception of owner Ford, has been Thomas. The buck has to stop somewhere. Fans have decided that's on Thomas's desk.

Thompson, Richard—May 17, 1937; battlefield commission for Patterson lieutenant.

Now that Oakland County crimebuster L. Brooks Patterson has stepped aside, Dick Thompson runs the prosecutorial show.

A graduate of Wayne State University Law School, he spent nine years in private practice before joining his mentor Patterson as his chief assistant. Thompson played second fiddle for some 16 years before Patterson decided to step away from the government forum. When Patterson did, Thompson's ascension was pretty well pre-ordained.

Thompson was challenged by attorney Jeff Leib, state Sen. Richard Fessler and Oakland County Commissioner Jack McDonald. Thompson continued with the "let's lock up the bad guys and throw away the key" message that kept his boss in office. Thompson's campaign slogan: "You don't have to wonder whether Richard Thompson can do the job as prosecutor. He's already doing it." Thompson won the primary with more votes than all of his Republican opponents combined, carrying every municipality but Southfield and Northville.

Tomlin, Lily—September 1, 1936; from Cass, with class.

One of the few actresses to make the switch from the television wasteland to high-class film and Broadway, she has an ability to translate daily life into art. From Ernestine (the nasal, obnoxious telephone operator) to greaseball Vegas singer Tommy Velour, her characters are all too real.

Tomlin's parents moved to Detroit's west side from Paducah, Kentucky. She graduated from Cass Tech High (where she was a cheerleader) and attended Wayne State University in 1960-'61. While at Wayne, she did a few parts at WSU's Hilberry Theatre. Detroit is a great place if you're a car designer, but not so great if you're an actress. So it was off to New York, where she paid the rent by working as secretary to a casting director. Tomlin did a couple of revues ("Arf and the Great Airplane Snatch" was among them) and did bits on Gary Moore's TV show before moving to L.A. and "Rowan & Martin's Laugh-In" on NBC, where she appeared from 1970 to 1973. "Ernestine" earned her recognition as a special talent.

She has gone on to major success on the stage ("The Search For Intelligent Life in the Universe"), a disastrous film role ("Moment by Moment" with John Travolta) and some Hollywood successes ("The Late Show," "Nashville"). When she returned to Detroit with "Search . . . " in 1988, she seemed to enjoy the homecoming. She took in the Thanksgiving Day parade and lunched with her old Cass Tech cheerleading pals.

Trammell, Alan (February 21, 1958) and Whitaker, Lou (May 12, 1957); the longest-running double-play combo.

Not long after second baseman Lou Whitaker and shortstop Alan Trammell joined the Tigers, a rumor arose that then-Tigers manager Ralph Houk might separate them. "Just because two kids have always played together," Houk teased *News* sportswriter Jerry Green, "doesn't mean they have to play together all their life." The Tigers knew better than to split a winning pair, of course. When Trammell and Whitaker took their places on the diamond for the Tigers on Sept. 9, 1977, Trammell was still a teenager. Whitaker was barely 20. They'll go into the '90s as thirtysomethings doing what they've always done: turning the double play.

The beauty of the partnership lies in their differences. Whitaker was Brooklyn-born, raised in Martinsville, Virginia. Trammell is a southern California boy. Whitaker sat out several games at the end of the 1988 season because of a dance injury. Trammell, however, is by far the more outgoing of the two. And how much are they together? When Trammell hit two homers in Game Four of the '84 World Series, Whitaker was on base for both of them.

Turner, Marilyn—see Kelly, John

Turner, Tom—October 27, 1931; the glue between labor's fiefdoms.

Except for the UAW's *Owen Bieber*, state AFL-CIO Secretary-Treasurer Tom Turner is the best-known labor chieftain in Detroit. He is a conciliator whose power comes from his ability to cajole, browbeat or beg union leaders to cooperate and do things his way. The labor federation includes about 725,000 members in the state. Some 60 different labor organizations representing plumbers, teachers, autoworkers, printers, public employees, steelworkers, lathers and bricklayers gather under Turner's AFL-CIO umbrella.

His is a tricky one because the AFL-CIO is not a union but a federation, albeit a large one. If a union boss decides to ignore the federation and get out—as the UAW did in the 1950s—there isn't much Turner can do about it. However, most union leaders have learned that it's better to hang together than hang apart in the anti-labor atmosphere of the 1980s.

An Army veteran of two wars (World War II with the Army Air Corps, the Korean War with the Army) Turner got into the labor movement as a member of the United Steelworkers, which he joined in the early '50s at Great Lakes Steel.

A decade later, Turner came to the Wayne County AFL-CIO as an administrative assistant to then-president Al Barbour. He took over as president of the Detroit chapter when Barbour died in 1968, remaining in charge when the Oakland, Wayne and Macomb county AFL-CIOs merged to form the metro Detroit AFL-CIO in 1969.

Since then, Turner's stewardship has been unchallenged. He has been re-elected every four years since 1972 with no opposition. He also carries clout in Detroit's black community, sitting as president of the Detroit NAACP from 1968 until 1970. He moved into his current job with the state AFL-CIO in 1988.

Although he's on television a lot, Turner operates most effectively behind the scenes, particularly in public employee strikes. He played a large role in solving the national Greyhound strike of 1983.

Turner generally can be found in the first row of any labor march, insulting Republicans, employers and anyone whose collar isn't blue.

U

Uchalik, David—December 15,1954; Eric Clapton, meet Jos. Campau.

He's proof that rock 'n' roll hasn't lost its sense of humor. This Hamtramck lad sired the Polish Muslims, whose following threatens to reach beyond cult status. He's expert at putting rock's standard lyrics through his own special prism. "Surfin' USA" becomes "Bowlin' USA." "Love Potion Number Nine" becomes "Love Polka Number Nine." "I'm a Travelin' Man" became "I'm a Travelin' Pope." The Muslims made sure they did that one in their "Popestock" extravaganza to celebrate the arrival of Pope John Paul II. Downtown's St. Andrew's Hall or any of the small Hamtramck rock bars fill up on Muslim nights.

The band was originated in December 1981 as a gag. A thief stole equipment from Uchalik's band, the Reruns, so he and pals got together and did a benefit. It caught on. The band's ever-changing personnel has included a lawyer, an ad man, an industrial designer, a physician's assistant and a tax assessor.

V

Vainisi, Jerry—October 7, 1941; Lions' future?

If *Russ Thomas* is the Lions' past, Jerry Vainisi may be the team's future. On the heels of the Lions' embarrassing 4–11 season in 1987, owner *William Clay Ford* woke up from his nap long enough to realize something had to be done. He put Vainisi in charge of football operations, which means Vainisi will pull the lever on drafts and trades. It is the only time Ford has given any indication that Russ Thomas wasn't going to live forever. Perhaps in a few years the Lions will fly. So, perhaps, will cows.

A football junkie of the highest magnitude, Vainisi turned pro in the Chicago Bears' bookkeeping section, working his way up to v.p. and general manager by 1983. The Bears won the 1986 Super Bowl under Vainisi's stewardship, which should have given him some job security. He was best friends with coach Mike Ditka, and the team appeared on the brink of becoming a football dynasty. But Mike McCaskey, a Bears owner by virtue of the fact that his mother is George Halas' daughter, was apparently not of the "if it ain't broke don't fix it" school of management. Vainisi got the gate not long after a Bears playoff loss to the Washington Redskins in early 1987. Some speculate that McCaskey was threatened by the Vainisi-Ditka juggernaut.

The Lions hired Vainisi as general counsel, which means he kept an eye on legal affairs for the franchise even though he didn't have a license to practice law here. Obviously, he could have cared less about Michigan jurisprudence. He received a promotion to vice-president for player personnel in 1988.

With Thomas readying himself for retirement in a few years, a favorite game is guessing his successor. Will it be Vainisi?

van der Marck, Jan—1929, date not available; keeping current.

As curator of 20th Century art for the Detroit Institute of Arts, you might say van der Marck is the DIA's "man of the moment." A native of The Netherlands, he received his education there and at Columbia University. van der Marck made stops at museums in Minneapolis and Miami before DIA director *Sam Sachs* brought him aboard in 1986. He was one of Sachs' first hires and is rumored to carry a great deal of influence at the DIA.

Van Dusen, Richard—July 18, 1925; power at the bar and at the GOP.

He's the No. 1 man at Dickinson, Wright, Moon, Van Dusen & Freeman, a century-old Detroit law firm with more Harvard and University of Michigan law grads than anybody can count.

A former all-Big Ten football player at the University of Minnesota, Van Dusen joined the Dickinson-Wright firm fresh out of Harvard Law in 1949. He has never worked at another firm, but made the shuffle from Dickinson to the halls of government more than once. In 1954, at the precocious age of 28, Van Dusen was elected to the state House of Representatives from Oakland County. He made such an impression that the Republicans had Van Dusen run for attorney general in 1956. He lost, but only by 52 percent to 48 percent. The GOP appreciated the effort.

Throughout the '60s, Van Dusen was included in *George Romney's* inner circle: as a delegate to the constitutional convention in 1962; as a member of the governor's staff during Romney's first term; and as undersecretary of Housing and Urban Development under Romney during the Nixon administration. The HUD job included a limo and plenty of black-tie dinners, and had Van Dusen rubbing elbows with all manner of Washington movers. Van Dusen left Washington just before Romney did. The going-away soiree was attended by former CIA director Richard Helms, George Shultz (secretary of state under Ronald Reagan) and U.S. Supreme Court Justice Potter Stewart. It's good to have friends.

Van Dusen is still somewhat active in politics, but his main activity nowadays is running Dickinson-Wright, which lists 180 attorneys and takes up four floors of the First National Building in downtown Detroit. (In 1992 Dickinson-Wright will move to the new One Detroit Center on Woodward between Larned and Congress.) The firm also has offices in Lansing, Grand Rapids, Washington—and Bloomfield Hills, so the Oakland County money doesn't have to travel far.

With his tie hitched to the top of his Brooks Brothers' shirt, Van Dusen doesn't always play it cool. He once got into a shoving match with a John Bircher in a downtown Detroit hotel during some now-forgotten function. From all accounts, Van Dusen's athletic 6'2" frame prevailed.

Vitale, Dick— June 9, 1940; hisonlypunctuationisthecommercials.

This former University of Detroit and Pistons coach has become a cult hero to some college basketball fans, a larynx run amok to others. As a hoops commentator for ESPN and ABC-TV, he narrates with gale-force enthusiasm. In Vitale's language a "glass eater" is a strong rebounder; "NBN" is nothing but net. He is the most unlikely of television stars. As the subtitle of his autobiography says, he's "just your average bald, one-eyed basketball wacko who beat the Ziggy and became a PTP'er" (Vitalese for Prime Time Player).

A native of New Jersey, he was an assistant coach at Rutgers when the University of Detroit persuaded him to come west as head coach. Under Vitale, U-D basketball came alive in a way it hadn't since Dave DeBusschere held court. Vitale's four seasons at Livernois and Six Mile saw him win 17, 17, 19 and 25 games. The latter team was the only Titan squad ever to play in the NCAA tournament. In an emotional matchup, the Titans were sent home by the University of Michigan squad.

Vitale's success was enough to attract the attention of Pistons owner **Bill Davidson**, who figured Vitale's charisma was just what the ailing NBA team needed. But what worked for college kids didn't work for highly paid professionals. Vitale was 30–52 with the Pistons in 1978-'79. When the team began the 1979-'80 season with a 4–8 record, Davidson decided Vitale had to go. That's the Ziggy. Despite his 34–60 record, Vitale was stunned. "I still didn't believe it," he wrote. "Even when the big stretch limo pulled up. Even when Tim, the chauffeur, let Davidson out of the limo and they came to the door. Even when the owner walked in and I invited him to sit down. But there were no doubts about it. This was strictly business. Gallows business."

ESPN, then a fledgling cable network, rescued Vitale. His language, mannerisms, and overheated style have made him far richer and famous than all but a few coaches—pro or college. "All I am really is the guy who got the axe, the coach who got the Ziggy," he wrote. "The limousine rolled up. The boss fired me. A little while later a guy gave me a microphone. I wasn't made from broadcasting school. But I happened to survive. Big deal."

Vititoe, William—September 19, 1938; his line is busy.

Michigan Bell's president and chief executive is so confident of his company's service that he lists his home number in the Detroit phone book.

Before taking over from longtime Ma Bell chieftain David Easlick in 1983, Vititoe networked at Indiana Bell, AT&T, and Michigan Bell. His company, one of Ameritech's five Bell subsidiaries (along with the Illinois, Indiana, Ohio and Wisconsin phone companies) did $2.2-billion in operating revenues in 1987. That's a lot of dimes.

Ever the good citizen, Vititoe is up to his switches in organizations outside the company. He chaired the Economic Club of Detroit and *Governor Blanchard*'s Michigan Strategic Fund. He also sits on the Comerica bank board. His cultural connections are good. He and his wife, Susan, hosted the Michigan Opera Theatre's opening in 1987. And he's a member of the Detroit Symphony Orchestra board.

Vlasic, Robert—March 9, 1926; a dilly of a company.

He proved pickles can both be funny and profitable. He joined his father in the family pickle business in 1949, taking over as chairman in 1963. Once in charge, the University of Michigan grad turned a regional Hamtramck concern into an American pickle behemoth. Remember all those pickle jokes that made the rounds in the '60s? They were funny, but they also translated into money for Vlasic's company.

Somewhere along the line he expanded into sauerkraut, relishes and peppers. Campbell Soup Co., the New Jersey-based food giant, thought Vlasic did such a good job that it bought the company for $33-million in 1978. Robert Vlasic was named Campbell Soup's chairman 10 years later, which means he commutes between the East Coast and his Bloomfield Hills home once a week. The job keeps him out of the day-to-day management of Campbell Soup, however, since a chief executive officer is on the premises to put out the fires. A large stockholder (about 864,000 shares), he watches out for his own interests and those of the family that founded the company.

Vlasic still keeps in touch with business around town, though he doesn't intrude much on the company's daily operations. He was chairman of the board of trustees of Henry Ford Hospital, the first non-Ford to hold the job.

Vogel, Steven—see Schervish, David

W

Wagner, Tom—July 28, 1938; "T" is for Bird and Taurus.

As general manager of Ford Motor Co.'s Ford division, he's in charge of peddling the company's bread-and-butter autos: the Escort, the Taurus, the Thunderbird and others. With the Thunderbird named *Motor Trend* Car of the Year for 1989, and with the Taurus still selling well, that's a fun job to have. Ford sales rose more than nine percent (to 1,527,504) in 1988. Before getting his current job in March 1988, he was Edsel Ford II's boss over at Lincoln-Mercury. As general manager there, (1985-'88) he presided over intro of the Merkur Scorpio and XR4Ti. Before that, Wagner made the rounds of district offices in Milwaukee, the Twin Cities, Louisville, Los Angeles and Washington, D.C.

Wahls, Myron—December 11, 1931; at home on the bench or the piano bench.

This Michigan Court of Appeals chief judge pro-tem is probably the most visible jurist in town. A favorite trick is bringing Wahls aboard a social event as a piano player. One could conclude that the host or hostess was humoring a powerful judge, but that isn't the case. Wahls is good enough on the keyboards to have accompanied jazz great Lionel Hampton on a European trip in 1988.

Educated at the University of Michigan and Northwestern University Law School, he was practicing law when Governor William Milliken appointed him to the Michigan Employment Security Appeal Board in 1969. Unfortunately, Wahls continued to practice law after he got the appointment, which is a no-no. That breach of ethics became something of an issue when Wahls ran against state Attorney General *Frank Kelley* in 1974. Given Kelley's long history of electoral success, Wahls probably would have been beaten anyway.

Wahls didn't have much time to pine, however, because Milliken appointed him to the Wayne County circuit bench within two months of the defeat. And it was Milliken who appointed him to the Court of Appeals in 1982.

Waldmeir, Pete—January 16, 1931; *News* curmudgeon/columnist for life.

He's the craggy presence at the *News* who spends a lot of ink deflating overfed egos in this town. His usual target is *Mayor Young*, but others have felt his sting. They include *Free Press* publisher *David Lawrence Jr.*, Detroit public schools former chief Arthur Jefferson and about half of Young's appointees.

His dad, Joe, tended bar. Like the *Freep's Neal Shine*, Waldmeir got into the business as a copyboy. He sat out the Korean War as sports editor of the Marines' Parris Island newspaper, appropriately named *The Boot*. After serving Uncle Sam, he rejoined the *News* covering high school sports, but worked his way up to more prestigious jock beats. He replaced Doc Greene as sports columnist when Greene slid over to the news pages in 1964. Eight years later, Waldmeir made the Doc Greene shift from sports to news.

One of the best media stories of the '80s was how Waldmeir announced he was joining the *Free Press*, then did a snappy dress-blue about face. *Freep* publisher Lawrence signed Waldmeir and took him through the newsroom on a Thursday. *News* publisher Robert Nelson was dispatched by Evening News Association chairman Peter B. Clark to retrieve Waldmeir. For reasons clear only to himself, Waldmeir backed out the next Monday. His new deal included plenty of money and a contract that runs until the end of time. He's famous around the halls of the *News* for spatting with *News* managers, but they can't do much unless they buy Pete out. And that would practically take a new stock offering.

"They say you should be nice to people on their way up because you'll meet 'em again on your way down," he's fond of saying. "Well, fuck 'em. I ain't coming down."

Warfield, Robert—November 29, 1948; one 4 the '90s.

Warfield heads Channel 4's news department, and helped turn it into a major force. He talks fast, gesticulates freely, and is anything but the Cool Hand Luke type of broadcast executive bred in the labs these days.

A graduate of Eastern Kentucky University, he began college as a 5'10" shooting guard on the basketball team, but finished on the academic side only when a knee injury wiped out his hoops career. Warfield joined Channel 4 in 1979 as an assistant news director, not long after Post-Newsweek bought the place. He was promoted to news director in January 1982, then got his vice-presidential stripes (v.p. news) in July 1984. *Alan Frank* won the general manager's job at Channel 4, but Warfield was given additional responsibilities in March 1988 — v.p. news/director of broadcast operations. That put the news, engineering, community relations and labor relations departments in Warfield's tent.

Nobody would accuse Warfield of being a shrinking violet. He is highly charged and is known around the station for his volatility. He regularly appears on lists of Detroiters who'll be running the town in the coming decade.

Was Brothers, a.k.a. Was (Not Was), .a.k.a. Don Fagenson (September 13, 1952) and David Weiss (October 26, 1952); funk poets.

Here's proof that talent and persistence can win out. After years of noodling around recording studios with modest success, the band's ship came in with their 1988 LP "What Up, Dog?" Their twisted lyrics and funk beat caught the attention of the *New York Times*, most of Europe and just about anybody with an ear for the bizarre. Nobody else but this band can sing a song like "Somewhere in America Is a Street Named After My Dad." Weiss once told *News* rock critic Susan Whitall: "Pop music is the last refuge of poetry in the post-literate era."

There were dozens of rock 'n' roll rats in Oak Park High School's Class of '70. Most of them are probably dentists and accountants by now. Fagenson (the band's musical brains) and Weiss (the lyricist, who did a stint as jazz critic at the *L.A. Herald-Examiner*) stuck with it. Fagenson's son can claim partial credit for naming the band. He'd point out objects and say "Brick, not brick." Their first album "Was (Not Was)" went nowhere on the charts, though it did gain an audience among the hip. Their second LP, "Born to Laugh at Tornados" had (as did "What Up, Dog?") a rather strange assortment of guests: Ozzy Osborne, Mel Torme and *Mitch Ryder*. Critics didn't know what to make of it. Their work was, well, strange.

A failure, however, turned into a success. Geffen Records, which had done their second album, told them to rid themselves of the band's two black lead singers (Sir Harry Bowens and Sweet Pea Atkinson). Weiss and Fagenson refused on principle, so the band was cut off without pay. Chrysalis Records had a slightly more egalitarian outlook on the band's racial/musical composition and let loose with the group's third LP.

Two hit singles later ("Spy In The House of Love" and "Walk the Dinosaur") have Geffen wondering if somebody at the label made the wrong call. Bonnie Raitt sought out Fagenson to produce an album, as did singer Carly Simon and the B-52s. The good guys—the locals, in this case—have won out.

Yes, we know these guys moved to L.A. Roots are the thing. They're Detroit (not Detroit).

Whipple, Kenneth—September 28, 1934; he assembles cash.

As all of Gaul was divided into three parts, so is Ford Motor Co. The automotive group makes cars and trucks; diversified products makes a range of goodies from satellites to Jack Nicklaus-designed golf courses; and the financial services group—Whipple's fiefdom—makes money out of money. It makes loans to car buyers and owns several financial institutions, a source of stability in the cyclical auto business. And it's profitable. Ford Motor Credit Co., the second-biggest finance company in the world, made $2.9-billion from 1980 to 1987. Chrysler Corp.—the entire company—made $5.7-billion, or only about twice that.

A graduate of Massachusetts Institute of Technology, Whipple joined Ford in 1958. He rose through a series of finance jobs, becoming president of Ford Credit in 1980. His first non-bean-counting gig was a biggie: He became a vice-president for corporate strategy in 1984. Two years later, he was the surprise choice to succeed *Robert Lutz* (who went to Chrysler a couple of months later) as chairman of

Ford of Europe. The thinking was that Ford needed somebody with strategic smarts to run its European shop. (The problems were two-fold: too much production capacity, and a half-dozen automakers each weighing in with about 12 percent of the market.) He ran Ford of Europe for two years, doubling its profits from $559 million in 1986 to $1.1 billion in 1987. Whipple's reward was his current job, which he got in March of 1988.

Whitaker, Lou—see Trammell, Alan

Whitman, Dr. Marina v.N.—March 6, 1935; GM's minister of economics/ranking company female exec.

As a group v.p., she oversees the General's public relations, industry-government relations, environmental activities and eco-nomics staffs. Another way of putting it: She's ultimately in charge of dealing with the pesky lawmakers and reporters who occasionally make life miserable for GM. She also commands the group that camps out in the crow's nest and monitors the economic weather.

She springs from an intellectually rich family. Her father, the late John von Neumann (hence the v.N. in her name) was one of the 20th Century's top mathematical noodles. Before his death in 1957 at the young age of 53, he had developed theories which helped in the development of computers and atomic power. His pals Edward Teller and Robert Oppenheimer were frequent house guests. "I was 15 before I realized that ours was not the normal way of life," Whitman wryly told a reporter.

Young Marina graduated from Radcliffe, where she ranked high-est in her class, and subsequently jumped through additional intellec-tual hoops at Columbia University, where she earned a master's and doctorate in economics. With that impressive pile of sheepskin in her purse, she lit out for a long career in government and academia. Throughout the '60s, she taught at the University of Pittsburgh, where her husband still sits as an English professor. She adminis-tered Phase 2 of Richard Nixon's wage-price controls before return-ing to Pitt. When *Roger Smith* recruited her as the company's chief economist in 1979, she was only the second woman v.p. in GM history. GM's board gave her a promotion in 1985, adding the public affairs group to her domain.

When she's not doing her job, there are board meetings to attend:

Manufacturers Hanover Trust, Procter & Gamble and Princeton University.

Wholey, Dennis—(birthdate not available); dry, talented and flourishing.

In these days of the Geraldo Rivera genre of TV trash, Wholey stands out like Alistair Cooke at a skinhead meeting. Guests on Wholey's nighttime gabfest, produced from Washington, D.C., by Detroit's Channel 56, are treated with a measure of respect and dignity.

Before he joined Channel 56 in 1980, Wholey's career was in shambles. He had worked as a talk show captain at Channel 7, but had a tough battle with booze that even got him arrested in New York City for disorderly conduct. Realizing that anybody who got busted for aberrant behavior in Manhattan had to be fairly far gone, Wholey took stock of his life. He visited the Rev. Vaughn Quinn OMI, the Roman Catholic priest who specializes in helping alcoholics recover. The new, dry Wholey even persuaded Henry Ford II to take calls from America one night—the only time the late mogul ever consented to such a thing.

"LateNight America" became a hit on PBS stations across the country. And when he wasn't in front of the camera, Wholey was turning lemons into lemonade. He wrote "The Courage to Change: Personal Conversations About Alcoholism," which spent six months on the *New York Times* best-seller list. The tome is a fascinating, often frightening, look at how a variety of people—many of them well-known—handled their alcoholism. It included tales of how rock star Peter Townshend and writer *Elmore Leonard* beat the bottle. The book was successful enough that he took a couple of years off from TV to write two others.

He got back into television in 1989, this time from Washington. The only reason the new "LateNight America" wasn't broadcast from Detroit is because Wholey figured he could round up a better variety of guests from the capital. But the show remains under Detroiters' control.

Wilhelm, Elliot—March 3, 1950; screening room impresario.

The city's film cognoscenti owe him a debt. Were it not for Elliot Wilhelm and the series of high-quality films he and the Detroit

Institute of Arts show each weekend, they would have few options. And this town would surely qualify for status as a cinematic wasteland.

A native west-sider and the son of a heart specialist, Wilhelm started showing movies at the now-defunct Wayne Cinema Guild in the late '60s. The Detroit Institute of Arts, knowing a good thing when it saw one, enlisted Wilhelm and used his film sensibilities to program a series in the DIA's auditorium beginning in January 1974. Now Wilhelm's films—which might be something by Akira Kurosawa, Jean-Luc Goddard or the late Rainer Fassbinder—are well into their second decade. Wilhelm's little experiment, in fact, became the most successful program of its type in the country—even more successful than similar programs run for sophisticated San Francisco and Chicago film buffs.

For maybe 600 regulars, Wilhelm's show is the cultural experience of the week. Altogether, about 1,000 filmgoers drop in each weekend. The gatherings have a clubby feel. If a bomb were to go off on a Friday night, the town's average IQ would instantly drop a few points. One sure way to identify a Detroit intellectual is to look for one of Wilhelm's familiar DIA film schedules hanging on the refrigerator door.

Williams, Charlie—June 22, 1947; power in the pipeline.

He's probably *Mayor Young*'s most trusted aide. Williams runs the Water and Sewerage Department, the one stick Detroit holds over suburban communities that would like to divorce themselves from the city. They can't, because Detroit built the regional water and sewerage system way back when and still controls it. Some 77 burbs send their sewage to Charlie Williams, and another 110 get their H_2O from him at wholesale. The latter figure accounts for 42 percent of the state's population.

Born in Camp Hill, Alabama, he grew up amid depressing poverty on the city's north side. His mom's ADC check bought the groceries. But he graduated from Pershing High in 1965 and grubbed his way through Wayne State University, working in various city Recreation Department programs. City hall beckoned in 1977, when he was named deputy director of the Department of Public Works. He's had a number of impressive stopping places since then: director of the city's Public Housing Department (1978 and 1980);

Mayor Young's politics assistant (1980); Housing Department (again) until early 1982; personnel director through 1983; then water and sewerage chief since 1983. He replaced Charles Beckham, who eventually went to prison on racketeering charges growing out of the Vista corruption case. Along the way, he got himself a law degree from Wayne State (1980).

If Young has groomed anybody as a successor, it's this guy. Young entrusted Williams with the chairmanship of the Cable Television Commission. It was Williams who commanded the mayor's troops on Devil's Night in 1987 and '88. He is citywide coordinator for the 911 emergency system. And he is treasurer of the Mayor's Re-election Committee. But Young is so secretive, we may not know what he really intends for Williams until—and if—it happens.

Williams, Robin—July 21, 1952; comedy unchained.

This Bloomfield Hills native went on to create some of the best television of the '70s with his manic "Mork" character on ABC-TV's "Mork and Mindy." As the '90s approach, Williams appears to be on the verge of creating some first-class cinema as well. A strong performance in "Good Morning, Vietnam" (1988) was followed by a knock-out appearance in "Dead Poets Society" (1989). His rendering of English teacher John Keating may well earn him an Academy Award nomination and has proved he can do something besides tell jokes.

Williams, the son of Ford Motor Company vice-president Robert Williams, grew up on an estate in Bloomfield Hills. John Campbell, who taught the comedian history and wrestling at Detroit Country Day School in the late 1960s, remembers Williams as "shy, quiet . . . an excellent student, and a tough little athlete."

He eventually moved to California, where he attended two colleges in the San Francisco area and worked the comedy clubs of Los Angeles. If Williams was shy as an adolescent, he was everything but by the time he hit network television as "Mork" in 1978. Williams practically secreted jokes as the space character who landed in Colorado. The audience loved it, but ABC-TV and the show's producers tampered with the formula, moving it from Thursday to Sunday and trying to provide a serious spin on William's performance. It almost killed the show, which eventually died a natural death in 1982. Williams also gained a reputation as a Hollywood party animal. In an effort to keep himself away from the Hollywood street scene, he lives on a 600-acre ranch outside of San Francisco.

Williams hit the big screen in 1980 as "Popeye." The movie earned him some nasty reviews, and had critics wondering if Williams could make the stretch to film. But he kept working at it. His performances in "The World According to Garp" (1982), "Moscow on the Hudson" (1984), and "Club Paradise" (1986) earned kinder critical notices. The only question is whether the movie-going public will accept a Robin Williams who doesn't do jokes every 15 seconds. If "Dead Poets" is any indication, the answer seems to be yes.

Williams, Ron—June 10, 1951; filler of media vacuum.

The media business, like nature, abhors a vacuum. Because of Williams' *Metro Times*, Detroit has what Boston, Chicago and New York City have: a free-spirited publication that covers political and artistic issues the big daily newspapers are too unhip to cover. Would the *News* or *Free Press* have the guts to run gonzo journalist Hunter S. Thompson's ravings, or cartoonist Jules Feiffer's primal screams? Probably not. Besides, where else does one find where Karen Monster or the Junk Monkeys are playing next weekend?

A Royal Oak native and 1969 grad of Royal Oak Dondero High, he landed a BA from Antioch College and knocked around the Midwest as a newsman/public affairs commentator at a half-dozen public radio stations. He worked at Chicago's *In These Times* when a light bulb went off in his head: Why not do the same thing in Detroit? The reasons for not doing so were articulated numerous times by everybody who advised him: Detroit hadn't had an "underground" publication in years; advertisers were afraid of the spiked-hair set; too many suburbanites could care less about left-wing political issues. Williams ignored the advice and plunged ahead. Says Williams: "We were too naive to know this couldn't be done."

Filling the paper with slightly overwrought political ravings and sophisticated musical/artistic coverage, he has done all right. By 1988, the weekly had a free circulation of 75,000 and revenue of $1.5 million. He might have made a mint catering to the idiot Birmingham trendy set. But what fun would that be? In an era when journalism has become increasingly corporate, some readers appreciate a publication that bleeds for what it believes in.

Williams has branched into typesetting and whatnot with Metro

Graphics. He wears a suit and tie to work and has cut his hair. He has even impressed some ad agency types enough to grab a Chevy ad or two.

Wilson, Ralph Jr.—October 17, 1918; shuffling off to Buffalo on Sundays.

He owns the Buffalo Bills football team, but his lakefront mansion is on St. Clair, not Erie, in Grosse Pointe Shores. Wilson runs a hodge-podge of businesses besides the Bills. His ventures include four television stations across the United States; an insurance agency; an auto parts company; a highway construction company; thorough-bred horses; oil- and gas-drilling ventures—all of which he controls from a suite at the Renaissance Center. None of 'em, except for the Bills, are showstoppers. But stack 'em up together and you've got some money. It's all privately held, so Wilson's true wealth is tough to figure. He bought the Bills franchise for $25,000 in 1959. Nowa-days, *Forbes* estimates a football franchise to be worth at least $60 million.

Not a fameseeker, despite having signed the paychecks of O.J. Simpson and Jack Kemp, he generally lays low and away from news-paper reporters.

Wilson, Tom—October 8, 1949; it's all net.

Pistons chief exec Tom Wilson minds the ledgers while general man-ager *Jack McCloskey* tends the on-court crew. Wilson is also the organization's chief salesman and sees to it that the buckets translate into bucks big enough to match the salaries.

There was a time when Wilson didn't have much to sell. When he joined the team in 1978, the Pistons dribbled out a miserable 30–52 performance. But now that the team is hot (1989 NBA champion-ship), selling isn't as difficult. The team set a National Basketball Association record in 1987-'88 by drawing 1,066,505 fans—the first NBA team to break the magic million mark. Now, the only trouble anybody has is getting out of the Palace's crowded parking lot after the game—and even that's improving.

Wilson's marketing abilities have contributed slick ads and a de-cent TV/radio presentation. Wilson himself does color commentary on Pistons PASS broadcasts. With his wholesome good looks, Wil-son could pass for a game show host. He should be comfortable in front of a camera. He gave Hollywood a shot early in his career, doing about 40 bit parts before realizing that he wasn't the next Robert Redford. While living in L.A. he picked up a marketable skill working for the Lakers and Kings. He works on his wholesome, healthy appearance in running shoes, and negotiated two *Free Press* marathons.

Winograd, Bernard—December 31, 1950; manager of a very large portfolio.

Zillionaire *Al Taubman* doesn't manage his zillions alone. He gets help from Bernard Winograd, president of Taubman Investment Co. and Al's right-hand man.

A Detroit native, Winograd joined Bendix Corp. as W. Michael Blumenthal's executive assistant. When Blumenthal left Bendix for Washington, D.C., and a job as President Jimmy Carter's secretary of treasury, Winograd went along for the ride. But he was back at Bendix within a year as director of corporate communications (1977-'79). When Taubman found him, Winograd had already served as treasurer of the company for four years. If Bendix chief William Agee hadn't screwed up and lost the company to Allied Corp. in a hostile takeover, Winograd might be Bendix president by now.

Winograd's brother, Morley, ran the state Democratic Party from 1973 to 1979.

Wonder, Stevie (a.k.a. Steveland Morris)—May 13, 1950; Detroit's longest-running rock act.

He was introduced around the fledgling Motown Records organization by Ronnie White, who was one of *Smokey Robinson*'s Miracles. Motown founder *Berry Gordy Jr.* made millions off that handshake. Wonder, blind since birth, broke onto the charts at age 13 with "Little Stevie Wonder/The 12 Year Old Genius." "Fingertips," the single from that LP, went to No. 1 on the *Billboard* lists. Now people are talking about Wonder—seriously—as a future mayor of Detroit.

If Wonder were a baseball player, his stats would put him in the Babe Ruth/Hank Aaron category. "Fingertips" was only the first of 15 Wonder albums in *Billboard* magazine's Top 40 LPs from 1963 to 1985. Four of those albums were recorded before Wonder was 20. (Imagine having a Greatest Hits record at age 18!) Wonder received an allowance until he was 21, when he collected about $1 million in royalties. That sounds hefty, but he reportedly made some $20 million for the Motown organization. Burned by that experience, he negotiated to have his own company, now named "Brave Bull."

What set him apart from childhood artists who are destroyed by early fame was the fact that Wonder kept growing artistically. He learned new production techniques, mastered new musical instruments, stretched himself. "Innervisions" (released in 1973, 58 weeks on the chart) netted him five Grammy awards. "I Just Called to Say I Love You" (1984, from the film "The Woman In Red") won him an Oscar.

Mostly, he is noted around Hollywood for his meticulous craftsmanship. "Songs in the Key of Life" (1976) was so long in the making that he took to wearing a T-shirt that said "We're almost finished." It also stuck around on the charts for a long time: It stood at the No. 1 spot for 14 weeks and netted him another five Grammys. (The album also helped him financially. It was the first of a package that guaranteed $13 million over seven years, plus a generous royalty cut.) Wonder even improved former Beatle Paul McCartney's popularity. Their "Ebony and Ivory" tune ran seven weeks on top of the chart, which is how long "I Want to Hold Your Hand" stayed at the top. The only Beatles single to surpass it was "Hey Jude," which stayed there for nine weeks.

Wonder's civic activities include heavy involvement in the successful effort to make the Rev. Martin Luther King Jr.'s birthday a national holiday.

Woodworth, Fred—November 12, 1940; he specializes in trust.

This Detroit lawyer is among the anti-trust heavies at the Dykema Gossett law firm. As this book was written, the Federal Trade Commission was trying to force Woodworth's clients—area Chrysler dealers—to open on Saturdays. Woodworth was doing his best to see that didn't happen.

Woodworth has a habit of brushing up against literary heavyweights when he isn't in court. He was editor of the *Cranbrook Crane* while a student at Cranbrook in the late '50s. One of his charges at the newspaper was writer *Tom McGuane*, who later went on to great success as a novelist/screenwriter. "The columns were the funniest I've ever read," he recalls. "They were called Mother McGuane's Helpful Hints." After graduation from Amherst,

Woodworth went on to the University of Michigan Law School, where he roomed and drank beer with **Kurt Luedtke**, who later went on to become an Academy Award-winning screenwriter.

After U of M, Woodworth joined the U.S. Justice Department's Anti-Trust division, and the Federal Trade Commission. He took what he learned and returned to Detroit in 1972, when he signed with Dykema Gossett.

These days he's heavily involved in bar association activities. He was president of the Detroit Bar Association in 1983-'84, and later treasurer of the State Bar of Michigan in 1989. He's still tight with McGuane, who dedicated *To Skin a Cat* to Woodworth. That makes Woodworth about the only lawyer in Detroit who has made the acknowledgement page of a major fiction work.

Wrigley, Al—June 28, 1933; the best unknown automotive journalist.

Wrigley is Detroit correspondent and automotive editor for the weekly *Metalworking News*, which reports on companies who twist metal for the auto manufacturers. From dozens of inside sources he has cultivated for 25 years, Wrigley wrests details about what cars will be made of and look like two, three or more years hence. How does he do it? As secretive as automakers are about future products, they must clue in their suppliers about what they'll be doing. Wrigley works the supplier/manufacturer network, then breaks it for the automotive community to read.

He grew up milking cows and working the farms of Indiana. A graduate of Indiana University, he signed on at *Metalworking News* in 1965. His longevity gives him a huge advantage over journalists who foolishly think they can parachute into town and break auto stories. "It's nothing more than having been here longer than most people," Wrigley says modestly. "When young people ask for a little advice, I tell them 'When you find something that you like—stay there.' Too many journalists move around. They end up never having developed those special contacts. That can hurt their overall careers. There are some that can do it (move around)—but very few."

Y

Yaffe, Fred—March 2, 1933; hyper-energetic ad maverick.

This Detroit ad community fixture runs a Southfield agency that bills $20-million annually. The big accounts include ABC Warehouse ("Knowwudimean Vern?"), Art Van Furniture and Channel 2.

A Brooklyn native, Yaffe allegedly became interested in the Midwest while listening to a University of Michigan football game on the radio. "Where is this place, Michigan?" he wanted to know. He wangled his way to Ann Arbor, where he sold Fuller brushes and worked as a short order cook. Between the bristles and the bacon he earned an MBA, long before business school became hip.

In the ensuing 30 years, he has run (or helped run) a variety of agencies including Yaffe, Stone & August through the 1970s, and Barkley & Evergreen, which became so upset when he left in late 1980 that five lawsuits were filed as a result. For awhile, the shingle read Yaffe and Berline. These days it's Yaffe & Co.

His first wife was Lanie Pincus, who went on to fame but little fortune as owner of the London Chop House. His second wife, Katherine, is an ex-Playboy bunny and daughter of state Rep. John Fitzpatrick. Yaffe and his wife met when she worked in cottontails and Yaffe handled the club's advertising. With Yaffe acting as her campaign manager, she ran for Detroit City Council in 1969. She placed 22nd—far out of the money—but won a husband. She had better luck as a candidate for the City Charter Commission. Nowadays, she operates a string of fast-food restaurants around Oakland County under various flags.

Yaffe believes in the "Kentucky windage" theory of advertising. "That means that after all the research, ratings and studies are finished, someone still has to make a judgement on whether the advertising campaign that has been prepared will work successfully. The difference between a good and a great agency is the ability to feel which way the wind is blowing and then make the proper judgment."

Still loyal to U-M, he was once governor of its booster club. His bi-annual party, on the eve of the Wolverine-Ohio State game, is a classic: In 1987, he rented the Franklin Hills Country Club (the town's most expensive) and had White Castle hamburgers and fast-food chicken catered.

Yokich, Steve—August 20, 1935; Bieber's heir apparent?

There are those in the union movement who think the auto companies and the union ought to become pals. Steve Yokich, the UAW vice-president in charge of its Ford department, is skeptical. Referring to Ford's executive bonus plan in 1987 that fattened executive paychecks by an average of $30,000, he said: "For every brilliant decision the executives made in 1986, they made another dumb decision, and this one tops the list."

Even without his bargaining clout, Yokich would pack a punch. He directs the Michigan Community Action Program, which means politicians must chat with him when they come hat-in-hand looking for UAW political funds.

A former tool-and-die maker and a third-generation UAW member, he ran UAW's Region One, which includes Detroit's east side, neighboring suburbs and the Thumb. As a young union man on the rise, he received a lot of joshing from UAW types who believed one needed a little gray on top before one received any respect. One regional director dubbed him "2004" — the year Yokich faces mandatory retirement. He got the union's Ford post in 1983. And there isn't much kidding about his youth, because he isn't a kid any more.

Now that Yokich is on the other side of 50, he seems to have mellowed. He has never called a national strike at Ford. Although he was said to be a candidate to replace Doug Fraser as UAW president, he couldn't say enough good things about *Owen Bieber* when Bieber got the job. There are those at Solidarity House who say Bieber would very much like to turn over his office to Yokich when Bieber leaves in 1995.

Young, Coleman—May 24, 1918; Hizzoner.

Easily the most controversial figure in this book, his political future is under serious consideration at this writing. His popularity waxes and wanes month by month. As of spring 1989, pollsters had given Young only an even chance of returning to Manoogian Mansion. But if Young's shaky status turns out to be juiced-up wishful thinking by his opponents, it won't be the first time.

Young is an enigma in some ways. He's a master of one-on-one dealings, and he can play to a crowd, but he spends an unusual amount of time dealing solitaire in his room. Some have accused him of being arrogant, but he has extensive experience as a victim of other people's high-handedness.

Born in Tuscaloosa, Alabama, Young migrated with his family to Detroit's Black Bottom as a child. There is a lot in his past that explains some of his latter-day attitudes. Whip smart as a youngster, he was denied admission to a Catholic high school because of his race. As a serviceman during World War II, he was detained for three days because he sought to get a cup of coffee in a white officers' club. Young got a job with the U.S. Post Office, but was discharged for trying to organize a union.

Most significant of all is how he was forced to sit out his prime years because of his answers before a traveling unit of the House Un-American Activities Committee. The group came to Detroit in 1952—ostensibly to investigate Communism. Instead of cowering before the panel, Young gave as well as he got. He told the HUAC unit that "you have me mistaken for a stool pigeon," and gave them a lecture on un-American activities. Said Young: "I am fighting against un-American activities such as lynchings and denial of the vote." That made him virtually unemployable during the '50s.

The '60s were much better, however. He worked as an insurance salesman, but abandoned a promising career in that arena for one in politics. He made it to the Michigan Constitutional Convention as a representative from Detroit's east side, then was elected to the state Senate. There he fought for civil rights and kept his eye on the mayor's office. As a member of the state senate, he was legally barred from running in 1969. Young didn't give much backing to black candidate Richard Austin, who eventually lost. Young's own ship finally came in in a tight 1973 race against Police Commissioner John Nichols.

There is a lot of weight to place on the positive side of Young's balance sheet. He is smart, loyal to his friends, and has kept the city afloat where other mayors might have failed. The Police Department is far more reflective of the population. On the negative side: He's stubborn, and he hasn't built many bridges to the suburbs. The city has been brought to the brink of ruin by crack cocaine, and there are questions whether he might have done more to prevent that.

The paradox of the Young years is visible on any tour of the city that includes a neighborhood and a downtown jewel. Decay and delight. Ruin and renaissance. The gap between the two is incredible. Whether Young could have stanched the city's loss of middle-class blood will be one for the historians to decide.

Young, Shirley—May 25, 1935; GM's consumer watcher/tree shaker.

Remember when a Buick was a Buick, an Oldsmobile was an Olds and everybody knew the difference? Things changed for GM in the 1980s. Buicks, Oldses, Cadillacs—and even Chevies — started looking alike. That may not be the only reason GM's market share dropped from 44.5 percent in 1980 to 35.9 in 1988. But analysts say it's a good part of the reason. Shirley Young's gospel, which she has preached since GM hired her in mid-1988, is that consumers should know the difference. The people who hear it sit on GM's executive committee—a powerful set of ears, indeed.

Young's dad, a Chinese diplomat, was murdered in the Philippines by the Japanese during World War II. She picked up a Phi Beta Kappa key and an economics degree from Wellesley in 1955, joined Grey Advertising four years later, then rose to the presidency of Grey's marketing subsidiary. While at Grey, she acted as a consultant to GM. Company brass felt they needed her expertise full-time when she presented a six-page paper on "brand equities." She summed it up this way to *Forbes* magazine's Jerry Flint: "A brand is like a friend. Levis are my friend. I know what they're like. Chevrolet is like my friend. McDonald's is like my friend. You just don't tamper with that."

Although she's a newcomer, the word around GM is that she's taken very seriously.

Youngblood, Hal—November 5, 1929; WJR's Mr. Erudite.

Detroit's best evening talk show host is an actor, playwright, broadcaster and opera freak. His 8 p.m.-11 p.m. "Nighttime Detroit" show, often preempted by sporting events, mixes serious talk and froth. Discussion may range from German philosophers to the future, when he brings *Cleo* the astrologer on to chat with guests. If you're looking for talk such as "The Commies are coming, the Commies are coming," which seems to be a big deal in Detroit talk radio, you'll have to turn the dial.

A native of Tennessee, he was an anchor and news director at WKBW-TV in Buffalo when WJR brought him to Detroit. He has left a brainprint on the station. He was *J.P. McCarthy*'s longtime producer, assembling the celebrity guest list for McCarthy's morning show and his midday "Focus" program. He was known as the ultimate second banana because he filled in for McCarthy when J.P. was away, but he also gave the place a shot of erudition. Youngblood separated from his 21-year marriage to WJR when he left for New York's WNEW, but he reconciled four months later. "I just couldn't have an impact," he said. He did at WJR, and still does.

Yzerman, Steve—May 9, 1965; another Gordie Howe?

Detroit Red Wings center/captain Steve Yzerman runs counter to the perception that the Wings are nothing more than a collection of bad actors who can play hockey. He's the last guy you'd expect to be caught driving drunk. All he does is play hockey. His jersey number (19) is the one you'll see youngsters wearing most often in their seats at Joe Louis Arena. He may not yet be the best player in the National Hockey League, but Yzerman ranks no lower than third, not far from L.A.'s Wayne Gretzky and Pittsburgh's Mario Lemieux. His nickname, "Silk," sums up his style of hockey: smooth.

Yzerman has better breeding than many players and fans of the grind and bump sport. His father, Ron, is a high-ranking official in the Canadian government. Red Wings general manager *Jimmy Devellano* drafted Yzerman as a first-round pick (fourth overall) in 1983, the same year Bob Probert (drafted third by the Wings), Petr Klima and Joe Kocur (both drafted in the fifth round) came aboard. Jimmy D. believed the 19-year-old would lead the team to a Stanley Cup championship some day. Devellano may or may not be right, but Yzerman wasted no time showing his stuff. He was still three months shy of his 19th birthday when he appeared in the '84 NHL All-Star Game. His 87 points in his rookie year immediately put him in an elite club with Wings greats such as Gordie Howe, Mickey Redmond and Marcel Dionne—the only other Wings ever to rack up a better season.

Yzerman hasn't lost steam. He collected 102 points in 1987–'88, and would have had more if a knee injury hadn't sidelined him in the final 16 games of the season. His 1988 knee injury was front-page stuff. The *Free Press* played it like the loss of, say, Gandhi. The man's thoughtfulness was demonstrated in the open letter he wrote to the fans who sent him cards and letters. Imagine Kirk Gibson doing that. In 1988-'89, Yzerman became the fifth Wings player to score 50 or more goals in a season. (Redmond was the first.)

There was grousing among fans that he makes more than a half-million bucks less than Gretzky and Lemieux, but Yzerman isn't hurting. His pay in the 1988-'89 season was close to $400,000, and he does ads for the metro Detroit Ford dealers. That's enough to finance a new home in Grosse Pointe. When he's not on the rink, Yzerman hangs around with linemate Gerard Gallant.

Z

Zaret, Eli—March 17, 1950; Channel 2 revival, sports division.

He sounds like an auctioneer with pebbles in his throat and Lithium in his bloodstream. Somehow, it's a decent medium for scores, highlights and sports analysis.

Zaret, a 1972 graduate of the University of Michigan, made his name in, of all places, FM jazz radio. "Sports With Eli" on WJZZ-FM introduced the world to his unique-toned rap. A stint at white rocker WRIF-FM led to the first nationally syndicated FM sports show (ABC) and called him to the attention of Channel 4, which helped him adapt to television in 1980. Station execs were smart enough to start him out as a weekend anchor before promoting him to the main sports slot on the 11 p.m. news. He also hosted the Tigers pre-game show, probably the most visible sports gig in town. When WABC-TV hired him in 1986, Zaret appeared to be on the road to network stardom.

But a big fish in Detroit, where sportscasters are taken seriously, can be utterly at sea in New York City. There are many voices in the Big Apple, and sports isn't the center of the universe that it sometimes seems in Detroit. Zaret's ouster from WABC-TV a little more than a year after he got there is a classic illustration of why the television news business isn't for the faint of heart. When Capital Cities bought ABC and its New York affiliate, bringing in its own man as general manager, Zaret's contract was bought out.

Eli returned a humble man. Now that he's on the lower-rated Channel 2 newscasts, people don't talk about him as much as when he hosted Tigers pre-game shows and bantered with George and Al. But that could change. WJZZ's ratings weren't much, either.

Zeff, A. Robert—February 7, 1934; megabuck lawyer.

He may be the richest attorney in Detroit. A lifetime of winning multi-million-dollar personal injury awards and investing wisely have given him a majestic lifestyle. He has a home on Henry Ford II's old street in Grosse Pointe Farms, a winter home in Florida and a private jet to get him there. Defense lawyers cringe when he enters the courtroom—not because anybody would mistake his legal acumen with Oliver Wendell Holmes', but because juries have a tendency to believe what he says.

Zeff's career after graduation from the University of Detroit Law School took off more like a space shuttle than a dragster. Zero to 60 slow and painful, then watch out! Defense lawyers cuffed the rookie around a good deal until Zeff learned his lessons. His highest marks are in the emotion-packed closing argument.

Plenty of lawyers can sway a jury, but few have invested the rewards so cannily. His constantly changing investments have included a jai alai palace in Connecticut, a hotel in Paris and oil wells in parts unknown. During the mid-'70s, he marveled to friends how he made several dollars every time one of his wells sucked a few more drops from the ground — without him having to work for it. His scheme to transport industrial waste to Africa did not meet with much approval from the city's black power structure.

For awhile, it looked as though Zeff was going for the society trade. He represented Cristina Ford, Henry Ford II's second wife, in her divorce from the auto titan. He performed a similar function for Bobby Poselius Ford when she split from Henry Ford II's nephew, Walter. From time to time, Zeff has hit social functions and made a fine appearance: He's tall, square-jawed, perpetually tanned. But society bores him. One wonders which world he'll try to conquer next.

Zimmerman, Rod—December 30, 1952; CBS's eye on Detroit.

He was the first guy sent into Detroit after CBS bought WWJ-AM and WJOI-FM in spring 1989. One of his first acts was to steal the Detroit Lions from WJR-AM, the sports powerhouse. While that may not seem like a great acquisition with the Lions losing at the moment, Zimmerman's gamble will certainly pay off if the Lions ever start winning again. And with the Pistons also on WWJ-AM, the station is beginning to challenge 'JR as the area sports biggie.

A graduate of Southern Illinois University, Zimmerman signed on at CBS as an account executive at WBBM, the broadcaster's Chicago outlet. He rose to general sales manager in 1985 before CBS sent him to take over here. With CBS's history of making all-news radio stations work, you can bet Zimmerman will do great things here.

Zurkowski, Roy—October 10, year unavailable; brother, can you spa a dime.

One of the few locals to attend the wedding of Maria Shriver and Arnold "Conan the Barbarian" Schwarzenegger, Zurkowski and a partner bought the Vic Tanny chain of health and fitness salons in 1962 from Vic Tanny himself. (Yes, there really was a Vic Tanny, but no longer. Tanny died in 1985 at the age of 73.)

Chicago-based Bally Manufacturing Co. bought Zurkowski's company in 1983 for about $140-million. Nothing much changed after the buyout: Zurkowski still runs the show. There is gold in fat, apparently. The clubs contributed about $700-million to Bally's sales in 1988.

The fitness business has been good to Zurkowski financially, and in other ways. Tall, seemingly devoid of fat, permanently tanned and ridiculously rich-looking, he may be the most handsome male chronicled in this book. He and his wife, Lucia, were close pals of Henry Ford II and his wife, Kathy. Now that Henry is gone, they remain close to his widow. Kathy and the Zurkowskis, in fact, were seatmates when Kathy accepted a posthumous award for her late husband at Orchestra Hall in 1988. Cardinal Szoka has been known to call on the Zurkowskis when the church needs a buck or two.